About the Author

E T Laing has travelled to work abroad since the 1970s. His main work is in aid to developing countries and his specialisation is in the economics of ports and shipping. But you will find little about that in this book, which is about the places and the people, not the work.

In some cases names have been changed, for obvious reasons, and the order in which events happened has been slightly rearranged, but all the events described happened.

The chapters sometimes draw on more than one visit, but the years in which the main visits took place were, in alphabetical order: Albania 2008, Angola 1992, Australia (Memories of Tasmania Revisited) 2009, Azerbaijan 2004, Bangladesh 2002, Belize 1988, China 1995, Croatia (Sunset in Croatia) 2007, Dubai 2000, Dubai (Another Twenty-Hour Night) 2004, Egypt 1997, Eritrea 1996, Estonia 1996, Georgia 2007, Hong Kong 1998, Hong Kong (Night Flight) 2000, India (The Real India) 1993, India (Mumbai) 2002, India (The Taj Mahal Intercontinental) 2004, Java 1990, Kazakhstan 1997 and 2009, Korea 1971, Latvia 1995, Malaysia 1992, Mexico 1971, Moscow 1971, Mozambique 2003, Mozambique (Another Tropical Paradise) 2003, Nigeria 1988, Pakistan (After the Election) 2008, Philippines 1980, Philippines (The People's Power Revolution) 1983, Philippines (Hash House Harriers) 2002, Romania 2008, Russia 1971, Sierra Leone 1996, South Africa 2004, South Korea 1985, Sri Lanka 2004, Tanzania, 1991–2011, Turkmenistan 2004, Turks and Caicos Islands 2005, West Pakistan 1971.

E T Laing was born in Northern Ireland, educated at Oxford University and lives in London with his family.

Acknowledgements

With many thanks to the members of the East Finchley Writers group – in particular, Carola Groom (the Chair), and Ralph Goldswain, Lillian Chavert, Phil Black, Harold Karton, Shirla Philogene and Indu – to whom I am greatly indebted for criticism, suggestions, comments and encouragement; and also to Ray Kershaw for his always helpful suggestions and support.

FAKIRS, FELÙCCAS AND FEMMES FATALES

Tales from an incidental traveller

by E T Laing

Bradt

First published by the author on lulu.com in 2010 under the title *Travel to Work in Seventy Countries*

This revised edition published 2012 by
Bradt Travel Guides Ltd
IDC House, The Vale, Chalfont St Peter, Bucks SL9 9RZ, England
www.bradtguides.com

Published in the USA by The Globe Pequot Press Inc,
PO Box 480, Guilford, Connecticut 06437-0480

Text copyright © 2012 E T Laing
Copy-edited by Shelagh Boyd
Text design and typesetting by Adrian McLaughlin
Cover design: illustration and concept by Neil Gower
                    typesetting by Creative Design and Print

ISBN: 978 1 84162 439 6

British Library Cataloguing in Publication Data
A catalogue record for this book is available from the British Library

Production managed by Jellyfish Print Solutions; printed in India

Contents

Introduction

You can talk to the people of a country, starting with the taxi driver on the way in from the airport. You can listen to them and laugh with them. You can watch their sunsets, smell their cooking and walk in their hills. You can discuss their politics, and football. Knit it all together and you have the soul of the country.

This book is based on many of the 70 or so countries in which I have worked, often far off the tourist trail. The pieces follow the principle of 'show, don't tell'. You will read about a Chinese Red Guard recalling the day when, at 14, she saw her *own* parents led out into the village square to be sentenced in their dunces hats; about a young Indian confiding to me over long lunches that although he was looking forward to his arranged marriage, there was a problem, which was that she was 'rather plain'; about a tiny babushka on a Russian market stall reaching up and kissing me again and again on the lips in front of a cheering crowd when I bought one of her leather jackets for $12; and about the blood pouring from the head of a man being lashed with an unwound metal coat hanger in an Angolan police station for the same crime that had just been committed on me.

You will read about the baleful influence of politics and politicians, especially in the countries ruined in the name of communism; and how the idiocy and self-interest of their rulers strangled their economies and left them twisting in the wind – in the 'stans' of the Soviet Union, the dumping grounds that were paid to test their rulers' bombs; the gerontocracy of Egypt where the power and the secrets are kept close to the chests of the old, like pharaohs who live forever; the ruination of Tanzania by a good and well-intentioned man; the impoverishment of Turkmenistan by a president who promised every family a Mercedes; and the law of the jungle in Sierra Leone's civil war, in which a commander called Savage asked his soldiers to go to look for human hearts and they brought back a sackful to eat. There are also descriptions of how I avoided death, more or less narrowly – in India, Mexico and Nigeria.

Along the way I meet the dirt-poor (the fakirs of the title), the feluccas of Egypt gliding down the Nile at sunset and, everywhere, the femmes fatales – from the Nigerian girl who raised the bar to new heights of predatory sensuality as she sashayed across the patio of a hotel swimming pool, to the Natashas of Dubai.

The travel is covered warts and all, with disasters and miseries as well as high points. I recall that sinking feeling at my first sight of the icy cold and windy city centre of Seoul, Korea, in the 1970s, with its brutalist concrete buildings and a stench of boiled cabbage, garlic, urine and fish, knowing that I was going to be spending four months there. An even lower point came when staring at my passport lying in a wet ditch where it had been thrown by Nigerian soldiers – about 17 years of age, garlanded with guns and ammunition belts, armour-plated with muscle, and drunk – as they squatted in a huddle, deciding what to with us, miles from anywhere. Maybe Jan Morris got to the heart of the matter when she said that the miseries of travel are 'the salt that gives them flavour'.

I focus often on the pleasures of travelling alone – travel is undermined by company. Accompanied, you talk to those you know; while unaccompanied you turn to those you don't. A couple, or a group, looks inwards; or you look out as a couple, not as yourselves, and shared experience is often an illusion. My most powerful memories – of sunsets, misty eyes at airports and brief but intense friendships with people I will never meet again – are from journeys alone.

1

Dubai

The road between Dubai, the richest of the Emirates, and Ras Al Khaimah, the poorest but still very rich Emirate where I am working, is a six-lane corniche, straight as an arrow. On the right are a hundred miles of pure yellow desert: on the left are a hundred miles of pure turquoise sea. Above – an electric-blue sky and a fierce sun. In England I drive slowly, but here I drive at over a hundred miles an hour. On the cassette player the plangent voice of Joan Baez, pure as crystal, is singing 'Diamonds and Rust' at force-nine-gale volume. The cassettes sell for a dollar in the local stores. As I drive I see nothing on the road in front, except the slight shimmer of a heat haze. Very occasionally camels walk off the desert and cross the road. Car drivers, their concentration lapsing in the sparse traffic, hit them once or twice a year. It is instant death for both. The camel's legs are swept from underneath, and its body hits the bonnet and then the windscreen. But this danger is not sufficient to deter me. There is a feeling of freedom in the warm air rushing past.

In the evenings, I drive south again, the sun slowly setting over the sea, the windows open, a country music channel playing on the radio. I know that I am approaching Dubai when, ten miles out, the road starts to widen, from three lanes to four, to five and finally six lanes. The traffic gets heavier, but the speed hardly falls. We drive almost bumper to bumper at what seems like 75 miles an hour – I steel myself and take my eyes off the road for a millisecond to glance at the speedometer, and, yes, it *is* 75 mph – along the stretch of road that has held the world record for the number of accidents per kilometre. Many of the cars have their hoods down in the searing heat, and some rich brats, even at this speed, perch dangerously on the back seats of their sports cars, laughing as the wind tears at their hair. As we enter Dubai neon lights start to stream past us – first, car showrooms full of gleaming Lamborghinis and Maseratis and later shops, restaurants and nightclubs. Their names flash past: Mr Dollar, Big Spender, Oxygen, Boudoir, Scream. I wind the window down for a moment, and am assaulted by the banshee wail of a wind-tunnel gale as the iron snake of cars careers onwards. Then suddenly the red tail-lights come on in front; we brake and gradually slow to join the queue as we reach the centre of Dubai.

I find a parking place close to a cluster of nightclubs. I lock the car and my spectacles steam up as I emerge into the humid night air of the city where much of the vast wealth of the Middle East is now spent. The buzz on the streets is electric. Designer clothes shops – glitzier than Singapore's – alternate with street cafés where Arabs lounge over hubble-bubbles; men are shaved on the street, crowds of sunburned young Westerners spill out of pubs into the street, and Arab, Indian and Western music booms out of the bowels of the nightclubs. A girl in black robes, with only her eyes showing though a burqa, gives me a smile and unexpectedly says 'Hello'. And everywhere, at least at night, you see the Natashas, the Russian girls who are to be found wherever there is money.

Fifty years ago Dubai was a pearl-fishing village. Then the Ruler did something very simple. He tore up the petty rule books, permit forms, taxes and regulations, and made Dubai an easy place to do business in an authoritarian and difficult region. Fifteen years later Dubai had won it all. The old Middle Eastern commercial centres of Bahrain and Beirut were toast. Dubai was the new oasis of freedom, wealth and worldly pleasure. The city was already rich when the oil price was $9 a barrel in 1998. By 2008 it was $130.

By day, Dubai is a now a city of clean-lined modern architecture, much of it Islamic, almost all of it white, alongside modern sculptures of steel and glass. Inside the buildings, black-suited girls move silently in offices lighter, brighter and whiter than anywhere else. The Arabs know only modern. When we were sitting in Georgian and Victorian parlours 50 years ago they lived in the desert.

My contact there was Stanley, a Geordie who had moved to Dubai 40 years before, soon after finishing technical college in Gateshead. His voice, manner and appearance had been preserved in formaldehyde. His hairstyle was an unaltered tribute to Johnny Cash, and his wife Martha had coils of hair from Little House on the Prairie. They owned a small villa outside Dubai, and travelled once a year to see their children in South Africa and Australia. There was a flushed energy and old-world friendliness about Stanley and his expat friends when I met them in the pubs and at the British Club; it was borne of success. Had they stayed at home they would have been playing dominoes over their pints in the pensioners' club behind the long abandoned Consett steel works.

Their great love was barn dances, and Stanley was keen to take me to one of their dance evenings, which were held three times a week. At first I was able to escape with the valid excuse that I was being taken out to a round of restaurants and pubs after work. And later in the evenings, finding heat in the city centre unbearable, I liked to go a little north, to the beaches. Even though the nights were still hot, and the evening sea breeze brought little respite – only the warm air of a hair dryer – the temperature was a few degrees lower than Dubai's, and around 10pm families started to arrive on the beach. By midnight, banks of Mercedes were parked for miles along the shore, and down on the sand the women sat in black robes with covered faces, next to the fathers and children in Western clothes. There in the moonlight they lay looking out to sea, or played volleyball on the beach, the young mothers included; they jumped and shrieked just like any other girls, as if their black robes did not exist.

But the day came when I could not avoid the invitation to an evening's dancing, and Stanley and Martha, dressed up to the nines, drove me over to The Club. It was in a plain hall that took me back to the annexe at our village Presbyterian church where they ran an unsuccessful youth club in the 1950s – chairs folded against the walls and an old gramophone on a table. There were about 15 regulars there when we arrived, mostly English and Scots, in short sleeves and with welcoming smiles for a visitor. Almost all were elderly, at least in spirit. It was holiday time and the evening started with the reading of some messages from absent regulars.

"Here's one from Nancy and Bill. They write that they are having a wonderful time in Singapore."

"And I wonder what they are getting up to? Eh?" asked the reader with a wink, and the others batted back some saucy seaside postcard double entendres.

The formalities over, the gramophone scratched into action, and the first dance was a valeta, which I recalled from school dances. I was, of course, hopeless and, after a little discussion, they decided to entrust me to the youngest woman there, who was also the best dancer. She was an athletic-looking girl with thick cropped hair, a strong jaw and just a little of the Salvation Army about her. As the next dance started she placed my hand round her waist and I was surprised to feel, just a couple of inches below the soft curve of her hip, an unexpected layer of taut packed muscle. It turned out later that she was the gym teacher at the British School.

She tried hard to get me to work out the steps, but in vain, and it started to become clear to her that it would not happen. Then at a certain point her patience ran out, and giving me a little smile which said 'well, this is not working: let's try another approach; and... hold on to your hat', she abandoned the rule that the man leads, tightened her grip, and, taking full control, started to propel my unresisting body powerfully around the floor. I am probably one of a very few men to understand what it must be like for a girl to be swept off her feet; and it may have been the strangest and most unexpected sensual thrill of my life. Even stranger, I thought on the drive home, was its having taken place in an empty desert with this little band of people from a distant land and a half forgotten time.

Stanley and his like had built Dubai. But always under the directions of that select few of the Emirates' Arabs that worked, and a meeting with Stanley's director was essential. He had arranged one for me, and was slightly concerned that I might commit an unintended faux pas. The director was the fourth son of The Ruler.

"Make sure you're well dressed, and just be... a little careful."

"OK, will do... is there anything in particular I should be wary of?"

"No. I think he'll be OK with you. But no jokes. He'll give you about ten minutes."

"Anything else?"

He hesitated.

"Well, one thing I'll tell you: he's a good-looking bugger." This was praise indeed; a Geordie of Stanley's generation would normally think it improper to raise such a subject.

The director's secretary's office was cool and spacious with a black marble desk in the centre of the room, lit from above with a narrow-focus halogen light which gleamed on her lustrous black hair.

"Your good name sir? And may I have a visiting card?"

I gave it to her.

"Thank you, sir. I will do the needful." She took it in to the adjoining room, and returned a minute later, saying, "Sir, His Excellency will see you now."

His office was furnished entirely in white, with the exception of the steel of the minimalist furniture, mostly Bauhaus classics, Barcelona and Wassily chairs, and cream leather sofas. But it was the director that made the greater impression. For the hundredth time I thought, where do these looks come from: the perfect skin, the clear eyes and the hair shining with animal health? And how do they get those robes to radiate that immaculate whiteness? They were living in the desert only two generations ago.

The director's manners were those of a solicitous Italian cardinal.

"Is it your first visit?" He seemed pleased to find that I had been there several times before.

"Excellent. I hope your hotel is comfortable."

There was another five minutes of formal pleasantries; then a gear change to a more businesslike tone.

"What do you need?" he asked.

I listed the information I needed.

"It will be with you on Wednesday."

He signalled that the meeting was over with a gracious but distant smile.

I had rarely spoken to anyone who seemed more from another universe. So perfect and unworldly do the Arabs look in their white robes that I usually manage to suppress the thought of how disappointingly they fall off their pedestal when occasionally seen in Western clothes. Their model for immaculate Western taste in smart casual appears to be John Travolta.

The Arabs and British are far outnumbered by the infantrymen of Dubai – the Indians, Pakistanis and Filipinos who make up 80 per cent of the population, and run the hotels, restaurants, shops and construction sites so well. The food in Dubai is better than anywhere on the Indian subcontinent. But now a different type of Asian is moving in – the businessman. The old managers were British and Americans; but they became expensive, and are being replaced by South Africans and Bulgarians – and Asians with gold bracelets. I listen to one in my hotel foyer, a squat unhealthy-looking man with thinning hair and a soft stomach showing through his partly unbuttoned silk shirt. He was shouting in an insistent voice into his mobile.

"Right...I need the e-mail addresses of everyone that's important. And I need them now...What's the name of that man in the Ruler's office? You know the one, he's my friend...Find out...no, I don't know what he's called...Do you know if the VIP suite is booked? You know, the one I usually stay in. I need something good for meeting important people...Don't pay more than half price: tell them I always get a discount...Oh, hold on...I have a call on my other mobile..."

He listened irritably to the other phone, then cut the conversation dead with an abrupt "No way."

Then, returning to the first phone, "No, it's OK, it was just my wife... She's busy spending all my money..."

He leered pointlessly into the receiver. The phone call over, his mask of specious charm fell instantaneously, to be replaced by a look of sulky vacancy. The phone call had brought out sweat marks in the armpits of his shirt, and the smell of sweat mingled with the reek of his perfume.

Most fascinating of all the new tribes, however, is the Natashas. I had watched a group of them coming out of the entrance to one of the clubs on the first sweltering evening. Tall, with bones like sabre blades, and blessed with that silvery unassisted blonde hair, the Russian girls are in a league of their own for improbable beauty. At first they look like northern Europeans, but there is a slightly unearthly aspect about their pale snow-dweller eyes. Part aristocrat, part hardened tart, they look straight through you if you do not smell of money. They give the impression that they could have been supermodels or businesswomen had they wished. But there will be things of which we know nothing. Everyone is mesmerised by the Natashas, their minders and their controllers; everyone has stories, often deeply unpleasant.

My work was almost complete. I had all the information I needed and had met everyone on my list apart from one – Mr Jackson, the director of the Ras al Khaimah Development Bank. He had been due to return from his month's holiday in England two weeks before, but had not yet arrived.

Two days before I had to leave I went to see Mr Edwards, the Ruler's adviser. He was the man responsible for my being there. He had been in the Emirates almost as long as Stanley. A handsome silver-haired Welshman, he was immaculately dressed, not in the customary English business uniform but in the fresh lightweight linen jackets and blue shirts worn by Americans who stay at Browns when in London – men who work with and understand very large sums of money. Pleasant and intelligent, he was anxious that I should make a courtesy call on The Ruler of Ras Al Khaimah to let him know how the work had gone. As with Stanley, he was concerned that I should make a good impression and he warned me in particular not to contradict any statement of The Ruler. "Find some way round it, if it comes up," he advised.

We arrived at the palace on my final day and were ushered into a vast room of extraordinary opulence, even more so than that of the Director in Dubai. The Ruler did not have the good looks of the Director, but had an even more commanding presence.

He asked how my work had gone and I replied "Very well," assuring him that I had everything I needed.

"And how have you got on with Mr Jackson?"

It was the only question I was dreading.

"Well, unfortunately, I have not been able to meet him. . . He has delayed his return from leave for two weeks."

"Oh, well, you must stay to meet him."

"Well, unfortunately, I can't stay beyond today." I had hesitated, but it was my only possible reply.

The Ruler's eyebrows rose theatrically, by a full two inches.

"But you must," said the Ruler.

Mr Edwards, normally so relaxed, looked as if a heart attack was imminent. I thought as fast as I could, and this is what I heard myself say.

"The reason I cannot stay is that I have a holiday arranged in Italy with my wife, starting on Friday. It has been arranged for weeks."

His posture became even more erect, and he raised his forefinger.

"You must change your plans. You will bring your wife here instead, and we will show her hospitality she has never known while you wait to see Mr Jackson." I glanced at Mr Edwards, thought quickly, and started to wing it.

"I must explain my problem. In the West, unlike the Middle East, the power of women has grown and grown over the years. I deeply regret that in our country the wife's wishes now come first, and. . ." I continued to improvise in that vein, breaking Stanley's rule – no humour. The Ruler listened.

There was a short silence

He shook his head, feigning astonishment at this sad state of affairs, and then asked me if he thought our report could be completed without seeing Mr Jackson. On my assurance that it could he wished me well on my holiday.

I heard later that Mr Jackson didn't arrive for another ten days.

At the airport on my way out, the check-in queue hadn't moved for 20 minutes. Behind me was an oil industry worker in his mid 50s. Paunchy, heavily tattooed, wearing thick coke-bottle spectacles, his hair combed like Stanley's, he was also a Geordie. He had a ruddy open face and an engaging boyish grin. As we waited in the slow-moving queue he kept up a constant commentary.

"Why aye, it's always the bloody same here. In fact it's getting even worse. Everything is getting worse. . . Women have no sense of humour any more. . . you try to chat to them and they ring the police on their mobiles. . . And the bureaucrats are getting more stupid, like the ones at the check-in desk here." He had raised his voice in the hope that they would hear.

"Bloody bossy officials." He took a swig from his beer can.

"The next thing will be that they will find that beer makes a hole [pronounced 'who earl'] in the ozone layer. . . and ban drinking."

His monologue was on a tightrope over the border between wonderful and dreadful. Somehow – it was difficult to pin down why – Dubai was one of the places in which it was acceptable.

He stopped in mid sentence: he had noticed two Russian girls who had joined the queue. They had taken advantage of the airport's air conditioning to revert to their grey furs and high leather boots, and had entered a new league of intimidating glamour. He said, in a quieter voice, "Jesus. Take a look at that." But it was not quietly enough. The girls heard him and impaled him with icy glares. At the same time two tall white-robed Arabs in the first-class check-in queue turned to glance at the girls. Their eyes widened but they showed no other reaction and said nothing. A Lebanese businessman looked up irritably from his mobile, then returned to his texting. Six hours from now we would all be back in our separate worlds.

As I board the plane I think back to that first feeling of freedom in the warm air rushing past the open window of my car in the empty landscape. But when I reached the centre, Dubai City, there was an emptiness. There is only one thing that the Arabs, the Stanleys, the Indians, the Asian businessmen, the young professionals and the Natashas have in common – it is not their city. Even the Arabs don't belong there: their grandparents were nomads and they themselves went to school abroad, in the US or England. Rootless, they may be most at home in the airport arrivals hall, watching for their luggage to appear on the carousel. It seems doubtful that anyone will ever come to love Dubai as Mumbai, Lahore, Bangkok or even Hong Kong is loved. There is no melting in the pot; like insoluble chemicals the tribes will never mix.

2
The Taj Mahal
Intercontinenal, Mumbai

I awake to find rain lashing against the windows of the hotel. Looking down I can see that the road at the entrance below is flooded. Taxis are ploughing through the water, sending spray in all directions, and hotel staff are dashing out into the rain with umbrellas. The promenade is almost deserted, although a few stalls are still manned by drenched figures in shorts, flip flops and yellow tarpaulins. The only person moving down there is a man with no legs propelling himself through the water on a wooden trolley. He is shouting at the sky. He seems mad, but the stall holders speak to him and he occasionally takes a package from one of them.

The weather, however, is of little concern as it is Saturday. I have no reason to do anything much today, and the Taj Mahal is a good place to be on a morning like this. It is a hotel to come to, not from. I walk down to buy the newspapers and sit over a long breakfast, breaking my rules by having cake at the end.

Later, I wander around the hotel's shopping arcades and the cluttered bookshop where I have bought many cheap reprints of books I regretted not having read over the years. The hotel is not quite as comprehensively grand as might be expected. As the stately home of Indian hotels, it has retained little oases of shabbiness within its opulence, perhaps to distinguish it from the hard modern smartness of the Sheratons and Hyatts. It had been built by an Indian, J N Tata, a century ago after he was refused entry to Watsons, then the best hotel, and 'Whites only'. Tata had his revenge, as Watsons has long since closed, and the Taj is now the acknowledged social centre of Mumbai. When I am with Indians they point out who is who around the lobby.

Returning to my room, in the lift I feel a tug at my trousers. I look down and see a little boy, about three with sweet doggy eyes.

"Uncle, are you a ghost?" he asks me.

His father looks alarmed but I smile down and say, "Why do you ask?"

"Your eyes are a funny colour"

"That's just because I'm from another country. Everything else is the same except for our eyes – and feet, of course."

"What's funny about your feet?" asks the little boy, wide-eyed.

"It's a secret. Shsh." I put my finger to my lips.

As he leaves the lift he looks back, giggles and says, "I think you *are* a ghost."

Back in my room, I have a feeling of 'undone homework', a sensation that used to afflict me more on Sundays than Saturdays when I was a child; so I sit down and bring my notes up to date. It is still raining but starting to clear. If it stops I will go for a stroll around the Gateway, which is right under my window.

The Gateway is Mumbai's best-known monument, and the site where passengers from the P&O liners disembarked in colonial times. It was also where the 'fishing fleet' used to come ashore. The fishing fleet was the 'cargo of damsels' – daughters of the British, resident in India, that arrived in the cool months from November to January in the hope of catching a husband. Just out of Roedean and Cheltenham Ladies' College, the girls plunged into a round of polo, tea dances, parties and pig sticking, and by the end of their visit many were engaged. The hotel bookshop has sepia photographs of them stepping ashore under parasols in their Edwardian frocks, with that beautiful hair, and the sun sparkling on the crystal-clear water – very unlike the damp spectacle outside the window today. Those who failed to find husbands were called 'returned empties'.

By mid afternoon the rain has stopped, the flood has subsided and sightseers are starting to gather outside. Up in my room the canned air has been drying out my skin, and I feel restless and in need of exercise. I am in India, and I have been sitting in a hotel all day. I have never sat in a hotel all day.

I walk down to the hotel entrance, past the little army of Sikh doormen, some over 6'6" tall, and out to the Gateway.

The Gateway in this weather is not attractive. Once honey-coloured, the stonework is now drab, and under a low sky in a fine drizzle of rain and salt solution it seems ugly, square and lumpen. The slate-grey sea behind it is torpid, and its sluggish waves heaving and slopping against the seawall seem tired. India's is an old civilisation, and even the sea looks over-used.

As I walk, the crowd is getting denser. Groups of young mothers with rolls of fat overflowing from their saris – plump jolly parrots I once heard them called – chatter as their children play. Some have spread blankets on the ground despite its being damp, and there is a smell of wet wool in the air. Along the promenade, courting couples look out to sea, pleased to be at Mumbai's great landmark. I am surprised that all are Indian: there are no foreign tourists. The postcard sellers are irritating me now and I start to sweat in the humidity.

I see a small, pale, nondescript man staring oddly at me. He has an ineffectual look and a sickly wan ghost of a smile. Then he steps forward, pulls out a knife and cuts my throat from ear to ear. . . My whole life does not flash in front of me. The last spasms of my brain home in only on those closest – wife, son, daughter – and then back to my father and mother who died so long ago, sparking the next thought, that this is like an Oscar acceptance speech. So typical, just another silly joke. . . My last thought of all was of the saying 'find me a man whose mother died before he was 15 who is not a comedian'. I never thought the obvious. . . 'it's too late now'. The pain is like. . .

Black.

This happened, on 13 August, 2004. Except that in the final half-hour I was replaced by someone else.

At the same time as I had been deciding to go downstairs and out to the Gateway, Uzer Patel was making his way there from his home a few miles away. He was a disturbed young man of 25, short, plain and recently unemployed – and said to be prone to fits of temper. He had just stabbed and killed his father after a quarrel, and had decided that he would now go further and make himself famous. He had cleaned his knife, sharpened it, dressed up and set out for the Gateway. When he got to that most public and famous of places, he was going to kill a foreigner in front of a crowd.

Arriving at the Gateway he looked around for a foreign face. At first he could find none, and he started to stroll amongst the crowd. It seemed he was going to be unsuccessful, until at last, out of the crowd came two striking-looking girls with exotic almond-shaped eyes. They were in fact Indian, but from the state of Manipur near the Burmese border. The Manipuris' features, often very beautiful, are Mongolian. The two girls had come to Mumbai looking for work. They were the closest he could find to foreigners. He followed them for a few yards and, walking in front of them, cut the first girl's throat, and then turned on her friend. The friend survived with 500 stitches, but the first girl died within seconds.

I had never got to the Gateway. At the very last moment, I decided that I didn't want to be pestered by the card sellers and to be noticed as the only foreigner down there. So on a whim I broke my rule of never staying in a hotel all day. I had a good excuse: the weather had been prohibitive. I would just go for a swim later in the hotel pool, a highly atmospheric pool surrounded by a craggy stone wall and rambling plants.

As I walked through the entrance of the swimming pool an hour later, I saw the staff looking at a horror film on a huge television screen. A girl was lying on the ground in a hideous pose, her throat cut wide open. Another girl, covered with blood, was being held up by onlookers. A crowd was screaming.

I remonstrated with the staff, saying, "That's a grisly film to be showing in the afternoon."

"No, sir, it is not a horror film. It's the news and it is something that has just happened outside the hotel."

3

Eritrea

The camels were sprawled, knees tucked under, along the shore in the shimmering heat haze. In profile they were like throwbacks to prehistory, deeply unbeautiful but aloof, noses held high. They were chewing busily with their rubbery lips, but were otherwise motionless in the unbearable heat. A goatherd flicked each of them with his stick, summoning them to join another group of camels that were already roped together along the beach and being loaded with boxes of vegetables and dried fish. The camels that had been disturbed raised their heads to the sky and bellowed out their unearthly guttural groans of misery. It must have been the sound of the mediaeval caravanserie. Then, grunting and moaning as if in pain, they hauled themselves to their feet and ambled over to join the others, where they stood shuffling, saddle bells clinking, exhaling and stamping in discontent as they were loaded up as beasts of burden.

Until they moved, they seemed the most ungainly of creatures. Then on the command they glided forward – and were transformed. They eased into a light lope, and as they gathered speed, all four legs started to leave the ground, their front and back legs on each side moving – unlike other animals – in parallel with each other rather than in contrary directions. By the time they reached 30 miles an hour, they seemed to be levitating, weightless, as if on the moon.

Within minutes the caravan was a speck in the distance along the beach. Eritrea has almost a thousand kilometres of untouched white sand and placid warm sea. There must be few places like it left in the world, but no developers have set foot on the Eritrean coastline. Tourists might be enthralled by the dizzying descent from the misty mountains of Asmara, the inland capital to the west, along hairpin bends and sharp drops to the arid desert of Massawa where we had spent that week. But they would not be enthralled by the twisted wrecks of tanks cluttering the landscape and the hundreds of tiny trenches still littered with the bleached bones of the fallen fighters. The Eritreans have been at war with their neighbours, the Ethiopians, for 30 years.

It is the sparest of countries, like a distant planet where a hardy form of life has survived without water or sustenance. There are shortages of everything in Eritrea – flour, sugar, sorghum, millet and teff. We were there to build up the port to bring in the aid cargoes, because although there was a cease-fire they were producing almost nothing.

As the camels disappeared, the men ambled back from the shore. Massawa is one of the hottest places on earth, with a furnace-like average maximum temperature in June to August of 104 degrees Fahrenheit, and the wiry Giacometti figures walking back towards us in the heat haze looked skeletal, sculpted down to bare minimalist essentials, their bony limbs burned like mahogany.

Their women had been waiting for them under the thorny trees where they had been herded for a little shade. They were dressed in robes and some in veils, but not the black purdah of Muslim Asia. On the contrary, their cloths were in arrestingly beautiful colours – dusty blue, primrose and sunburst orange – with every last watt of luminosity extracted from them by the fierce sun overhead.

Some of the women looked old before their time, but others looked dazzling under the electric-blue sky against the sand and ochre monochrome of the landscape. As we came closer, we saw that their eyebrows and lashes had been blackened with heavy kohl, making their eyes glittery and mysterious, an effect heightened by their sensual purple lips and dark-blue gums which they prick with thorns dipped in charcoal dye to make their teeth appear whiter. Their arms and hands were patterned with henna, and their noses and ears studded with gold bangles. Their voices, in contrast with the peremptory harshness of Arabic, were melodic, and as they walked away past us a musky smell of frankincense wafted in their wake. It was the smell of Arabia. But the scene was more biblical than Arabic.

There was a primitive beauty there; and there was also a dark side. Almost all of the women are circumcised – and by the women, not the men. They believe it makes their men prize them more. They are forced into marriage while still children, and they die, on average, at 44. They are taught early to ululate, the mysterious, intense, unnerving sound of communal mourning, in which the women open their throats wide to expel their grief straight from the soul, vibrating their tongues from side to side to throw out a shrill keening scream, like hot fast-bubbling water, that swells eerily in the air and shuts out all other sounds. Unique to the tribes of Africa and Arab countries, it is a high, clean sound echoing back to the beginnings of time – the sound of lamentation, the loss of a child, the body of the warrior being lowered into the grave, the fall of the sacrificial knife and the dark unfathomability of the Bacchae. The women of ancient Greece are thought to have ululated at the moment when a sacrificial animal's throat was cut.

We wandered off along the beach as we had no meetings with the port that morning. We had brought our swimming trunks. But when we dipped our feet in the water, it was not just warm, but scalding. We saw children swimming about ten metres out and mimed, 'it's too hot for us'. They laughed and replied in English, "You have to run through the first ten metres." And they were right. We splashed over the shallows into the deeper water which was still above blood temperature, and we floated for a lazy sybaritic half-hour until the sun became too hot.

The port offices we worked in most days were in an overbuilt echoing building set up by the Italian colonial rulers in better times. The large empty rooms had an atmosphere of sepulchral gloom, and the staff were not the most open of people, at least at first. They had spent much of their lives lying in foxholes, staring out over the desert past their rifle sights, and they now dressed with a military but old-fashioned neatness. Untouched by Western fashions they looked, as in old sepia photographs of young men in the two world wars, much older than their years – with smart cream shirts, well-pressed beige slacks and well-polished leather brogues. They spoke surprisingly good English, which they had kept alive in the trenches. We had seen the maids reciting the English names of the days of the week in their classes behind the hotel, and writing them in their exercise books. The port kept neat records in the same sort of exercise books – stationery was scarce. They were wonderful to work with and by the end of the week their mistrust of us had thawed.

In the evenings we ate in the old quarter of Massawa, a mediaeval Arab rabbit warren of dusty alleyways, closed shutters, heavy wooden doors studded with copper bolts and an air of dead secrets. When their war finally ends it will surely be rebuilt into an irresistible tourist attraction, but then, far from being reconstructed, it was still scarred with thousands of bullet holes after a ferocious attack by the Ethiopians that had almost destroyed the town.

It was a strange location for a restaurant that no-one in Eritrea did not know. It was stranger still that this best restaurant on the coast was outside in the open air on a dirt street, under a corrugated-iron roof, with old plastic seats and rickety tables, cold strip lights with insects buzzing in their silver glare and the acrid smell of smoke. But it was crowded every night with locals and a scattering of foreigners. Although it sold no alcohol the waiters would bring it in from round the corner if you asked. At first the waiters looked dirty, but the black stains on their white overalls were just charcoal from the cooking. The only thing on the menu was fish cooked in Yemeni fashion in a clay oven, blackened on the outside but memorably wonderful inside, served with their local bread, *enjera*. The temperature in Massawa is unusual in being as high at night as in the day, and the heat of the ovens made it even worse. Our foreheads glistened and our shirts were damp as we ate, feeling the bodies of scrawny cats rubbing against our legs as they prowled underneath the table on the lookout for leftovers.

We were sad to leave Massawa. We drove out on the Sunday afternoon, past the thorn bushes, boulders, salt pans, goats, flimsy shelters you could see through, and the debris of wrecked tanks; and then out into the desert. On the outskirts of the town we passed a group of locals rebuilding the railway that had been damaged by the Ethiopians. They were working without tools or machinery, on their holiday without pay. It was a wonderful thought, but we doubted if it would be much more useful than the old bucket cable way the Italians had built in the 1930s to bring goods up to the Imperial Italian Army which was invading Ethiopia. An hour later we reached the foothills and the road up to Asmara.

About halfway up the mountain road our Danish engineer nudged me as I was dozing and pointed to a man at the roadside. "I think that man is over two thousand years old," he said. He was wearing a simple orange robe, ramrod straight with an aquiline profile. He was leaning on a stick and looking down to the plain below. He might have been an illustration from the pages of the Book of Exodus.

Our arrival in Asmara brought us relief at last from the relentless heat: at 7,000 feet above sea level the average temperature was only 60 degrees Fahrenheit, and it was there that the colonial rulers had decided to live and build a provincial Italian town – now preserved in aspic. It was a town of pavement cafés in the strong but dull colours, angular shapes, dark polished wood and chrome of 1930s Art Deco, housed in white Italianate buildings; a town of espressos and cappuccinos from glass cups in the mornings and the afternoons; and a town of the sunset *passeggiata*, when the young girls and their mothers dressed to be seen, and to kill, on their evening strolls through the main square.

But not much else seemed to be happening in Asmara. The Eritreans had been in another world for 30 years, fighting rather than working and living. We visited the local Chamber of Commerce, and looked at the little display of Eritrean goods in the entrance. There were bobbins of sewing cotton, scrubbing brushes, candles, matches, mangles, detergents in outdated cartons, screwdrivers, loofahs, mousetraps, wrenches, hairbrushes – most in wood or metal, devoid of colour. It resembled a corner hardware store in Jarrow in the 1940s, more like a museum than an exhibition of the best they could do. But they seemed unaware of this. Their exports that year totalled only two million dollars, less than the value of a terraced house in inner London today. About a third of Eritreans were living abroad and they were sending back over a hundred times as much money as their annual exports earned.

We called at the government offices, which were the main employers in Asmara, along with shoe-makers. The top jobs in the ministries had all gone to those who distinguished themselves on the front line in the war, brave men who had survived great hardship before becoming civil servants. They spoke English well – they had probably doubled as teachers in the trenches – but now they seemed in a time warp, unconcerned that the country had forgotten how to make a living. "We have our friends abroad, and they will help", they said. And for a time they were right. At first, they were greatly admired for their heroic resistance to their intimidating neighbour, their fierce independence, and their dedication to reconstruction after their long war.

But a short time afterwards I was disappointed to hear that hostilities had broken out again. I thought, 'after all the Eritreans had gone through, those Ethiopians go and start it all again. . .' The Eritreans had told us how cruel their enemies were, strangling the captured young men with piano wire, and throwing others down dried wells to shatter their bones. But then I was shocked to hear that it was the not the Ethiopians but the Eritreans that had restarted the fighting – over the border boundaries. Brave men they may have been, but now the war was over they were stubborn, mulish and dysfunctional. The war was everything to them. I had watched the older men in the coffee bars. Dressed in the brown and grey sports jackets of English schoolteachers after the Second World War, they greeted each other by holding hands then lining up their shoulders and bumping each other three times like elephants. It was the old soldiers' greeting: that is how they saw themselves.

Later, the government took over the industries such as they were, closed all the newspapers, put most of the journalists in jail and fell out with the UN peacekeepers. It is now one of the most closed countries in the world; they have been called the North Korea of Africa, second from bottom on the World Press Freedom Index, below Turkmenistan and Burma. Nobody in this long-suffering country had wanted more war, more ululation, except for their leaders.

4

Nigeria

My first sight of what was to come in Nigeria was three women brawling like hippos at the first-class check-in desk at Heathrow airport. The subject of the dispute was several huge boxes tied with rough twine. Two hefty, exotically dressed ladies with massive hips were labouring to heave the boxes onto the check-in weighing machine. Another was trying to pull them off. All three women plus the check-in staff, also Nigerian, were screaming at each other. Their menfolk stood to one side, intent on something more important. Like their women they were expensively dressed, in well-cut suits. They had powerful bodies, thick bull necks, profoundly masculine, deep, sonorous voices and immaculate English. After five minutes of ill-tempered skirmishing, one of the men turned on the women and shouted at them. His tone did not leave open the possibility of dissent. The noise subsided, the ladies looked sheepish, the boxes were taken off, and the queue started to move forward again.

Three days later, I was on the road between Lagos and Port Harcourt. My mission was to see some shipping agents about a project to barge cargo up the River Niger, after which I was to travel north to the landlocked French-speaking country of Niger. I had a Turkish companion, as I was told not to travel alone. The Turk had been in Nigeria for 20 years. A quietly composed man in his late 40s, with an unsmiling manner but a deeply dry sense of humour, he had run large construction projects all over the country and was clearly capable of looking after himself. As we drove towards the border, on a highway through dense jungle drenched in tropical rain, he reclined in the back seat, and told me about how things worked in what is the most corrupt country in Africa. He said that he welcomed the break from the chaos of Lagos.

All went well until we crossed the state border from Lagos into the state of Bendel. The Turk called it cowboy country, and it was only one mile over the border that we saw our first roadblock, Nigerian style. Lying across the road were two thick planks, penetrated by about a hundred six-inch nails, pointing upwards. We stopped the car, and from behind a tree trooped about ten young men. They signalled to us to wind down the window, and we were addressed by a good-looking young spokesman with heavily exaggerated charm.

"Good afternoon, gentlemen." His voice was deep and confident. "I welcome you to the state of Bendel and trust that you are having a pleasant journey. . . I wonder, however, if I could just check whether you have paid your licence fee for your car radio?"

The driver said yes and showed his receipt.

"Ah, yes, but unfortunately this is the fee paid to the Lagos licensing authority. While here you have to pay to the Bendel authority. . . Well, you know this is a *very* serious offence. . ." There followed a short silence. Then he resumed.

"We should strictly be accompanying you to the local police station, but maybe as an alternative you might like to give a small contribution to our local community fund."

The Turk, who had been looking relatively unperturbed during this exchange, silently put his hand in his pocket, and handed them a few notes.

"That is very kind," the community leader beamed. The planks were hauled to one side and they waved us through, wishing us a good journey.

This happened six times in the next 20 miles. The amount given depended on the degree of menace, which varied in each case. On the sixth occasion, the leader of the welcoming party was about 6'4", foul-mouthed and visibly psychotic. He screamed in the driver's face, spraying him with spit, then opened the door and pulled him out by his neck. For the first time I saw the Turk pale, and a large donation was volunteered. We carried on in silence. The Turk did not speak, and looked fixedly ahead. I asked him if he had been frightened. He did not turn to look at me; he kept looking ahead, and said "Yes."

By early evening we reached the Port Harcourt Hotel.

The most memorable entrance I ever saw occurred in the patio bar at the Port Harcourt Hotel swimming pool. The girl was a prostitute by profession. First to enter were two high-slung battleship breasts, apparently in mid air. There followed a brief gap, and then the initial sight of the slow-moving, heavy hips – swaying, dipping, undulating in several separate but exquisitely synchronised orbits below a slender waist. Next, the whole body sashayed into view, articulated into interlocking and slowly revolving sections – legs, hips, waist and breasts suspended from broad, powerful shoulders. But the full impact was delayed until the appearance of her neck and head – held high, proud and predatory. Pure witch queen, eyes rolling in an absurd caricature of sensuality, her imperial bearing crowned by a knot of scarlet and dark-green bandannas piled up above her head, superb against the deep-brown skin. She stopped; arrogant, poised. . . and surveyed the surrounding tables. Her eyes turned slowly, swivelling like a gun turret rounding on its target. They fixed for a second on mine. I felt like helpless prey, a timid stewpot missionary, but her gaze had already swept elsewhere. With an almost imperceptible shrug of her powerful hips she resumed her progress across the pool, and took her place at a table with two other girls. The rest of the guests turned back to their conversations.

I sat with the Turk over a drink. Like every man in the bar our eyes drifted continually towards the girls. Each and every glance in their direction generated an instant response, the girls' antennae enabling them to lock into immediate eye contact. They held your eye until you returned to your conversation.

The Turk left to go to the toilet; and two girls materialised instantly at our table. They were almost as striking as the witch queen, and went straight into overdrive flirtation. I said that we were busy today, but assured them that maybe tomorrow... When the Turk returned they retreated to their table.

The mistake I had made was not to conceal the number on my room key. So half an hour later, when I had barely returned to my room, there was a knock. I opened the door and there was one of the girls who had come to the table. She had a wide smile, enormous teeth, sensual pneumatic lips and technicolour makeup, looking more formidable than cheap.

"Can I come in?" she asked. I made a second mistake, saying I was busy just at the moment, underrating her facility with English.

"What? *So-o-o* busy you can't leave it for an hour to enjoy yourself?"

Her theatrical look of incredulity implied that the white man's priorities were beyond laughable. On the other coast of Africa they call the white man a *muzungu*, which means a busy bee, rushing around with his little bits of paper. I carried on the banter but felt pale in the glare of her presence. She seemed to give up, but then tried one final gambit,

"OK... but could you do me a little favour; it's really hot; could I just come in for a quick shower."

All this time her foot was planted in the door, and her face was a few inches away, her eyes level with mine. Her neck was rather thicker than a

European girl's. She was about cruiserweight, and it dawned on me that she might actually be physically stronger than I was. I racked my brains for an escape route, but without success until a group of Dutch sailors arrived in the corridor and she transferred her attention.

Later, I had to go north, to be taken unofficially over the border into Niger, to save air transport costs. I was sceptical, but persuaded. A Lebanese who had lived there for ten years was going to look after me.

I met my Lebanese protector in Kaduna, in central Nigeria, where he had lived for many years. I spotted him as we drove up to his house, wearing a smart yellow shirt and well-pressed brown trousers, with a short neat haircut. He knew how to look after himself in Kaduna, but it turned out that he rarely left the city; and once off his own territory, he became increasingly uneasy. He missed his wife and small daughter, and had a wallet full of photographs. His favourite picture, which he showed me often, was of his daughter standing with a wan smile in a sunlit back yard in Kaduna. She was about eight, and, with her aquiline nose, beaky appearance, a yellow bow in her long dark curls and a shiny satin pink dress, she looked out of place and uncomfortable.

It soon became clear that rather than his looking after me, the reverse was going to be the case. He seemed pleased to have a stranger to talk to, to confide in about life's disappointments. Two pieces of information he divulged, and repeated many times, were 'Life is tirribil', and 'A reech man, he can leeve anywhere and be happy'. But most of all, he feared 'those girls'. Sitting in the open bars on the first evening, he lowered his voice and disclosed to me the fundamental difference between the young African girls sitting there, aged 13 and upwards, and girls in Europe or at home.

"The European girls," he told me, "will sleep with you, up to a point. But... these girls here... they want *nothing* except sex, and *all* the time!"

He seemed to blench as he contemplated the fate that could befall him if he let his guard drop.

The journey to the border of Niger took two days. By the second day, we had left any connection with Western life far behind; we drove for 300 miles without passing a shop or a restaurant.

Fifty miles before the border, we were stopped by five soldiers. They were about 17 years old, armour-plated with muscle, bull-necked, heavily armed – and drunk. One waved his gun vaguely in our direction and told us to get out of the car. His eyes were dead, like clouded glass, not quite human. His dress was superficially smart, but deeply grunge in the detail.

"Passport, white man," he grunted. He looked blearily and unsteadily at it, sneered and dropped it into a ditch. Then they went into a huddle about what to do with us, looking up at us from time to time.

I once knew a very insecure man whose reason for wanting to marry was that he feared falling sick in his flat and not being discovered until after he died. This was the first and only time a similar thought occurred to me. Nobody, absolutely nobody, had any idea of where we were; it would take weeks after our disappearance for anyone to get close to the trail.

The soldiers in their huddle seemed not to be reaching a conclusion. I suddenly heard myself say in a clear voice:

"Can we have our passports back?"

The leader looked distracted and confused by a question he had not expected. He hesitated. I went on, "Is there a problem?" to keep the initiative. Then I manufactured what I hoped looked like a big smile. He seemed to puzzle for a second, and then turned away and grunted assent. We picked the passports out of the ditch, got into the car and drove off, too drained to speak.

We drove for another 50 miles, and crossed the border into Niger. Its capital, Niamey, is quiet, formal and dull. It has a French town hall, a library, an Alliance Française and a museum. Within a day I was missing Nigeria.

5

Hong Kong

Hong Kong is like nowhere else on earth. You look up from your 40th-floor window, and see no sky. All you see are higher buildings towering over you, a forest of glass and steel. The best of it is superb – especially the bank buildings of I M Pei and Norman Foster side by side on the waterfront. There is a riveting ethereal beauty about the centre of Hong Kong around sunset. It is the cool beauty of an architectural photography book – dehumanised, depersonalised, but hauntingly memorable in certain lights.

Then you look down. The roofs of the 30-storey buildings below you are strewn with refuse, and the backs of the buildings are stained, mildewed and neglected. Further down at ground level the street scenes have a touch of *Blade Runner*'s decaying ultra-modern megalopolis. Wander into a street-corner 7-Eleven at 2.30am and you will find razor-thin young couples in sunglasses queuing alongside tieless city bankers, pale with exhaustion, and moon-faced old men in string vests and baggy shorts. Rotting fruit and vegetables lie in the street bins waiting for morning.

'Quivering grey, intelligent without purpose, excitable without love... a heart that certainly beats but without humanity' was E M Forster's description of 19th-century London. But with the exception of the greyness it could be Hong Kong today.

For the young and clever, Hong Kong is a deeply exhilarating place to work. The salaries are sky-high, leaving most people with money to play with; and that is what they do. For the Chinese, for whom gambling is in the blood, Hong Kong is a re-creation of paradise on earth. For the ten years up to 1998 they were able to bet sums of which they never dreamed, and almost always win. Everyone, just everyone, plays the stock market; and even very ordinary people buy up apartments in Europe and the US as well as Hong Kong. Even the more cautious British expatriate salaried staff have become millionaires.

But there are downsides. They earn their mega-bucks and work in modern temples of glass and steel, but they go home to cramped apartments which cost more than in London. Few own a car, culture is thin on the ground, and television is woeful, making British soap operas seem like works of Sophoclean profundity. Even their football is not their own. The pubs are packed in the early hours of Sunday morning for live English Premier League games. There is little time to read.

What they do is work and drink – both with high-octane intensity. The working day is 12 to 14 hours. Then they decamp to the bars – maybe stopping first for an hour to crunch their six-packs in dayglo lycra leotards in shiny gyms. By 9pm the bars are heaving with casually dressed alpha-male bankers and lawyers and 30-something black-suited girls – Hamishes and Ruperts; Carolines and Virginias; and Lo Fats and Lap Tops. Most seem single. All are high on networking.

The high priests are the investment analysts and financiers, almost all under 40. The Westerners among them are straight out of Tom Wolfe's masters of the universe – the cream of Oxford and Cambridge, Harvard and Yale; but a new breed. In the past they would have been firsts in classics, destined to be university professors, writers or revered public servants at Foreign Offices or Treasuries. But today they may have studied astrophysics before turning to make money – in the style of Billy the Kid. Expensively dressed and highly intelligent, they speak a language from Tarantino films... "Wow... Holy fucking shit...!" The smart style is high-speed cynicism. They hoot with laughter at anything uncool in the banking world. High on money and success, they tell rapid-fire tales of financial scams, scandals in high places and banking widows.

The only product is money. It is ten years since Hong Kong produced anything much, but since then it has lived high on the hog from the profits from the factories which moved over the border into Guangdong, the source of most of China's exports. It is said that China opened its economy to the world in the 1980s, but only Hong Kong noticed. The profits from its economic colony have been astronomic.

Everything is reducible and reduced to dollars. As I walk to work I listen to a passing tourist bus. A frail Chinese girl in a black suit is pointing out the sights with a robotic commentary... "On the left is the convention centre; it cost US$500 million. On the right is the Grand Hotel; it cost US$800 million. And the building ahead cost a billion." No details, no background, only prices.

But this was 1998, and something was happening. The machine had been stalling for the last year, as in other Asian countries. It was the so-called Asian crisis. The Hang Seng index of share values had collapsed from a peak of 16,000 to 7,000; property prices were down 40 per cent from last year, and the negative equity trap was far deeper than it ever was in Britain. Tourism, especially from Japan, had collapsed; and recession was now official. The bankers were leaving their offices a little earlier, at 8pm rather than 9pm, to adjourn to the bars.

We met one group of bankers in a busy bar. It was theirs; they had bought it – because they could. And what did they talk about that evening in 1998? Not just turmoil, disaster, collapse and economic meltdown, but – literally –

about the end of the world. The bankers were not depressed by the impending apocalypse. They were visibly excited, exhilarated. Their knowledge of geo-politics was stunning – it had to be to manage their portfolios. They rattled through the doomsday scenarios. They started with Japan going into deep recession. The domino consequences were that China would devalue; therefore so would Hong Kong, thus ending its role as a financial centre. At the same time, other economies outside Asia – Russia, South America – would collapse. Meanwhile the world tensions would grow. North Korea would send more missiles over Japan; and China would start to throw its new weight around, maybe over Taiwan. But the Armageddon would probably be engineered by the wild cards, the loose cannons – the new super-rich Islamic militants, and the Russians, bankrupt (remember, this is 1998), but with enough nuclear weapons to blow up a galaxy. These weapons were now in the hands of unpaid generals, desperate for income in the ruins of their economy. One apocalyptic scenario has the Russians selling the missiles to the Islamic militants; another sees them simply going out to take what they want at gunpoint. Hong Kong's bankers are funny, very funny, on these subjects.

As the apocalypse loomed, the flavour of the month in 1998 was 'downside scenarios'. The banks were losing money and 'reviewing the quality of their loans'. In our office we were working on a 'due diligence' report for a big bank on an investment in a port, and they were unhappy with our draft – not because it was lacking in thoroughness, but because it was lacking in pessimism. They sent it back, asking us to test increasingly gloomy scenarios. I heard Jamie, our exasperated Hong Kong Director, talking to them on the telephone.

"Come on, you asked us to give you our opinion, and our opinion is that it's a winner, it's a slam dunk."

Pause. He listened to the response, miming incredulity for our benefit.

"What! You want us to assume what?! Negative growth for ten

years?. . . Er. . . Why not a hundred years?" For once he was ignoring his own advice; the Chinese don't like sarcasm.

There was a pause, while the banker at the other end of the line spoke at length.

"Because it won't happen," was Jamie's curt reply.

Another pause. Jamie held the phone away from his ear, and then responded:

"Well. . . would you like us to look at the impact of the coming of an ice age? Come on!"

Pause.

"How about a large comet hitting earth; or the sun going out. Would that keep you happy?"

He put the phone down and said, "Let's get out of here." It was only 8pm but it was Friday, and we piled into a taxi, and up to the steep narrow streets of Lan Kwai Fong, the heart of Hong Kong's social life, with its dense warren of expensive bars, restaurants and clubs. By the time we arrived the crowd, ties removed and computers slung over shoulders, was already spilling out on to the cobbled streets.

The air seemed charged on those weekend evenings – animated faces glowing with rude health from a combination of the frenzied pressure of work and weekends sailing. The music boomed from inside the hottest club, Insomnia. Although workaholic, the last thing the Hong Kong financiers are is dull. They often seem to know more about what is happening in London than I do.

Later in the evening I find myself talking to a young physicist who had later done an MBA and switched to financial services. As the alcohol took effect he also turned out to have a fair grounding in philosophy, and homed in on a theme that kept recurring that year with a drink-fuelled attempt to form a coherent theory of the universe around the thoughts of Gordon

Gecko – 'greed is good, greed is right, greed works'; 'if you need a friend, get a dog'; and the lawyers' more blood-chilling 'eat what you kill' (it was the year after the film *Wall Street* had been released). The young of Hong Kong were carried away by the thought that making money was the key to happiness, not just for themselves but for everyone. Rarely can so much brainpower in a few square kilometres have been concentrated on a single thought. It is possible that most of them didn't even want the money itself, having little time to spend rather than make it. They just wanted to be there in those glorious years in that centre of the world.

But here we come to the fascinating thing: with the benefit of hindsight they got everything, or almost everything, spectacularly wrong. It turned out that the world economy was not on the brink of collapse; it was back on its feet and flourishing again within a year, and not one of their fears materialised. The hiccups since then have been caused not by their too-clever-by-half apocalyptic scenarios but by a textbook trade cycle in 2001, followed by SARS, bird flu, 9/11 and now the sub-prime mortgages. Not one of them was forecast. All those words, all that theorising from all that brainpower – for nothing.

It is one in the morning when the others at last hail a taxi, but at the last moment I decide to walk back to my hotel on my own. There is light drizzle as I stroll down the hill. Emptied of people Hong Kong is even more beautiful, its steel and glass sculptures floodlit against the skyline. But at street level the lighting is a harsh yellow. Cleaning trucks go about their business as the last lights go out, and the metal shutters of late-night food stalls come juddering down. A few nylon-shirted engineers, the old colonials of the 1960s, and lonely ponytailed travellers can be seen in the windows of late-night internet cafés. It is not their city. In the early hours of the morning Hong Kong is Edward Hopper territory – a city of buildings, not people.

I call at an all-night 7-Eleven for a carton of milk, and wait behind an elderly Chinese couple. What could they be doing out at this time, I wonder? They look left behind, lost, oddly anonymous under the towering bank buildings. The Chinese grow old very visibly in a warm climate. The colour fades from their hair and skin; their skin wrinkles and dries, like old tortoises; their posture sags and the light in their eyes goes dim. It's no longer their city, but nor does it belong to the invading tribe I had just left at Lan Kwai Fong – now asleep for a few hours in their short-let apartments.

6

South Africa

We rarely walked on our own after dark in Pretoria. Although the leafy avenues with their sweet earthy smell of damp vegetation and the warm lamps coming on in the windows of the old Dutch colonial houses made our strolls home deeply evocative, there were cold faces watching at the edges of the streets. And so we walked each other home like boy and girl; and in that first fortnight, apart from being robbed of $1,000, I emerged unscathed. But a UN employee working alongside us was less fortunate. In the centre of Pretoria a man in a hood pointed a gun at him and told him to hand over his computer. He resisted, and when the gunman pulled the strap off his shoulder he dragged it back. The thief put his gun to the man's head, shot him dead and walked away – in full view of hundreds of bystanders, at midday. No-one dared stop him.

I found out about this from Solomon, our driver, on the way to the airport to return to London.

"So maybe you were lucky to lose only $1,000," he said.

"Yes, maybe I was... What a way to die. Can you imagine his thoughts in those last few seconds – that this was the way it was going to end...

And what do you think would have been in the mind of the gunman. Hatred of Whites?"

Solomon, who was black, was happy to talk about this sort of thing. He considered the question carefully, as he often did. I watched his face in profile, illuminated by the oncoming cars. It was like a mask, compact and composed. Solomon was below average height but his natural grace and erect posture gave the impression of a tall man.

"No, I don't think so. He probably wouldn't have felt much emotion. He had probably been in jail for a time. The thing you have to understand is that when they get out there is little chance of getting a job, and. . . he would have been ice-cold. You get like that in jail, believe me."

"What do you mean?"

He hesitated. "Well, I was in jail for a time." He kept his eyes fixed on the road ahead. We had known Solomon for a week. He was studying to become a lawyer.

"What for?"

"It was supposed to be robbery. It was a mistake."

So ended my first fortnight in South Africa, arguably the most beautiful country in the world, with its warm terracotta landscapes, its laterite earth, and air softer around sunset than anywhere else; a country of wonderful cool interiors, Dutch no-nonsense interiors, with echoes of Vermeer in the colour and design. The weather in summer is glorious, but best of all to a melancholic Nordic mentality such as my own are the brilliant frosty winter mornings; the chilled evenings when the old stone hotels light log fires; and the spring with the flowering of the heavenly pale-blue and mauve jacaranda trees.

The Dutch guesthouse we were staying in was homely and warm, with ochre walls, old blue and orange pottery, crackling wood fires in winter, a garden lush with southern hemisphere trees and bushes – and a perfect duck.

It was a mandarin with plumage of iridescent chestnut browns and oranges and blues, with a sheen that might have been touched up with fresh gloss paint a minute ago. Everyone laughed when they saw it; it was such a flawless creation of nature.

Our Afrikaans landlady was proud of her duck and said that everyone who had ever visited talked about it.

She fussed over us with the over-eager friendliness that dates back to the days South Africans felt excluded from the civilised world. In her 50s, dressed in tasteful blues and greens, she had a finely boned face, but a slight tightness around the mouth, into which you might read the sadness of a people whose forebears were resigned to dying in a distant land, or, less charitably, the tiniest hint of dog-trainer callousness. She had taken a liking to us, and asked us constantly what she could do to make our stay more comfortable. We assured her, truthfully, that her home was a pleasure to stay in, but she persisted, and it was in desperation that I suggested a tiny indulgence.

"Just one very small thing: would it be possible for the maid who comes to our rooms in the early evening to put the electric blanket on setting number 3 rather than 2, as the nights are getting very chilly?"

The landlady was delighted at this opportunity to improve her already impeccable standards, and summoned all her staff. They stood in front of us – all black, all dressed in pinnies and mob-caps and all with downcast eyes – as the landlady scolded them for not looking after the 'gists' properly. As the poor girls began to slink away, she explained to us, still within their hearing, that:

"A good ticking-off is good for them; it kips them on their toes."

Every evening we rang for our taxi, to take us to a pre-selected restaurant. I had asked our landlady if taxis there were safe.

"Absolutely. Very safe."

"So we should be able to get one on the street outside?"

She looked aghast. "Good gracious me, no. Never get into a taxi on the street. No, just let me know when you need one and I'll give them a tinkle. They'll be here in a jiffy."

At first I had argued that we should walk, as there were often five or so of us, and it seemed a crime not to walk through those tree-lined avenues and spectacular homes that raised suburban living to an art form in the balmy evenings. But everyone had their stories of the consequences of not playing safe. The commonest crime at that time was car-napping at the owner's gate. As the driver reached his fortress home he would slow down, and sound the horn to alert the servant inside to open the steel gates. But just as the gate was opening two men would appear on either side of the car, guns pointing through both side windows. If the owner was lucky he would lose only the car. Others would lose their lives. Solomon told us of more dangers: feral children descending on cars stopped at traffic lights, hunting in packs; and Aids sufferers who believed that sex with a baby would cure them. "What percentage of the people could believe a thing like that?" I asked. As usual, he applied some thought and replied, "Maybe five per cent."

But the feeling on the streets was not so much of danger but of hopelessness and alienation. Men stood staring into space at street corners, in drab clothes, devoid of style, so unlike the clothes of blacks in Europe and the US where all the kids want to dress 'black'. The South Africans are the unhappiest looking blacks I have seen, with the exception of Niger. I recalled a brief stopover I had made in Durban in 1994, when I watched the black intellectuals on television discussing the future and their new freedom just before Mandela became president. Even in those heady days there were few smiles. How could they not have been damaged after what had gone before?

In the second week we moved to Johannesburg, or at least its new suburbs. Johannesburg had once been the prosperous financial centre, but the businessmen have now decamped with their offices and residences to the outskirts, to Sandton and other new suburbs. And here there are no people at all on the streets. There are coldly modern buildings, sleek German cars, upmarket shopping centres and wonderful restaurants – but no people. It is as if they had dropped the neutron bomb, the weapon of the 1970s that was designed to kill people without destroying property.

By this time I could not stand taking a car everywhere, and I started walking to the restaurants and pubs in the evenings, occasionally dragging a few people along with me. Edwin, a civil servant working on transport policy, was fascinated and said:

"We are watching you keefully and keeping rikords. We'd lake to discourage people from using cahs. You are the first tist kise of a White who walks in the city. We're very interested to see exictly how long you'll lest." All with a cheery smile.

South Africans are obsessed with the state of their nation. The Mandela years offered hope, and now, more than ten years on, things had turned out, on balance, rather better than most had feared. But a deeply corrosive problem was starting to surface. Unlike our kids at home, who are now colour blind, the young South Africans are not. We watched them on Friday nights queuing for the clubs outside the university, healthy human stock, corn-fed statuesque blonde Dutch girls and boys with their limpid pale-blue eyes; solid capable people, bred from ancestors self-sufficient on their homesteads; illustrations of vitamin and protein excess. Contrary to the old caricature of the repressed colonial, the South African young are well-mannered and open, mixing easily with adults – the polar opposite of the skinny-necked kids from the estates past the end of our streets in London with their pale pastry-dough faces. The problem, however, is that good jobs are, as in most places in the world, difficult to find, and the white children discover that after finishing the university they are locked out of jobs by the policy of BEE (Black Economic Empowerment) – 'positive discrimination for the bleddy blicks', as one blonde young man explained disdainfully. The pros of this policy may only slightly exceed its cons. It will leave a long legacy of bitterness.

As we drove on to the airport, I tentatively mentioned a verdict I had read in a newspaper leader about the first ten years. The article listed the achievements and failures, and concluded that 'all things considered, things have turned out not too badly, but the sad truth is that our blacks and whites don't really like each other very much'.

Solomon smiled and said, "There is something in that."

To pass the remaining time I watched the cars on the freeway and observed that most of the very expensive cars were driven by blacks. There were also a lot of shiny new fast minis, driven by women. Solomon said, "Yes, they are popular with the rich blacks' wives." Then he added an observation I will always remember.

"You know, black people resent other blacks getting rich even more than they resent the whites. It's a bad flaw in our character."

Had I been writing the leader article I might have started my notes. . . 'Beautiful place; damaged people, both blacks and whites; projected recuperation period for psychic scars, 30 years'.

7

China

Like many things in China, our visit started with a banquet; and like many banquets it had a purpose, a hidden agenda, a political agenda. We were there to evaluate a loan that a bank was considering making to a port, and the Chinese wanted the money. But we had to advise the bank on whether the port would be able to pay it back. If there was such a game as 'Chinese Political Chess' the banquet might have been an opening gambit called 'testing the gullibility of the foreign devil'.

It was presided over by the two directors of the Wuhan port authority – one plump and epicene with thinning hair and a fleshy handshake, and the other tall and coldly good-looking in a black polo-neck and cashmere jacket. The food was spectacular, and mercifully devoid of the turtle bile and chicken's feet with which the Chinese tease foreigners. But the evening was prolonged by welcoming speeches of unedited off-the-shelf paragraphs about the 'great achievements' of Mao and the 'pragmatism' of Deng. "We will cross the river by groping the stones," they told us. "It matters little whether the cat is black or white, as long as it catches the mouse." The need to say it first in Chinese and secondly in English via an interpreter made the evening even longer.

Towards the end of the banquet our team leader asked about our programme for the week. We had sent ahead a long list of the people we wanted to talk to. A minion arrived with a schedule, and the interpreter read it out.

"Tomorrow you will visit the Sparkling Lake Pavilion; on Tuesday you will visit the Yellow Crane Tower; on Wednesday you will visit the Snake Mountain; and on Thursday the Great Bridge over the Mighty Yangtze."

It was five days of sightseeing. They had clearly decided that the last thing they wanted was the foreign devils talking to anyone who might not toe the party line. Our team leader, Bill, who had been basking in the warmth of the reception, thanked them effusively for their hospitality. It was left to me to spoil the party.

"Although I of course look forward to seeing these famous landmarks, I am afraid that we will also have to talk to a lot of people while we are here."

"No need," the plump director replied. "We've prepared all the information you need."

I thought 'how could you know what we need?', but I said, "The banks, unfortunately, have protocols that require meetings."

The word 'protocol' seemed to do the trick. It was a word they understood.

"We'll see what we can do."

By the next day they had partly relented and had arranged a tour of the port and the city.

Wuhan in the 1990s must have been amongst the most dispiriting cities in the world – a sprawling mosaic of smokestack metal-bashing industries, covered almost permanently by a thick low cloud which made the all-pervading smell of coal more acrid. With its bleak buildings of grey concrete, it could have been any of a hundred cities in China, only more so.

The Chinese have never distinguished themselves at urban design, except perhaps in the inner courtyards of their old traditional buildings, which can have an austere beauty especially in winter when bathed in the amber glow of the low afternoon sun behind the bare branches of the trees. But in Wuhan almost all of these old buildings had been torn down since the cultural revolution, and the impersonal factory-like structures erected in their place seemed to speak of the contempt the Communist Party had for the people.

Most dreary of all were the narrow streets of unremitting cheerlessness in the centre of the city, where the sour smells of neglected drains rose into mile after mile of tiny shops cluttered with old-fashioned mangles, scrubbing boards, treadle-powered sewing machines, black sit-up-and-beg bicycles, vulcanising equipment, fly catchers, metal kitchen utensils, dark lacquered wood, old metal typewriters and pre-war style school exercise books.

The docks when we reached them were like a throwback to South Shields after the war, commemorated in black-and-white photographs of rusting steel coils, grey-painted cranes, smoke-blackened buildings and dockers aged before their time. The Wuhan port staff were helpful, answering our questions as best they could, but language was a problem and much of the afternoon was spent trying to identify their main cargo, which had been translated to us as 'magnificent plate'. Half a dozen translators were summoned but couldn't help, and we left, still puzzled. At the end of the meeting they proudly handed us 'the information'. They had tried hard, but the information – including the early history of the port under the Ming Dynasty – had little relevance to what we were doing.

By late afternoon our hands and feet were cold and we were pleased to be heading back to the head office with the Chinese who had been with us all day. The offices were gloomy, institutional, dusty, and badly heated, but as we all gathered round the stove with rosy cheeks and wet noses to drink glasses of warm water there was a collegial atmosphere as we flapped our arms together like penguins to get the blood moving.

Our interpreter was Miss Lee, a pleasant motherly girl in a padded jacket and the Chinese quarter-length nylon stockings that cut into the skin just above the calf – probably the least attractive garment ever designed. She missed her children but told us that she was happy to be with us as 'the success of our project comes first'. She was known to sing like an angel, and that was the reason that our second evening ended in a Karaoke bar. Most Chinese men sang well in deep, military voices, but when Miss Lee sang, whether marching songs or opera or the falling cadences of Chinese pop music, there were always crowds in the doorways.

Later in the evening, we stumbled on the fact that the Chinese, none of whom had ever left the country, found foreigners, and especially their noses, extraordinarily ugly. They also thought that we looked very old. Encouraged that we thought this interesting rather than insulting, the locals went round the table telling each of us who we looked like. Our Danish engineer was thought to look like James Coburn, and another like President Clinton, and they picked up on my receding hairline to call me. . . Mister Shakespeare. The evening was going well, so I thought, why not, and said to Miss Lee:

"What did you think about Tiananmen Square?"

She didn't blink. "Do you mean whose side was I on? Well. . . maybe I am ashamed to say it. . . I, and most of us, were against the students in the end. You see, they were mostly teenagers, anti-everything. . . clever, but they know nothing. Of course they were right to protest. But we remembered the days when the schoolchildren took over in the Cultural Revolution. They sent the doctors to work in the fields and replaced them with so-called paramedics, who were only students. We didn't want to go back there again. Everything just stopped working. There was no medicine, no transport and in the end a cabbage cost a week's wages. . ."

"So what did you think of the Red Guards?"

"Oh, I was one." She must have been a little older than we had thought. "We thought it was great for a while. We arrested our teachers, and had no lessons. And we sat around talking all day, and decided everything. But then it went too far, especially when they sent the doctors away... Then one day they brought my mother and father into the town square. They were both teachers. The leader of our Red Guard group, who was the worst bully in the class above us, said they were capitalist roaders. They made them wear dunces' hats and pushed them around. I didn't feel so good then."

"Were they badly hurt?"

"No, but some weren't so lucky. The children killed some of the teachers they didn't like"

"What about the military uniforms they made you wear?"

"Oh, they didn't *make* us wear them. We thought it was cool to wear... do you call it army surplus? We combed the shops for old army coats."

"And the Chairman Mao tunics?"

"We weren't made to wear them either. They were just what was cheap and available in the shops."

Meanwhile, the port directors had decided that they trusted our good intentions. They gave us a list of the best people to see, and we set out in a combi van with Miss Lee, Mr Wong, of whom more later, and our minders, Mr Zhu and Mr Su. Seconded from the People's Liberation Army Mr Zhu and Mr Su were flinty-eyed and razor-thin ex-soldiers. We were told that they were there to look after us, but we knew that they also had to report on our movements. They spoke almost no English and kept their distance until a few mornings later when they suddenly shouted at the driver to stop the car. As the car ground to a halt Mr Zhu asked, through Miss Lee, "Can you use a Kalashnikov?"

"What?... Um, no."

"Would you like to try?"

In the firing range, which they had spotted from the road, I was equipped with an alarmingly heavy Kalashnikov rifle and ear pads. "*Don't* take them off. You could be deafened for ever." They pointed me towards a dummy dressed in a US GI uniform about a quarter of a mile way and said, "Can you see the red heart pinned on its chest? That's what you have to hit." The recoil of the gun was like a horse kick, but for reasons unknown, I apparently hit the heart time after time. Mr Zhu and Mr Su were impressed, in fact so impressed as to ask for the rest of our stay for continuing advice on a composite perfect female, assembled from the characteristics of women in other countries of which they had no knowledge except from very, very scarce films. The first draft combined blonde Scandinavian hair, French dress sense, African behinds and American 'morals'. Miss Lee, whom Mr Wong was later to call 'a jolly good sport' was happy enough to translate.

Mr Wong was our secret weapon. He was from the new mandarin aristocracy, selected as a young man from the cream of the Chinese civil service to be fast-tracked in English before a posting to London as a spy. His English was possibly superior to ours, but wonderfully outdated. It was as if the Chinese authorities had sought and achieved perfection in all respects in the training of their spies, with one flaw. Their models were precisely 40 years out of date and Mr Wong's conversation was studded with 'shall' instead of 'will', 'I say', 'splendid', 'chum' and even 'topping'. He had been at the London Embassy at the time of the incident in the 1980s when the diplomats broke out and attacked people on the street with meat choppers. But he had left the civil service and set up a small company which was part of our team.

On the second morning we were driving to some meetings and I asked Mr Wong who we were going to see first. As usual he paused for thought before constructing his reply.

"Well, the port management have given us an approved list of interviewees. We are scheduled to meet them over the next two days. However, the selected gentlemen would paint for us a rosy picture which would be wholly at variance with reality. Consequently I have initiated my own investigations and we shall, instead, visit some well-informed gentlemen who can be relied on to present a more accurate and comprehensive assessment of the true picture." Needless to say, he was right.

Our hotel was comfortable enough, but lacking in charm, with hard surfaces, dark lacquered wood furniture and plastic flowers. The restaurant where we had breakfast was a vast barn with elaborate karaoke equipment in the corner. But it transpired that it had another role, which I stumbled across one evening when I passed the restaurant floor in the lift and heard a dull thudding. I opened the door and was assaulted by a wall of rock music. It emerged that twice a week the tables and chairs were removed to run a disco. The boys that night looked deeply dorkish, although the girls had picked up the details of the styles of the last ten years – Goth, punk and glam rock – rather well. But it was the music that was superb – driving heavy metal at frenzied steam-hammer gale-force power. It was clear that about half of the girls there, mostly those in leather hot pants, were commercial girls; but, packed to the doors, it gave the impression of being the centre of a small universe.

The next day I asked Mr Wong if he had seen the transformation of the dining room on the previous night.

"No, I was unable to observe the proceedings myself. However, Mr Zhu and Mr Su this morning informed me that they chanced upon the scene when walking up the stairs past the restaurant. Being curious, they entered and were confronted with scenes that implied the possibility of loose moral behaviour. They drew their conclusions and, of course, retired immediately."

The last night was almost a disaster. It was a banquet attended not only by the port staff but also by new and more senior people including the secretary of the Communist Party for the region, Mr Wu. He was a small wiry man in his late

60s with a hard face and ill-disguised contempt for the foreign guests. To test the foreigners, he proposed a drinking game, *Gambai*, in which you are challenged to sink a glass of beer and then put the empty glass upside down on your head to demonstrate that you have drunk it all. You then challenge some else at the table. Because there were always at least five times as many Chinese as foreigners, and the Chinese always challenge the foreigners, you end up drinking at least five times as much as them. But it was taking time to get us really drunk, and suddenly the interpreter announced that Mr Wu had challenged our team leader, Bill, to a chilli-eating contest. Bill looked up, seemed unperturbed and accepted; then picked up a chilli from the plate in front of him and ate it with apparent enjoyment. Mr Wu responded by eating three. His eyes were shining and he let out a sudden harsh laugh. Much of Chinese laughter has little to do with humour. It can show embarrassment or surprise. But in this case it denoted confrontation. Then, just as Bill started to reply by putting five chillies into his mouth, I recalled that Thai food was one of the great joys in his life. Mr Wu followed with five chillies, but looked stressed. Then Bill started slowly counting out his next response . . . 2, 3, 4. . . 11, 12, 13, 14, 15. . . He put them in his mouth and started chewing. Mr Wu looked aghast; his mouth twisted, and he rose and left the room. There were audible intakes of breath. Although it had not quite registered with us, the Chinese knew that he had powers of life and death over 50 million people and he had been humiliated in front of 30 people.

But politics are more important than even the top politician, and when the plump director asked us at our wrap-up meeting the next morning if our report would recommend the loan, and we said yes, all was forgiven. Although they kept their mouths zipped up we suspected that the Chinese were rather tired of politicians and felt some schadenfreude at the humiliation of a top man by outsiders.

"By the way," they said as we left, "we have consulted the Ministry of Transport in Beijing and found that a better translation than 'magnificent plate' is 'plywood and veneer'."

8

Memories of Tasmania

There was not a trace of a smile on the faces in the sepia photograph on Auntie Dora's sideboard. It showed a family of ten, sitting stiffly outside a farm. The date was around 1880 and the location was a hillside in northern Tasmania. Their clothes were heavy, the women dressed in high-necked black bombazine, the stiffened silk material favoured for mourning by the Victorians; and the men looked ill at ease in clothes that seemed to have been designed for other people. The children looked surly. All have the white irises and the morose look that was common in old photographs. They may have been from a first generation of immigrants, far from home, and aware that they would never return, never see their families again. The quality required to fashion a new life out of that harsh landscape was brute strength; and there was an air of silent toil in an unforgiving land, building homes for the next generation.

Next to it was another photograph, in black-and-white this time, of some of their great-grandchildren. They were my wife and her five sisters as little girls, with bows in their identical pudding-basin hair, surrounded by mothers and aunts in 1950s summer frocks, and their men folk in dark Sunday suits and ties, holding their beers. This time the children were smiling shyly in the sun with a *Last Picture Show* innocence. In this photograph you could sense that chatter had replaced the long-suffering silence.

We finished tea and said goodbye to Auntie Dora. Like most of the family she still lived within a few miles of where she had been born, and her neat three-room clapboard house had been one of the early stops on my first visit to Tasmania.

Outside, the sleepy town was silent in the late afternoon. The shops were open, but there were no customers to buy the outdated clothes, hardware, souvenirs and faded knitting patterns with curled edges that filled the shop windows; and there was only an occasional car on the roads which took us out of town, roads which led only to similar towns where not much happened.

Not that our visit had been dull. The previous evening I had had to be on my toes to face the inevitable Pommy-baiting – all well-intentioned, but the Australians are dangerously practised at improvising seven- to ten-word put downs, and it is difficult to match them. I recall the first time I met Pete, in London; as we walked towards an Indian restaurant I asked him politely, "Are you hungry Pete?"

"Hangry? Jees, I could eat the arse off a rag doll," was his reply.

Thirty years later, as one of the guests left the same Pete's BBQ, he said, "Thanks for the barbie, Pete. . . I'm sure you'll do better next time."

"No worries. Next time I'll have the women working, not just chatting. Anyway, just leave your money on the plite by the door."

But that afternoon the photographs and the empty streets sleeping in the sun had released a heavy surge of the common pool of nostalgic memories of small-town childhood – the seemingly endless summers, lying in long grass gazing at the sky, thoughtful and alone, or with friends whose names and faces are starting to fade like languages learned at school but never practised; the lazy hum of bees in the late afternoon and the smell on clothes after rolling down grassy slopes; taking shelter under trees, waiting for the sun showers to end and the sadness of wasted, wet and windy days; the autumn nights curled up warm in bed under the roof as the wind gusted and the rain spattered on the windows through the night, and mornings luxuriating late in bed as the sun danced through the leaves.

The melancholic mood deepened as we moved on along the coast to the boarding school my wife and her sisters had attended, and we sank into her memories of a Catholic upbringing – the smell of beeswaxed floors, the swishing of the black habits of the nuns approaching, the candles, holy water, incense, prayer-mat knees, catechisms and the Stations of the Cross. Is it possible that I wasn't there? In my mind's eye, I seem to remember catching, long ago, a glimpse of them through their classroom window on a bright spring morning, far from the home of their mainly Scottish ancestors – the old country of 'meanness, sophistry and mist'. There they sat, cross-legged on the floor in their gymslips, bows in their hair, little hands clasped together and eyes shining up at teacher at the piano, as they sang out "Jesus loves me, this I know, because the Bible tells me so. . .". Get those girls together now and they will soon be convulsed with laughter at the memories of the nuns all those years ago: Sister Purity who held a ruler above their chilblained fingers on the piano keys and brought it down sharply whenever they hit a wrong note; and beefy Sister Hortensia who administered the holy rites of the mortification of the flesh by spanking them on their bare bottoms – up to the age of 15 – when they were caught sneaking a look out of the dormitory curtains at the boys passing with their trannies. They say that in their mothers' era robes were handed out at bath times to prevent the girls seeing their own naked bodies, and talcum powder was sprinkled on the water to avoid seeing their reflections as they climbed in. Catholics have a much more deeply textured tapestry of memories, and more substantial doors to push against and kick open than Protestants. I always envy them their lighting of candles for departed souls on Christmas Eve.

These sentimental associations were now starting to get complicated, seen through a double filter, with my wife's memories of her own childhood being overlaid with those of my own first trip to Tasmania. When I first arrived there in the 1970s, Australia was still dozing in the 1950s. It was a country of evening slide shows of visits back to the old country; meat pies, coleslaw and tinned fruit; echoing restaurants with plain white tablecloths, quarter-filled with men in ties and ladies in wraps with their hair done for the occasion; and just the beginnings of knowledge of wine, advertised by stiff didactic tutorials, usually delivered by the husband, audible across the room.

As evenings progressed men and women separated like oil and water. It is natural law that almost two-thirds of women's conversation and over half of men's is about people. But back then in Australia there was an earnest *National Geographic* magazine flavour about the men's talk and an avoidance of much that was personal. There was, on the other hand, a deep knowledge of their local communities, fed by bookshops stocked with dull, worthy publications and provincial newspapers padded out with snippets of local history rather than news hot off the press. Dozens of little theme parks were just starting up around that time to create the 'authentic Australian experience', with grainy photographs of defunct timber and bark factories, pictures of heavily bearded men tied to trees waiting to be taken to Sydney to be tried and hanged for crimes like cattle duffing and horse theft, and tree names unhelpfully in Latin.

There was, and still is, an engineer in most Australian men. A broken machine was a source more of pleasure and challenge than annoyance, and all the men present would gather round to advise. Not that there was no humour, and there was a wealth of good advice to Poms on how to deal with sharks, snakes and spiders in dunnies. And then of course there was beer and sport, and beer and sport.

This was a country that was still deeply conservative. The old monarchist PM Menzies had gone by 1966; but ten years later the Australians voted to support the Queen's representative, throwing out Gough Whitlam, their most attractive, able and progressive prime minister. And they were soon to vote to remain part of the UK rather than become a republic. In those years there seemed to be a residue of uneasiness and bleakness still detectable in the Australian soul. What often came to mind was 'clubbable loners'.

There is much in Australian art that reflects a loneliness, melancholy, silence and most of all wistfulness for lost roots. A 19th-century painting, *Gold Diggers Receive a Letter*, shows a burly miner's mates looking over his shoulder tenderly and enviously as he reads his letter from home; and another, showing a man also reading a letter in a wooden outback shack is called *From a Distant Land*. One of the most popular paintings in Australia – the country's equivalent of Trechikoff's green Asian girl – is a triptych by Frederick McCubbin, showing three scenes at the same spot over 20 years in the 19th century. In the first panel, the young man and his new bride have arrived in a clearing in the woods, with a covered wagon loaded with their possessions. He is cooking over the fire, while she stares into the distance, contemplating her new life in this remote outpost. In the second picture, smoke is rising from a wood cabin which has been built between the trees, and she stands with their baby. In the third, there is only the man; and he is no longer young. A town can now be seen through a gap which has been cleared between the trees; but the man is now sitting alone, beside the wooden cross that marks his wife's grave. My wife's grandmother would have been the generation after the last panel. More modern pictures show sad Aboriginal stick figures under spectacular sunsets with skies of sulphurous yellows gashed by burnt oranges; and ethereal isolated figures in empty dreamscapes; and brooding silhouettes on sea shores, 'the indifferent waters lapping at their feet'.

But that was 30 years ago, and money had been good for the country since then. We moved on to Hobart, where the exteriors of the old colonial sandstone buildings have remained untouched – Hobart Gibson's City Flour Mills 1896, Telegraph Hotel and the Customs House. But inside, the massive old beams and the heavy stone walls of most have now been refashioned tastefully behind slabs of glass into design centres and life enrichment galleries selling 'The Art of Tea' and 'The House of Herbs' and 'Colour Therapy Centres'. We spent the morning in the Saturday market in Hobart's Salamanca Place, a weekly event which has retained the feel of the 1960s more than similar places in Europe, but the flavour is more of affluence than of Woodstock.

At the end of that afternoon in Hobart we called at the cemetery where my wife's father is buried. She finds his grave. He was a local sports hero who died young. She wants to be buried with him. We wander, looking at the other gravestones. Many are of friends and relatives from this small town. After half an hour we start to drift towards the car, but she walks back to her father's grave. She stands for a minute, then five, then ten. . .

Later we set out along the coast again in search of the evocative landmarks of our earlier visits. But the old deserted farms had been reshaped into busy up-market cheese centres and chocolate factories with bustling car parks. In the evenings a slight shadow was cast across the sisters' conversation by a small scandal in the family history that has come to light.

At the end of the week my wife stayed on in Tasmania, but I left for the mainland with two of my in-laws to drive up the east coast to Sydney. We passed through little beach towns with the same stores, Coles, K Mart, bottle shops and Woolworths – which is a prestigious store in Australia – and long rows of beach and surf shops with pick-up trucks piled with boards. There were a few irritations, like the huge television screens in every store where beefy presenters with orange fake tans and ice-blue teeth spouted blokish sports babble from morning to night. But for those who like beach life this coast looked as good as it gets.

We stopped for coffee at a café with a garden sloping down to a bay far below and watched the waves coming in. A group of half a dozen boys in their 20s were at the next table. They were nice-looking kids with wraparound sunglasses and spiky hair. They had the build of natural athletes – they were probably surfers – with the compact physiques that come from active outdoor lives, not gyms. They asked if one of us would take their picture.

"Is that OK?" asked Baz, my brother-in-law, as he handed their camera back.

"Beaut, mate."

On the way out Baz asked, "You're off surfing for the weekend, are you?"

"No, we're going up to our mate's town."

"Why, is he crook?"

"No, he's just died."

"Oh. . . I'm sorry."

"No worries. It's all good."

We walked to the car.

"What did he say?" I asked. "His mate just died and it's good?"

"It's what the kids all say today: it's all good. That's the way they like to see things. Remember, they used to say 'it'll be apples', or 'you sweet?'"

My last day was spent in Sydney, which may arguably have now become the best city in the world. I do the same things each time I go there: I take a walk through the botanical gardens behind the Opera House and then sit and watch the ferries sliding in and out of Circular Quay, the sun glinting on the water under a sky which has always been cloudless when I have passed through. This month the Jacaranda trees, with their heavenly mauve blossoms, were in bloom. Healthy good-looking office workers sat at outdoor cafés eating food that is as wonderful now as it was dull back in the 1950s. This year the locals, who always complained in the past that the clothes in London are so colourless, are all wearing black and looking good in it.

But even here, in this successful modern city they cling on to their history. Down in The Rocks – the first convict settlement, but later the first place to have its buildings gutted and lovingly restored – there is a little section of road made from the wood blocks they used when they first paved the dirt roads a hundred years ago; and beside it there is a little display with faded photographs. The thirst for memories is still deep in their way of life even now that they have laid their ghosts.

After I returned, I asked my children, now in their 20s, if they have strong childhood memories. Their reply was unexpectedly sharp. "No," said one, and left it at that. The other said, "Childhood memories are for old people." He said he thought things just happen at the time and the memories that come later are different things. Maybe they were kicking against the irritating adult claim that childhood days are the happiest of our lives, while children just want to be grown-up and do what they want. It is food for thought that nostalgia and déjà vu are flawed and second-ranked emotions – sentimental and saccharine. But the deep and lingering impact of the extent to which it is woven into the Australian way of life would suggest not.

9

Belize

It was pitch dark as we climbed out of the six-seater plane. The airstrip was deserted and the only building barely visible in the distance was a shed at the end of the runway. We started to walk towards it, but there were no lights inside. The only sound was of the wind in the palm trees. We looked back to gesticulate to the pilot who was turning the plane round to leave. High up in his cabin, his black face lit by a cold green sheen from his instrument panel, he silently shrugged his shoulders in reply to our implied question and took off again. As the sound of his engine faded into the night, we sat down on our suitcases, and Henry said, "What now?" We could hear the sounds of the ocean somewhere near.

Ten minutes later, a heavily built figure trudged out of the darkness. We could just see his ponytailed dreadlocks, long shorts and flip-flops. He was carrying two large fish over his shoulder.

"Hi, mun," he said in a deep noncommittal voice.

"Hello...um...would you happen to know if a man called Dave is around? We are supposed to meet him. And do you know a hotel called the Banana Heaven?"

"Yeah... It's still being built. But we've got a place for you. It's not five-star, in fact it's maybe not one-star, but Craig says he thinks you'll like it, mun. It's a boat ride over to the other side." He picked up our two bulky cases effortlessly and we followed him down to a jetty. We stepped into a small wooden boat and off we went, the heavily over-powered engine shattering the quiet of the night.

Belize, to the south of Mexico, is a lush, sleepy jungle on the edge of the Caribbean. Its sources of income through the centuries have been piracy, logging and drugs. In the 1980s the value of its marijuana crop exceeded that of its official GDP. And then came the big money. Belize was one of the first countries to go Thatcherite and open up to foreigners, attracting a cast of shady characters and the cream of the cowboy money in the region. The main front for money laundering was growing bananas on vast plantations. Several of the landlords were absent, in jails in Florida.

We had arrived in its capital, Belize City, two days before. It is a rambling, ramshackle town of clapboard houses and a mainly Creole population of 'mister cools' in dark glasses and baggy jeans, cruising the unmaintained streets in ageing American cars, their fins dipping lazily as they negotiated the potholes, their sound systems on full bass. Music boomed out everywhere, mainly reggae.

Everything of importance in Belize was plotted at the bar at the Fort George hotel, and it was there that we had arranged to meet Craig. We had come to see whether his banana port in the south could be dredged to take bigger ships. The Fort George's bar lived up to its reputation in the guidebooks – an eagle's nest of polished tropical hardwood, ship's brass and old maps. It was smoky, noisy and crowded with a cast of pure Conrad characters, shipping agents, traders, speculators and outlaws. At one end of the bar was a pallid German with an eye patch who had come there to plant kilometres of orange trees in the south, but, huge investment as this was, we were told that this was just a front for his real business there. "Don't go near him," we were warned. Holding court in a corner was a tiny ageing taxi driver in a baseball cap worn back to front. We later found that he was Skinny, and he had some mysterious monopoly power over taxis in Belize. And in another corner a tall Dane of extraordinary good looks, known to be a member of an international Marxist group with an unknown agenda, was talking to one of the Mennonites, who did much of the real work in the country. Presiding over the centre of the bar was Craig, grey-haired, handsome and overweight, with a winning Irish smile and easy bar-stool charm. "Good to see you at last," he said with a strong handshake. He was both welcoming and challenging; we were funded, not by Craig himself, but by the Overseas Development Administration, and Craig was wondering what sort of animals he had been sent. It became clear that he expected practical people, when he later asked, "By the way, can you fly a Cessna six-seater?"

"What !?... Er... no," I said.

Craig turned to a tall black man a few metres away, Delton, his regular pilot.

"Can you fly these two down to Big Creek tomorrow? They are going to stay at Bonnie's place at Placencia."

"Yeah."

In this country of studied cool, Delton was the coolest. The next day he walked us out to the little plane, closed the doors carelessly as if it were his car, fastened his seat belt and took off with no formalities or checks. On the way, looking down over the Belizean jungle, he told us that Craig himself had actually been nervous about flying in small planes when he first arrived, and to calm his nerves Delton had once stopped the engine at 5,000 feet, taken the keys out of the panel and thrown them out of the window. As Craig turned white he explained, "This is just to show you how safe this plane is," as he glided down smoothly to land a few minutes later with no engine power.

The hotel at Placencia was a set of beach shacks at the end of an isthmus, run by an American couple in their early 30s. They would probably return to the US in the end, but had no immediate plans, in fact no plans at all. Like many young Americans from the Midwest they were effortlessly practical, seemingly able to fix broken generators, radios, plumbing, anything – given a little time. They could tell you what weather was coming two days before. Dave had a greying ponytail, and Bonnie was a sturdy attractive woman whose face was just starting to harden; you could tell she had no children and probably believed she never would. But even they, so capable, seemed a little in awe of Clint, who owned the hotel, and made occasional visits from Florida. Clint was a tough customer, a heavily built, central castings Vietnam veteran, with a gravelly southern-accent voice and dark glasses. He was putting on weight. Most of his conversation consisted of assignment of degrees of seriousness to the problem of the hour. There were three categories: we were in shit; in deep shit; or, worst of all, in serious shit. The two companions he had brought with him, dressed in photographer's jackets with hundreds of pockets, hung on his every word.

Although there was a circuitous road that can get you to Placencia, few people used it. The guests arrived by water. They drifted into Bonnie's bar around sunset – travelling people, yachties and American drop-outs in their late 30s. Many of them had given up their jobs in the States for a year or so, and were no longer in a hurry to return; life was easy on this idyllic beach and the marijuana was cheap. Some travellers came from unexpected distances. In the first week, two Australian girl smugglers, aged about 25, came into the bar most nights. They were tiny, attractive and feminine, and very independent. They lived on their boat, which was anchored out in the bay, and sailed in and out of the inlets between Honduras and Belize by night. Shorter visits were made by wealthy, big game fishermen, tough-talking Hemingways.

Evenings were talked away in Bonnie's low-beamed bar, looking out to sea through latticed wood laced with vines, watching the sun setting and the lights coming on in the cabins of the yachts moored offshore, listening to the sound of the sea outside and the breeze blowing in from the ocean, jangling the shell chimes hanging from the bar. When the evening light died the barman brought out oil lamps, which made the sunburned faces and bronzed limbs glow in the subdued light, and made the whites and pale blues of their clothing seem luminous. The bar, decorated with sharks' teeth, driftwood and beach debris, was thatched with dried grass, which rustled in the wind. The music played was carefully hoarded, esoteric, country and rock music, most of which was unknown in England; but one better-known record stays in my mind from those evenings: it was Joni Mitchell's '. . . the wind is in from Africa, last night I couldn't sleep'.

In the days we worked out of Craig's huts beside the port. He was a big man in many ways. On our first morning he came out of his hut beaming, and shouted to his administration manager, "Earl, we've just been asked by the Minister if we can employ two of his cousins as drivers. So can you buy a couple of cars for them this afternoon? There's money in the special items account. . ." We were astonished to find that he had been a bank manager in Northern Ireland before he came to Belize to become a regulator, a negotiator with the EU over banana quotas, and a plantation owner himself. And then there was Mary, his beautiful wife, also Irish, and in her 40s. Every week, on the top floor of their colonial timber home, she served us wonderful food on bone china and Irish linen tablecloths, looking out over the water, candles flickering on the windowsills. Many years later a casual inquiry elicited the news that Craig had died – he was always overweight – and I found my eyes misting over as those warm, elegant evenings on the edge of the jungle with the tirelessly amusing Craig, and Mary in her pristine white cotton shirts and jeans came flooding back. During one of those evenings he asked me, "If I were to throw all this in and try to get a job back in London, how much would I need to earn to keep the same standard of living?" I mischievously said "About £200,000." But there was some truth in it. There are many sorts of paradises and this was close to one sort. Mary missed her children, but had no desire to leave her new home.

Not that much happened in Placencia except for the weekly dance just along the beach. It started on Friday at sunset and finished around 8am the next day – half a day of lazy Bob Marley records, marijuana haze and slow dancing. My problem there was Brenda, a tough middleweight of a girl who had run away to Belize City when she was 16 but had later returned to her family. Now the bad girl of the village, she would have been pretty if not for a 16-inch neck. And Henry had told someone to tell her that I liked her. So much of the Friday evenings was spent avoiding the attentions of Brenda, who would materialise from dark corners and drag me onto the dance floor. Wonderful as her dark-chocolate skin looked, there was something disconcerting about holding a girl whose unyielding flesh was contained by skin stretched tight as a snare drum.

Slowly, the warm, lazy exhalations of the jungle went to work on our molecules. Henry mutated a little and turned out to be rather a Conrad character himself. A fives champion at his public school, an orienteer, and a young man, like Lord Jim, of general ability, he spent much of his time diving in the muddy water in the port's channel, unconcerned by collisions with the half-tonne manatee fish that inhabited the murky depths of the mangrove swamps. But strong character as he was – he later rose to be the managing director of his engineering company – he gradually fell under the spell of Clint. A few 'man's crept into the end of his sentences, and then 'mun's, and by the fourth week he had a slight American accent.

On one of our last nights there we walked a mile along the coastal track to the next set of beach huts. They were more refined than Bonnie and Dave's, and run by a strikingly beautiful American couple with two equally beautiful children. All four had the same long blonde hair and honey-coloured skin, and were dressed in expensive-looking white calico that night. Their guests that evening, sitting around a patio under the stars, were from the British army, 2,000 of whom used Belize's hostile terrain for jungle warfare training. They included some of the officers' wives, and the field marshal of the British army. Some amiable banter started between the two heavyweights, Clint and the field marshal, and gradually they squared off to walk their very different wits against each other – the field marshal, with his precision-instrument dry humour, tight upper-class vowels and, presumably, a double-first in classics from Oxford; and Clint with his detached *Deer Hunter*'s drawl. The exchange was riveting. In the end Clint probably won by about 60 points to 40; but no ill feeling was detectable. The evening ended when Clint told his acolytes that they had to be up early tomorrow. "Yeah, man," they said.

"Where are you off to?" asked the field marshal.

"Hunting," said Clint.

"What for?"

"Crocodiles."

10

West Pakistan, 1971

A ship had slipped silently into the port entrance just after dark and dropped anchor in midstream. Everyone in Karachi seemed to know about it, and the atmosphere was combustible. It was rumoured that there were 600 mutilated bodies on board – West Pakistanis massacred in East Pakistan in the first weeks of the war that was soon to lead to independence for Bangladesh. If the rumour proved true, the vengeance would be terrible. There would not be an East Pakistani left alive in Karachi. In the few weeks I had been there I had seen the rage on the faces of the demonstrators. "Keep back," I was told as I watched the marches from the roadside. "If they see a foreigner you don't know how they'll react."

But when the sun rose the next morning the ship had gone. Whatever cargo it had on board had been unloaded in the dead of night; and we drove into the office on a normal day, past night workers huddled in heavy woollens around braziers on the edge of the desert in the cool fresh morning sun. The desert, which stretches for 500 miles north of Karachi, gets cold at night in the winter months.

As we opened the car doors the bearers poured out of the entrance to carry our briefcases the last ten metres to the vast open-plan port office where we were working; and as soon as I sat down the Coca-Cola wallah rushed over to me. He was a skinny youth, terrified of the world, and his duty was to dispense a maximum of two bottles a day to each member of the staff, and to keep a strict record. He asked if I would like my first drink. "A little later," I said. It was 8.15am. He appeared to have taken a special liking to me because he thought that I was interested in record players. It seemed that he had been told that there was a pile of *The Phonogram Monthly* magazines in the back of our car and thought they were mine.

"You have phonogram magazines, sahib?" he said, smiling, waggling his head.

"Er. . . no. . . oh, yes. . . I know what you mean. I don't, but Mr Hill has a lot of them." Mr Hill was the boss.

He looked disconsolate. "Oh, I think they are yours, Sahib."

"Never mind. If you are interested in records, I am sure that he'll let you borrow the magazines to have a look."

"But I am not wanting to ask the Mr Hill." The gap in status was too wide.

"OK, I'll get them for you. Are you thinking of buying a record player, or are you just interested in them?"

"I am. . ."

We were interrupted by the secretary, an elegant young woman, clearly from a good family. She handed me 20 pages of typing that I had given her the previous afternoon. It looked immaculate.

"Well, that was fast, Asma," I said.

"I hope it's all in order; and I have corrected some grammatical errors," she said with the slightest of reproving smiles.

"What!" I said, with theatrically exaggerated horror. "I didn't know I made mistakes."

"I will show you."

We sat down and she patiently explained the ten or so mistakes, with phrasing calculated not to offend – that, "In Pakistan we may use the auxiliary verb slightly differently." She spoke with a combination of authority and modesty, of distance and intimacy. In her mid 20s, she had the assured beauty of a woman much older than herself. She was correct on eight of the ten grammatical points.

As she glided away, the schoolroom silence that usually prevailed at the other end of the office, the Pakistani section, was disturbed. We had been separated into foreigners and locals because who sat in front of whom was a matter of sensitivity and Byzantine complexity in Pakistan. Don Hill, the project manager, a handsome laconic American, had learned about the consequences of tinkering with hierarchical distinctions early on, when he insisted, US style, that the locals, even the cola wallah, should call him 'Don'. They complied reluctantly, and from then on he was 'Donsir'.

The commotion at the other end of the office was caused by a visit from the Director of the port at which we were working. He strode into the room, threw a heavy report on the desk and began to give the local Pakistani project engineer a dressing-down. His voice rose, his face was suffused with rage, but his vocabulary was endearingly archaic. "This is totally unacceptable. . . I shall not beat about the bush. . . You must pull up your socks." The local manager stood with his head bowed, his expression downcast; but within a few minutes of the Director's departure, he had summoned his own deputy and was heard to administer the same dressing-down. It was part of office life in Pakistan. Everyone got their dressings-down, except for Asma.

Later in the day the Coca-Cola wallah approached nervously and asked if I had got the magazines yet.

"No, not yet. . . But I can see you are really keen. I'll go and get them."

I turned to look for the driver of the car with the magazines in the back, and found that, as usual, he was already looking at me. He was another reason for my feeling uneasy about what might have happened if things had turned ugly when the ship came in. He was a massive Punjabi with a low forehead and the heavily oiled hair of a 1950s rock'n'roll singer, and spoke little English. He wore mascara and when he drove the car his unsmiling doglike eyes watched me constantly in the front mirror. He came to the car with me and carried back a pile of the magazines to my desk. The Coca-Cola wallah had an expression of beatific expectation, but his face fell when he saw them.

"No, sahib, no. . . it is the phonographic magazines I am wanting." He struggled to find the vocabulary. ". . . the magazines with the ladies with no clothes on."

Pakistan was not a country with ladies with no clothes on. Every morning, just before we left for the office, we watched a Pakistani woman dressed in a black burqa, with only her eyes visible, leave the house opposite. Behind her were four little black tents in decreasing order of size – her daughters. We had asked the Pakistanis we had come to know, "Why do the women have to cover themselves so completely?"

They insisted that men would find it difficult to control themselves if the women were more exposed. And they were right. In the markets, Carol, the wife of one of our group, and blessed with an athletic rounded figure and blonde hair – was bumped into time and time again, from behind and in front and from left and right, some of the men feigning implausible losses of balance and grabbing on to her breasts to prevent their falling. They affected deep apologies, and giggled to each other as they wandered off – demonstrating with blinding clarity that not only does the burqa fail to prevent lustful thoughts, it does the polar opposite.

An eerier event occurred one weekend when we went to a deserted beach a few miles out of the city. After an hour or so, lying quietly sunning ourselves, we noticed heads peering over the sand dunes surrounding the beach. After a time a young man came down on the beach, and then another and another, and sat quietly in the sand. Very gradually they moved closer and closer until they sat in a circle around us about five metres away. All young, all silent and expressionless to the point of catatonic stupor, they sat cross-legged and stared at Carol in her bikini.

But strangest, and most disturbing, of all was the servants' party. As the honoured guests, we were seated on wooden chairs at the front. The food was wonderful and after it was finished the men began to dance. The music was a hybrid of Pakistani and Western pop music, and the men were dressed up in the height of fashion; that is, the fashion of precisely ten years earlier, with winkle pickers, heavily greased DAs and their best white shirts with the collars turned up. They danced together with the merry abandon of a cub scout troop allowed into an adult party. I whispered to one of our group, "They obviously don't let the girls dance"; but a minute later the men left the floor, the music switched into Asian, and out from the kitchen swirled about ten girls, aged, maybe, 12 to 15. The older girls must have been married already.

The girls were not just made-up, they were painted, like Kabuki temptresses – with heavy rouge and dark-red lipstick. Unlike the boys, their dancing was mesmerising, with undulating hips and snakelike neck movements; but most striking of all were the come-hither looks of their kohled eyes, heavy-lidded and deeply sensual, which locked on to the eyes of the foreigners. Pure jailbait. They were hardly more than children. Who could have taught them these movements? It could only have been their mothers, who beamed in pride at the back of the room.

The food in Pakistan was wonderful, despite our first cook's attempts to keep us away from it. He had learned recipes from his father who, he was proud to tell us, was also a cook. They were for the meals that English gentlemen had always preferred, like toad-in-the-hole, shepherd's pie, bread-and-butter pudding and jam roly-poly; so whenever he asked what we would like for our evening meal, and we replied curry, he always found a reason to make one of his English throwbacks. And when we finally leaned on him to produce a curry it was less than wonderful. What could we do? We did not have the heart to sack him. But fortunately he managed to sack himself. On the first day he had asked for 10 pounds to buy the day's food at the market, but on the second day it was 20 pounds. "Why so much?" we asked. His head waggled philosophically. "Prices are high these days." On the third day the prices were still rising. He presumably thought that the foreigners had so little idea of the value of money that they would believe anything. So on the day he asked for 100 pounds we let him go. We worried that we had missed something and that he had not in fact been fleecing us. But in the new cook's first few days we were pleased to find he needed only three pounds a day for food.

Karachi was alcohol-free, as we discovered on our first visit to a restaurant – an old stone building, with walls decorated artistically with old printing blocks. We ordered our food and then beers to go with the curries. There was a look of alarm amongst the waiters, followed by a short discussion and then the senior man, tall and with a turban, stepped forward with the bad news.

"I am afraid we do not serve beer, sir."

"What?" said Richard. Normally congenial, he was irritated. But the rest of us made the connection – that Muslim countries were often dry.

The senior waiter tried to placate Richard. "But, sir, we can offer you some special tea."

"No, I don't want tea, just bring me water."

"But sir, I can recommend our tea."

"Please, I. . . do. . . not. . . want. . . tea."

He was getting annoyed, but his wife was one step ahead. She patted her husband's arm. "Quiet dear," she said, and turning to the waiter, " I'll try the special tea."

Richard sat glowering as the waiter poured the amber liquid from the teapot spout until he saw the beginnings of a foamy head in his cup.

All such a long time ago. There was so much more. . . The war did get very ugly, but it never impinged on our lives as we had feared the night the ship came in. A few years later we heard that our client, the Port Manager, still in his 50s, had died at his desk, possibly of apoplexy. And 20 years later I walked into a café in Manila and there was the boss, Don Hill. He looked tired and too thin, but his sardonic humour had not faded. Of the Coca-Cola wallah, our mascaraed driver and the cook I know nothing. But only recently, 35 years on, I returned to Karachi and sat in a meeting opposite a neat white-bearded man in his 60s; he came up later and said, "We have met before."

I stalled, and said, untruthfully, "I think, maybe, I can recall. . . Was it. . .?"

He rescued me. "It was one afternoon in 1971. You came into our office to see the director but he wasn't in; so you waited and we talked about many things for a couple of hours. I was about 25 then. After that I always wanted to visit England. But I never did."

Asma I can see now as a grey-haired matriarch, still distantly beautiful in her late 60s, presiding over a large family in the Pakistanis' much-loved city of Lahore, or in the foothills of the mountains of the north. She would not remember me.

11

Sunset in Croatia

One afternoon, during a long working lunch on the Croatian coast, I fell just a little, and harmlessly, in love for a few hours.

She was an interpreter and had seemed aloof, frosty and slightly impatient with her work earlier in the day. But she lasted well through three hours of detailed discussion at the port offices and was pleasant enough by the end of the morning.

After the meeting finished a group of us went down to the harbour where we had heard that they were building a unique – or at least a first ever – ocean-driven organ. It was a simple structure in an Italian stone of blinding whiteness in the cold winter sunlight. It worked by absorbing the power of the waves to make a form of music, a haunting siren sound. Although this was her town she had not seen it before, and she said that it was good to have foreigners to talk to from time to time. She suggested that we adjourn to a fish restaurant that she thought we would like, in a cove just outside town.

Over lunch she removed her heavy spectacles and I saw that her sharp features were as attractive as I had suspected. Her eyes were an unusual tawny amber which seemed illuminated from inside. It emerged that she had set up an English school and working as an interpreter was an occasional sideline. She was still a little difficult to warm up, until I mentioned a couple of unusual events that had happened in London that year. They passed the others by, but I saw her eyes light up.

It emerged that she had stayed in London for a time in her 20s; and she asked to change seats and plied me with questions. Her own observations about her time in London came from unusual angles, and later she changed the subject to the atmosphere in her town during the war with the Serbs, usually off limits for the Croatians. We brought others into the conversation from time to time, but all I really remember from that afternoon was her. As the lunch drifted on past 3pm it was one of those lazy afternoons when I would have liked time to freeze. One of the things she mentioned was that an eminent visitor – a film director – had observed that the Dalmatian sunsets were the most beautiful in the world. And with fierce national pride she insisted he had been right. She said I should make sure I saw it, just before she excused herself to prepare lessons for her students.

A few hours later, back in my hotel, I noticed the light fading and, remembering her suggestion, walked out to a vantage point overlooking the bay. There, up amongst the rocks, the yew trees and the bleached stone of the cliffs, looking down over the islands that line the Dalmatian coast, there was something Homeric in the air, especially at twilight, with the last sunlight glinting off the sea. I stood there for a while thinking about the morning and the girl. The romantic resonances had left all my senses open wide as the sunlight faded. And suddenly there it was. . . taking me far back in time.

In that final moment of life when the dying spirit flares up for one last time and then slowly fades to a single intense point, when all the words and people and places have slipped away, the last memory calling me back into the past and beyond will be that of those haunting childhood sunsets, those wispy drifting clouds of red and pink streaked high up against the pale blue sky of Northern Ireland, a timeless, achingly lonely beauty at twilight. And here I was seeing it again, the sun settling slowly, as it did all those years ago, into a red globe out at sea, gradually falling below the horizon, until all that was left was a line of gold. For a minute or two the colours in the distance fade, except for a thin red contour along the top of the clouds; and then slowly new colours appear, as the clouds are underlit in a soft, dusky pink by the now invisible sun. I sat, chin in cupped hands, looking out over the water as the lights from the islands started to glimmer across the bay and a last small boat headed out to sea and darkness fell. A lighthouse started to blink in the distance along the coast.

There in the dark I wonder if I will see another of these sunsets again. If so, it will fade as quickly as tonight, almost flaunting its transience. It may be the closest I will come to the beckoning and ever-receding dream of happiness – unattainable, by its nature evanescent and deeply rooted in the sadness of the loss of childhood. Below, at the foot of the cliffs, I watch the water in the moonlight lapping soundlessly at the Croatian shore, as it always will, long after I am gone.

12
Moscow in 1971

"Your plane will be delayed," said the man behind Karachi's Aeroflot check-in desk abruptly, as if he was issuing a reprimand. No explanation was given. The time was 10pm, and the plane eventually took off at midnight – the next night. For the intervening 26 hours we were forbidden to leave the airport on the grounds that the plane could go 'at any time', and we sat on the floor amid women in black burqas and men in baggy pyjama-like robes and their vast packages tied with rough twine. By that time we – myself and a friend with whom I had been working in Pakistan – were wondering about our decision. We had changed our ticket back to London from British Airways to Aeroflot, who had offered us three days' free accommodation in Moscow. This was 1971 and few people made that journey.

Out on the tarmac the four-engine propeller plane towered over us like an old warhorse, scarred with dents and painted a fading battleship-grey. But our first sight of the inside of the plane was encouraging. At the top of the ramp stood an air hostess with the hourglass figure and bleach-blonde hair favoured in 1950s Pan-am brochures. Behind her was the door of a small compartment with a deep carpet, flocked wallpaper and red mafia-rococo armchairs with gilt cabriole legs. But this, alas, was not for us. It was for the VIPs of the classless society; and so we moved on down the aisle, past flustered traders and farmers heaving their massive parcels onto the overhead racks, until we found our seats, and – I hesitate to record this, fearing an undeserved loss of credibility – found myself looking at a goat on one of the seats in front of us.

An hour or so later the plane finally groaned into the air – it was one of their dreaded Tupolevs which fell regularly out of the sky – and flew off into the darkness. But by that time we were fast asleep.

We were woken from our sleep of the dead at 3am. The plane had arrived in Tashkent and we were to be fed. Unable to understand the Russian announcements, we fell in behind the crowd as they were marshalled out onto the runway to sprint through torrential rain to a people's eating palace, a bare, echoing hall where 250 meals were laid out. It was gristle on cold toast. Even after one and a half days without food, we couldn't touch it; nor did most of the other passengers.

Back on the plane we fell into another restless half-sleep, fitfully conscious of the straining of the propeller engines, until wakened by the early morning light. Even hungrier and thirstier, we asked for some water. The air hostess was helpful, but the Russians spoke no English in those days.

"War Tur?" She frowned.

"Water. . . wasser. . . drink." We hunted for a linguistic root in common, but no connection was made. We tried again.

"Water. . . aqua. . . hydro. . . eau."

The last word worked. Her stern face was transformed by a dazzling smile, and she returned five minutes later, proudly proffering two small but elegant bottles of water. We thought she must have brought them from the VIP compartment; and we had both gulped down part of the contents before we realised that it was eau de cologne.

We landed at Moscow on a cold, crystal-clear and sunny morning. At immigration, they saw that we spoke no Russian, and telephoned the customs chief. He arrived in a uniform like a field marshal's, his cement-mixer chest covered with medal ribbons. He said nothing but directed a granite stare at a point about two feet above our heads, examining the backs of our heads in the mirror behind us, a fixture which we found later to be standard at Russian airports. After about a minute he diverted his nerveless eyes directly into mine. "Remove all items," he said, pointing to our cases. At first he seemed surprisingly uninterested in our possessions – our Western clothes and books and even the little collection of semi-precious stones I had picked up in Karachi. Until he came to our report – 'The Karachi Port Development Plan'. He fished it out as if it were a kilo of cocaine, and opened it with a flourish. "What is thees?"

"It's a report."

"What is it concerning?"

"The port of Karachi."

He smelled state secrets. In the Soviet Union's maps it was standard practice for the ports to be shown a few degrees away from their actual coordinates, just in case the maps fell into the hands of Americans planning bombing raids. And so he began to read to the assembled customs officers. His voice was deep and sonorous.

"The port of Karachi has three options. It may dredge a new channel; it may extend into the Western Backwater; or it may acquire new land." He raised his eyes briefly, then looked down again and read on through the whole page. The attendant staff looked stern. He stopped again and impaled us with a fixed stare, as if expecting a confession. Then he resumed:

"There are several options for construction: they include sheet piles, caissons and piled concrete decks..."

About half a page later his voice tailed off. "You may repack your bags."

The Intourist hotel was adequate, if institutional. It had the box-like rooms of a hospital annexe, with metal rather than wooden fittings on the windows and skylights. We were greeted sourly by the *dezhurnaya* for our floor, a dough-faced Madame de Farge with a faint moustache who kept guard at the end of our corridor and held our keys when we were out. She silently handed us a cardboard notice in English, instructing us to rest until the Intourist guide arrived. This was not unwelcome, as the eau de cologne was still passing through our systems.

Our guide for the day was a sturdy woman in her early 30s, dressed in the clothes our mothers had worn when we were children – a windcheater, a heavy skirt, a felt hat with a feather and galoshes. She carried a long list of sights, with a paragraph of the same length on each. By this time we were realising that we had become part of a group. She counted us as if we were a school party, marched to the door and signalled to us to follow.

Outside the hotel the low winter sun brought a slight warmth to the air, but there was little to illuminate. Our first sight of Moscow was in line with expectations drawn from the many black-and-white photographs we had seen in the West – in the grey brutalist concrete buildings devoid of signs or colour or painted windowsills. Winter had not quite ended and there was no greenery, flowers or trees. Above all, there were no advertising hoardings or shop displays.

The first stop was the Kremlin and Lenin's embalmed body. Outside his mausoleum a long silent queue stretched out past the onion-domed towers beyond the gates. The faces, at the end of the biting Russian winter, were blank and pallid, but most of those in line were unexpectedly well-dressed – in sombre, sensible, almost funereal black and grey, but looking warm and respectable as they stood in the last traces of the tired, end-of-winter snow. There were no jeans and none of the cultivated scruffiness that had taken over European dress in the 1960s. Very few wore spectacles. Maybe it was better that way in Russia. We noticed that eyes attracted to our Western clothes slid quickly away. Meeting no-one's eyes meant avoiding trouble. They 'saw all but showed nothing'; and said nothing. The sound of the Kremlin was of silence. I hardly saw a smile that first afternoon.

As we left the Kremlin we were diverted to watch the new brides who, by tradition, came to lay their bouquets on the eternal flame for the Unknown Soldier outside the walls. The only Russian women seen in the West at this time were the burly women who won every field event at the Olympics. But here we glimpsed for the first time the beautiful Russian girls we were to see blossoming a generation later, after the end of the Soviet Union. A pity about the hair, though. At least half the young brides had chosen for their wedding day an offal-coloured henna or orange dye that had seemed to have gone badly wrong.

The next stop was the market – a long shed under tarpaulins with wooden trestle tables bearing a few small, blackened turnips, potatoes, beetroots, soil-caked cabbages and tins of cheap red caviar. The stallholders, in from the fields, and flushed red in the icy draughts, huddled in their thick peasant coats and rubbed their mittened hands together to try to keep warm. Standing too long in the cold amid the stench of rotting vegetables, our group was impatient to move on. But our guide's eyes were shining. To her this was heaven. She eventually bought two tiny beetroots, probably for soup.

Then on to GUM, *the* department store of Moscow. Its cavernous unlit shop windows were sparsely furnished with displays of matronly coats, outdated suits, wooden toys, old-fashioned record players, Russian watches, matryoshka dolls and fur hats that lacked the style of Julie Christie's in *Dr Zhivago*. One item stood out – it was a single Gibson guitar, alone in its window, and illuminated like an icon. We asked our guide if it was '*pokazukha*', an expression that we had learned meant 'window dressing, just for show'. For once we got a little smile of affirmation.

We ended the day in an Intourist restaurant, memorable for a one-hour wait to be served, and two waitresses brawling like ageing hippos in front of us, ending up on the floor, in a flurry of old army surplus pants, Rubenesque thighs and black suspenders.

The next morning Comrade Nyetova, as we had called our guide, was not due to arrive until 11am; and the Intourist notices told us never to leave the hotel without a guide. So we did.

We walked outside, hailed a taxi, and asked for "The Tretyakov Gallery?"

"Jawohl. . .no problema. . ." he said, almost dragging us into the cab.

"Where you leev at?" he asked as we settled in our seats.

"London."

He became very excited. "Ah. . . Americanos. . . dollarinos."

"That's right."

"Marks and Spencer's," he said triumphantly.

He drove off, but at the first traffic light took his hands off the wheel, and suddenly they were inside my pants. He tugged at the elastic and scrutinised the label. It was indeed Marks and Spencer's. We heard later that you could barter two or three pairs for a serviceable Russian camera.

Twenty minutes later he stopped at our destination, and there it was – a statue of Yuri Gagarin and a sculpture of a spacecraft on a concrete plinth. We nodded approval and waited for him to drive on. But this was as far as we were going. He chattered away in Russian with a big smile. He clearly had no idea of where the Tretyakov Gallery was, and after five minutes of non-communication we paid him and got out. As he drove off he shouted, "Bobby Charlton!" at the top of his voice.

We turned to walk back the way we had come, and spent the afternoon exploring the city on our own. Only as it was getting dark did we find from our little guidebook that there were eight Intourist buildings in Moscow and we did not know which was ours. Nor could we follow the tiny map. At a loss, we tried to ask a passer-by for help, and another, but the language barrier was too great. Then one took our problem to heart. She scrutinised our map and jabbered away in Russian. Then she stopped another passer-by; and then another; and soon there were ten on our case. More than that, the silent dour-faced Russians became excited, and were transformed by beaming smiles. Somehow they communicated that our hotel must be near some well-known building; and then they started to do charades, beginning with something like a 'close to?' mime. One mimed kicking a football. We shook our heads. We had not seen a football stadium nearby. Then another did an elegant impression of ice-skating. But, again no; if there was a skating rink near our hotel, we hadn't noticed. By then there were 20 people attracted by the noise; and one simulated a dive and then a breast stroke. . . and. . . yes, I remembered, I *had* seen a swimming pool across the road. "Yes. . . Da!" I shouted. Everyone clapped. They hailed a taxi for us and waved as we drove off. It was my first experience of something that was to recur again and again – the contrast between the dismissive coldness of their officials and the wonderful natural warmth of the Russian people.

We left for London the next day, this time in an Illyushin 62, the pride of their fleet. Modelled on the Western VC10, it was like a silver sculpted paper dart. They served us caviar rather than gristle and Georgian wine instead of eau de cologne.

At Heathrow, the customs, seeing we had come from Moscow, asked us to open our suitcases and we found that a quarter of our clothes were missing. We looked at each other and said almost simultaneously, "The *dezhurnaya*?"

13

Angola

Of the 200 countries in the world, the worst of all in the 1990s may have been Angola. When the Portuguese colonial rulers left in 1975, they committed economic sabotage as they fled. They smashed the machinery and poured liquid concrete down the drainage pipes. The next day a civil war started between the rivals for power, or more precisely for Angola's diamond mines, and it lasted for the next 27 years.

Despite the blinding equatorial sun overhead, there is a deep darkness about Angola – in the abandoned overbuilt colonial ministries, the self-flagellation of the statues in the Catholic churches, and the Iberian gloom in the sombre wood-panelled corridors of the old hotels; but most of all in the dour hopelessness in the faces in the crowds. Oddly, in Mozambique, the Portuguese colony on the opposite coast of Africa, with the same history – of colonial rule until 1975 followed by a long and bloody civil war – the people have retained their sunny, open disposition. But not in Angola.

I had been warned against visiting. A laconic American who had been there told me, "If you want a contender for the modern heart-of-darkness award then Angola's your country."

"Worse than Nigeria?" I asked. I had been there a short time before.

"Yes. A different class... Nigeria's got energy, but Angola has been brutalised into apathy. The attitude there is 'if you can't eat it, fuck it and if you can't fuck it, break it'."

Heedless of the warning, I visited this modern heart of darkness in 1992. My possessions lasted only a few hours. Four of us had flown into Luanda, the capital, on an early morning flight, and transferred to the domestic airport to go south, to Lobito, to work on the reconstruction of the local port. Ours were the only white faces in the airport, but the eyes in the crowds seemed to look through ours. The echoing, hangar-like building was coldly devoid of atmosphere. Other African airports are theatres of noisy, demonstrative reunions. But in Luanda there was only apprehension, and bursts of ill-tempered banter between the anxious waiting drivers. Almost all there were men. It was no place for women.

My troubles began when, jostled by the crowd, I found myself a few yards behind the others in a dark corridor leading to the departure lounge. Passengers continued to push into the entrance to the corridor, and I became uneasy in the crush. It was also unlit, and getting very warm, when half a dozen hands dived into my pockets, like little silverfish. I think they were children, but could not see well in the dark. I tried to react, but my arms were partly pinned by the crowd. The hands withdrew, but then came again. By this time my arms could not move at all. When I emerged into the light I had lost my clutch bag, wallet, tickets, passport, credit card, money, everything. The others had already passed through into the departure lounge; it was quickly decided that they would go on, and I would follow them the next day.

I called our local company office and its administration manager came out to the airport. He was an overweight toad-like figure with eyes like frosted glass – a Portuguese/Angolan mestizo who did not hide his contempt for his visitor. He did not bother with a greeting.

"You should have looked after your luggage," he said.

I thought, 'well, that never occurred to me', but said, "Why, does this happen often?"

"Yes, all the time," he sighed wearily. I wondered why, if that was the case, he hadn't met us to take us through.

He continued, "They'll have taken your money and cards but thrown away the rest. Do you want to look outside for it?"

So we cruised along the road out of the airport for an hour, peering into the foul-smelling garbage, which was piled a foot high. But there was no sign of my wallet, clutch bag or any luggage.

"Unfortunately," he gave the word heavy emphasis, "we need to make an official report"; and we set off to drive the few miles to the police station in a heavy Mercedes through the narrow streets of a shanty town of dehumanising squalor. It was a no-go area, as I discovered later, where outsiders are regularly killed with impunity by the embittered residents. To have gone there that morning, in a Mercedes with a foreigner, was apparently an act of insanity.

The police, heavily armed in combat fatigues, looked bewildered by the arrival of a white face, and asked us to wait outside. We stood in front of a long wall, painted khaki. The sun was already high and starting to burn at my forehead. Some bony, threadbare chickens picked listlessly at a pile of rotting banana skins lying in the dust. I heard a snuffling sound behind me. At first I could not see where it was coming from; then I looked down and saw, at ground level, a small iron-barred hatch about 6" by 12" at the bottom of the wall. A couple of dogs, imprisoned inside, were fighting for air, their jaws on the ground and their mouths pushed up against the bars. Then I looked down again. The faces on the ground were not dogs' faces. They were prisoners, desperate for air and light.

An hour later we were allowed into the station, and asked to wait in an anteroom. In front of me was a screen which started about three feet from the ground. As we waited we could hear the sound of a man pleading with the police in the next room. At first we could see only their legs behind the screen. Then, with a heavy thud, the supplicant was thrown across the room, and fell on his knees where I could see him, and also the bottom half of the policeman standing over him. The partition prevented the policemen knowing that he was being observed. The prisoner's expression was one of terror and his head was bleeding. He crawled into a kneeling position with his hands raised to protect his head. Then an unwound metal coat hanger hit him full across his face. He screamed for mercy, gibbering; but the wire came down again and again. Blood was everywhere. I could see all this just six feet way, as could my Portuguese companion. I looked at him, mouthing, "*What* do we do?" He looked ahead like a sphinx, and raised his finger silently to his lips . . . "Quiet." The man was apparently there because he had also been stealing at the airport.

After another hour the same policeman called us in. He was tall, long-boned and muscular. He shook my hand with impersonal courtesy. His hand was cold, and there was just a trace of blood on the back of his forearm, which was whipcord hard. He took my statement and typed it out efficiently; and we drove back to the office in the centre of Luanda.

A replacement passport, valid for one journey, was provided by the British embassy in a couple of hours. This was a routine occurrence.

I slept in the company apartment that night. A driver slept in the next room, as a bodyguard. All night I heard gunshots, and sometimes screams, maybe every ten minutes. The breakdown of law and order had made the settling of scores easy.

The driver took me to the airport again the next morning. Outside the departure shed there was an angry crowd of about two hundred trying to get their luggage accepted at a counter protected by an iron grill seven-foot high. Nothing was being accepted and the crowd was screaming violently at the men behind the grill. My driver borrowed some money from me and spoke to one of the men behind the grill. He handed over the money and was then allowed to throw my case over the top, and it was carried away to the plane. He then took my ticket for processing. An hour later he came back, close to tears. "The plane has gone, Senor," – with my case, and without me. They had not announced the departure. We telephoned my co-workers at the other end, and fortunately they were able to race to the airport in the south to collect my case before it was stolen. The next day I joined them on the third attempt.

Lobito, in the south, was attractive enough. But one incident stands out in my memory. We were invited by the Portuguese for lunch, which was fish caught in the bay outside. After lunch, the servants washed up and emptied the wastebins containing the bones of the fish and scraps from our plates; and one of them started to take the waste bags downstairs to the garbage bin across the street. As he left, one of the Portuguese took me by the arm and led me to the window; he said "Watch." The fish bones were dropped in the bin, and the servant turned to walk back to the house. The instant the door closed behind him five men of indeterminate ages, all in filthy rags, scuttled out from different directions towards the bin. The bones were snatched by the most violent of them – a wild-haired man with mad, glittering eyes. He tore at the bones with his teeth, as the others clawed at him. The Portuguese man watched silently, with neither sympathy nor amusement. He said, "It happens every time."

Later, back in Luanda for a final couple of days, I saw the better side of the capital. The Portuguese who lived there took us in the evenings to some of the cafés and bars that had resisted closure, dotted along the beautiful natural bay. The more expensive restaurants used by the Portuguese had a convivial atmosphere, heightened by the alluring features of the Angolan-Portuguese mestizo girls – amber-eyed, wavy-haired and open-smiled. It was not difficult to see how Luanda has been a holiday paradise for the Portuguese 30 years before. But even in the pretty bars out along the bay, with the evening wind blowing in from the sea, the talk was of robbery, carnapping and murder.

My final encounter was with a lady customs officer as I left Luanda airport for London. She was stocky, thick-necked and surly, and she guided me into a dark area similar to that where I had been robbed on the first day. She asked how much I had in dollars. I told her in poor Portuguese, "Not much."

"How much?" she repeated.

I refused to answer at first, then capitulated. "OK, $500."

"Show me," she said. Again I refused, then reluctantly pulled the notes from my (new) clutch bag. She grabbed them and turned to run clumsily towards a door about thirty metres away. I was being robbed by a uniformed civil servant in the national airport. But, weighed down by layers of fat, she was easy to catch before she reached the door and I pulled the money back out of her hand, shouting to draw attention to her. But no-one paid any attention, and she lurched off like a sullen wounded hippo.

I was more fortunate than my friends, who were body-searched for diamonds.

14
Albania

When you visit Thailand it is impolite to show the soles of your feet. And in China you must never give a man a green hat.

The 'musts' in Albania are more demanding. The customary law of Albania, codified in the 'Kanun', requires you to kill any man who has killed your closest relative. It is central to Albania's traditions that blood must be avenged, with no exceptions. And after you kill the man, you must roll his body over so that he faces the sky. Another obligation is to kill any man who kills a guest of yours. Women, though, have no such obligations. They are excluded from the Code with the horrifyingly dismissive 'a woman is known as a sack, made to endure as long as she lives in her husband's house'. But there are some exceptions to the absence of women from the honour code – the Kanun requires a bride's father to include in his daughter's dowry a bullet – 'the blessed cartridge' – with which her new husband must kill her if she is ever unfaithful. These obligations must be complied with, not just for social acceptance. They are obligatory under the Kanun – the Code of Lek Dukagjin – which was drawn up in the 1400s, banned under the Maoist dictator Hoxha but then revived with alacrity after the demise of communism in 1991, especially in the mountains in the north of Albania.

The obligation to avenge, of course entails an unending chain of murders, and a town in the north was reported to have had 600 blood vendettas in operation just a few years ago. There are only three ways out. The targeted man can remain in his house, where it is forbidden to murder him, for the rest of his life. Or he can retreat to a windowless 'tower of refuge', where he will climb a ladder to the first floor and then pull it up behind him, and where food and drink will be left outside for as long as he stays. Or the relative of the deceased can refuse to avenge blood – accepting social disgrace and being served coffee with a bullet in the cup as a reminder of his loss of honour. He will also be banned from borrowing flour. Living by this honour code is particularly important in the mountains, where the old have a blessing for a baby, 'May he live a long life and die by the rifle'. Dying in bed is not for a man. His goal in life should be to accumulate enough honour points before his manly death by the rifle to merit a good memorial.

I didn't know any of this before I visited Albania. In fact I knew almost nothing about the country, and asked a friend who had worked there for two months if he would recommend going there. He replied:

"Well, if you take your own water." He remembered having no water for days when he visited; and he also remembered waiting to start work until a Mercedes was delivered to the man in the government who had to sign the contract.

I went on to say that I felt I knew less about Albania than almost any country.

"Many people say that," he replied. "For example, can you name ten Albanians?"

"Um. . . Enver Hoxha and. . . oh, Mother Theresa."

"Exactly. These are the two that everyone gets."

"How about their history?" I asked.

"Well, think of Ruritania. Until the First World War Albania was part of the Turkish Ottoman Empire, and that is why most of the people are Muslims. Then when the empire fell apart they looked around for a leader. Lacking anyone with a strong curriculum vitae to serve as king, they offered the Albanian throne to C B Fry – an exemplary specimen of the English gentleman that was revered at the time throughout the Western world. He had played for England at both cricket and football, held the world long-jump record, excelled at Latin and Greek at Oxford and became a writer and journalist. He was also extraordinarily good-looking, working as a nude model to make ends meet when short of money; and he was an admirer of Hitler. The Albanians offered him the post of Charles III, but he refused.

"Instead they got King Zog who ruled them for 20 years, mainly with Italian ministers that he drafted in. And after his demise following WWII, the country closed its boundaries to the outside world under the Maoist dictator Hoxha, who withdrew into isolation not only from Europe but even from Russia, a country Hoxha considered too liberal. For 30 years it languished as the poorest country in Europe. During that time visitors to Albania were rare. Then, like everyone else in that region, they got their independence in 1991."

"But you still don't hear much about them since they got their freedom."

"Well, they didn't start well. Do you remember the pyramid schemes of 1998? When the Albanians were persuaded to join in a racket like the old chain letters we got as children? They were told that they could get rich by enrolling other people in the investment scheme, and then lie back and wait for the interest to roll in. Thrilled by the new capitalist world, and the perception that you could make money for nothing, they sold their farms and houses to invest in the pyramids, and for a couple of years lived a wonderful life. Until it emerged that nothing was being produced and their money was gone. Now a lot of their income comes from remittances by Albanians who have gone to Greece and Italy to work. In Milan they are supposed to have outperformed the local mafia in all the main fields – narcotics, murder and white slavery."

But I decided to go. It was only for a week, on a short contract to work on the ferry port of Durres to make it more attractive to tourists. My first impressions were dispiriting. As I joined the check-in queue for the late-evening Tirana flight out of Milan, I saw ill-fitting clothes, low foreheads, eyes close together and the stressed look of children past their bed-times; and I started to wonder if I would have trouble at the airport when I arrived. But the taxi drivers massed at the arrivals hall were polite and orderly, and the car that took me from the airport was nothing like the rusty Ladas of most ex-socialist countries. It was a Mercedes and, if not new, it was very comfortable. I also noticed that most of the other taxis in the rank were also Mercedes, and, although some were the old 190s tanks, most of them were polished up like children's bikes. On the way, I asked the driver why there were so many.

"Oh, you'll see... the roads are very bad here," he said in surprisingly passable English.

"So you need to hire a good car?"

"No. I own this car."

"Oh... that's great... so... they are subsidised by the government?"

"No."

We were approaching the outskirts of Tirana, the capital, on a brightly lit four-lane motorway, past modern warehouses and shiny car showrooms, very different from the dimly lit, dilapidated approaches to most ex-socialist capital cities. The conversation drifted on to other areas, leaving me feeling puzzled.

The next morning, I awoke to a crisp December day, sunny and fresh, and set out to walk to the office, along wide cobbled streets, past elegant middle-European buildings of weathered stone, parks, gardens and bright new skyscrapers housing the banks and agencies dealing with the money coming in from the EU, the European Bank and the World Bank. The government buildings in the centre had been renovated and painted in tasteful yellow ochres and terracottas, reminiscent of Italy.

But the centre of Tirana also had a style of its own. All around the outskirts you could see tower blocks of flats, every one painted in garish pinks, greens, blues, purples and yellows, like children's play-bricks. They had been painted on the orders of the mayor of Tirana, who had decided that the austere grey apartment blocks built under Hoxha needed freshening up with a splash of colour. The extraordinary fact is that the mayor was an artist by profession – extraordinary because tasteful these colours were not. They were like the colours in the council depots of Liverpool when I lived there in the 1970s. The mayor must have delegated the bulk paint order to subordinates and told them to go for the cheapest on offer.

Much of the time that week was spent waiting for meetings with government officials. If they were good they were busy, and we – the local director of a development bank and I – adopted the practice of sitting in espresso bars outside their offices, waiting to be summoned by mobile phone, to avoid wasting half of the precious time they could give us. The espresso bars were comfortable places to wait, always full of smart, bright-eyed, talkative young people – still with something of that 'bliss to be alive in that dawn' that had followed the collapse of communism, but which had now faded in other Eastern European counties.

As we waited we talked a lot, and I asked about the Code of Lek.

"Yes, it's still important, but much more in the northern mountains. You should go there. They have a wild beauty of a type that you won't have seen anywhere else."

I also asked him about the Mercedes' which I was still seeing everywhere.

"How come there are so many of these expensive cars when incomes are so low?"

At first he gave the same answer as the taxi driver, that the poor roads mean that they need solid cars. But after day or two of getting to know him better he opened up.

"About two-thirds of our cars are Mercedes," he explained, "and at least three-quarter of them are stolen. In fact, they are often stolen to order by gangs who also do arms and drugs. There are over half a million cars in Albania, but in some years less than ten are registered. . . There is no pretence that the cars aren't stolen, but nobody does anything about it."

He even knew the routes by which they come in.

"The cars from Western Europe are stolen at night and have already crossed the border into Slovenia by the time their owners have woken up to find their cars gone. They are then driven to the port of Rijeka in Croatia, to be ferried to the port of Durres, 40 kilometres from Tirana. Nobody stops them coming in. The Albanians love their Mercedes."

"Are they never traced?"

"Almost never."

He also elaborated on Albania's new role as a transhipment centre for Asian drugs coming into Europe.

In the evenings, we went to the area that had once been out of bounds to ordinary Albanians. It had been reserved for the dachas of the Politburo – austere and colourless buildings in a 1960s minimalist style favoured by Hoxha. But it had now been transformed into a rabbit warren of hundreds of little restaurants and clubs, with throngs of young people looking cheerful rather than cool. One particular event struck me. It was a group of maybe two thousand soldiers wandering back through the centre after a big parade one evening, hats tilted Russian-style on the backs of their heads, full of smiles and chatter – so unlike the scowling uncommunicative military in other countries. Some even recognised me as a foreigner and wished me a good evening.

I never managed to figure Tirana out – the combination of the murderous traditions, the non-existent economy, the Mercedes, the shady sources of income, the cheerful coffee bars and the cosy restaurants... My week there had been too short.

Back in London we have a builder who has worked on our house occasionally and one of his workers is a gentle giant of an Albanian who does plastering. He has been here for ten years, and sometimes we mischievously tease him about his unreformed Albanian views. Recently my wife said, "Tell us what you would do if your little boy turned out to be gay?"

He grimaced and replied, "I would strangle him... with my bare hands."

"Come on, that's a bit strong."

"No," he said, turning a little serious. "I would." The odd thing, or maybe it's not, is that he is a lovely man.

15

Georgia

The taxi driver stared morosely at the sleet sliding down his windscreen. We were waiting outside a new bank building in Batumi, a small town in Georgia. Huddled in his thick overcoat he was muttering under his breath, biting at his words. His engine was running but the car heater was not working. Then suddenly and unexpectedly he switched into broken English, clearly for my benefit. What he was muttering was:

"All these banks. . . for what?. . . nobody has any money. . . look at them in their stupid suits."

He was glaring with nothing less than hatred at the young bank employees moving around silently inside their warm comfortable modern building. He started to become incoherent, but the gist was ". . . The young all work in banks, speaking English. . . and stealing the tiny incomes of the old and computer-illiterate. . . who are jobless."

Georgia has no oil, which means that, post Soviet Union, it has nothing. There had been great hopes of the new president, Shevardnadze, the much admired White Fox of Soviet diplomacy; but he turned a blind eye to Georgia's traditional corruption and gangsterism and the country went into economic meltdown. The low point came when Russia closed its borders to Georgia's exports, even their beloved Georgian wine. And now that the Russian buyers have gone there are no real jobs – only jobs in the 'government'; and there is little to govern. Stalin, a Georgian himself, had said about the building of the new communist state that 'you can't make an omelette without breaking eggs'. Eighty years later Georgia is left with the eggshells.

Later that morning we drove through the wet snow, past hunched Lowry figures in black leather jackets leaning into the icy wind, down to the port. We were there to help someone buy it. The ports, like everything in Georgia, were for sale to the highest bidder. The bids, however, might not be high; the port we saw when we reached its gates was like a faded monochrome photograph of Glasgow in the 1940s, the wind whistling through banks of outdated East German cranes silhouetted against a gunmetal grey sky. There was little activity. The cranes had nothing to lift except scrap, taken from the dismantled remains of Georgia's abandoned factories.

My companion in Batumi was an urbane Georgian in his mid 30s, called Mikhail. He was part of the group trying to buy the port. He had been a doctor in Moscow before turning to finance. After the port visit he suggested that we should drive up the coast, as his home town was only 50 kilometres away, and on the way he said – everything in Georgia is unplanned and a surprise – "We will have lunch with my family... But we will pick up my father first." It emerged that his father had been the mayor of the town before the Russians left in 1991.

Mikhail's father was waiting for us outside the town hall. I knew it was him even before we slowed down. He was '*Homo sovieticus*', unreconstructed – a stocky, stern man with a chest like a bullet-proof jacket. You could guess immediately from his demeanour that he deeply regretted the end of Russian rule. His voice was hard and assertive; and his smile, if it could be detected, was wintry.

We arrived at his house which was dominated by a cavernous formal dining room, with seating for 30, in faded beige and gilt baroque, with the light blocked out by thick heavy curtains. It was icy cold. But we ate in a warm room off the kitchen. At the table were Mikhail, his father, two uncles, a nephew about ten years old and their driver. Apart from Mikhail they spoke no English at all. The women – Mikhail's mother, an aunt and their domestic helpers – proudly served us the traditional meal, which tasted even better than the aromas that had preceded it. But they did not eat with us.

Five minutes into the meal I was finding conversation difficult because Mikhail, normally such easy company, kept putting his finger to his lips. "Shh. . . Don't speak now." In the end he had to explain. We were already on the third 'toast', and you were not allowed to speak except in toasts. Even at family meals it is the Georgian custom to elect a toastmaster, and there were still over twenty formal toasts to get through. The first toast had been to 'peace', for which the assembled are expected to stand when they drink. The second had been for the 'the hostess', and the ladies had smiled happily in acknowledgment through the kitchen door as they busied themselves over the stove. The next was to 'our country and the defeat of all enemies' (sometimes all have to stand for this one); then to 'all that have passed away', to 'life' and to 'love'. And so on and on. On the most important toasts the men stand and drink 'to the end'. One of the toasts seemed to propose that Mikhail pull his socks up and carry on the Georgian traditions more enthusiastically.

Ordinary conversation didn't seem appropriate. But I kept trying, and in the end raised some tepid smiles by mention of the Georgian footballer Kinkladze, Manchester City's legendary dribbler.

After that lunch many things started to come into focus. It turned out that it was the Georgians who had brought toasting to Russia. Both Stalin and Beria, his second in command and a serial rapist and torturer, were

Georgians, and they deployed the practice of toasting to murderous effect. It was their habit through the years of the great terror to oblige the highest-ranked members of the Politburo to come to Stalin's dacha at nights and drink until incapable. Only Stalin remained sober, by emptying most of his glasses into a bucket under the table. But everyone else was obliged to keep drinking, and when they had drunk themselves into defenceless stupors he would extract their deepest secrets.

The scars left by the straitjacket of toasting are deep. For many years travelling in the former Soviet Union countries I had watched the delegates at long dinner tables, awkward, devoid of conversation, almost silent. The former Soviet Union is not a land of smiles. Like Mikhail's father the apparatchiks started their careers in Komsomol, and keeping their jobs depended on keeping their mouths tight shut. Deeply suspicious of anyone outside their families, they no longer function well outside a narrow trusted circle.

A few months earlier I had sat at an evening banquet next to a bull-necked lady engineer with a brutal haircut who earlier in the day had blocked everything we were trying to do. "You do not understand our countries... We disagree with everything you have said," she commented, before we said anything.

"Do you have children?" I asked as the soup arrived.

"Yes."

"Ah, how many?"

"Two."

" Oh, so have I. Mine are 18 and 22. How about yours?"

"A little younger."

And so on. It was like digging turnips from frozen soil.

Then, from the top of the table came the call for her to propose a toast. She rose, relieved to be released from the ordeal of dysfunctional private conversation, to don her public mask. She raised her chin and, her eyes blazing with contemptuous insincerity, declaimed:

"Two days ago we met as professionals from countries that are far apart... Yesterday we worked together... And tonight we have become friends... We have forged links which will remain strong... And tomorrow we will sign the protocol on international integration and cooperation... So let us drink to... Friendship [*druzhba*, how they love that word] across international borders."

Ordinary Georgians are warm and spontaneous, but the apparatchiks like our lady engineer hate us. They blame us, the Westerners, for the loss of their special Party members' shops, their annual holidays on the beaches of Odessa and their crumbs of power.

Our business in Batumi completed, we took the train over the mountains through the ever deepening snow to the capital, Tbilisi. Built on hills, Tbilisi was unusually beautiful that day in the snow with its winding cobbled streets and little timber-fronted restaurants lit up by what seemed like fairy lights. Like many of the capitals of the former Soviet Union, its centre is now a mix of old stone building and modern steel and glass. As we checked into the hotel, I noticed on the reception desk one of those English language news sheets you often see in these countries with impenetrable languages. Its headline was that Georgia's economic growth rate, albeit from a low base, was now amongst the highest in the world, above China's; and inside I read for the first of fifty times, that the World Bank's 'Doing Business Survey 2007' had ranked Georgia the *number one reformer that year.* It had jumped from 112th in the world to 37th.

Had I been transported into another world? What was happening in Tbilisi that made it so different from Batumi? The answer was that the Rose Revolution had happened – three years before – and Shevardnadze had at last been removed. Shevardnadze had been 76 years old while the new president, Saakashvili, was 37. Saakashvili's policies were whatever Shevardnadze's were not.

We arranged to meet the deputy minister in charge of the ports in a fashionable restaurant on one of the hills overlooking the city. Mikhail hinted that I should smarten up a little. He said, "Why don't you put on that nice blue tie?" – embarrassed to be fussing; and we arrived early to make sure of arranging a good table with a view over the city, with its famed churches bathed in moonlight. As we waited I watched a beautiful young couple at a candle-lit table by the window. They were in their early 30s, and I noticed that even they were talking in toasts. Maybe in their case there was some of the poetry that had been lost at my formal banquets.

The deputy minister arrived late. He looked like a builder, with a sweater but no shirt, a beer belly and unshaven. Mikhail had told me that he had been, in previous jobs, the deputy chief of the Treasury, the head of customs, a consultant and an academic. The deputy minister spoke some English and seemed devoid of formality so I asked him:

"How old are you?"

"Twenty-seven."

A few minutes later the finance minister came over to say hello: he was 32; then the mayor of Tbilisi, 38; and then the president's advisor, a very striking-looking girl about 30.

I asked the deputy minister about the port. "What do you want from the new owners? Commitments about employment, investment in modern equipment?"

"No. The highest bid gets it."

"Just that? What happens if they are criminals? Or Russian 'interests'?"

"We take that chance. We have discussed it. We think a high bidder will want success."

We asked him if they were going to sell everything.

"Yes. Three years from now the government won't be able to ruin anything, because it won't be theirs to ruin."

He explained the World Bank's ranking of Georgia as the top reformer. "It means it is just as easy to fire as to hire. It sounds brutal, but we think it's for the best."

The evidence suggests that he was right. A year later, Georgia's growth rate is even higher.

But – much as our taxi driver back in the snow in Batumi won't like it – it will be the boys in the banks that will inherit the new Georgia. The scar tissue clogging the thought processes of the old, lies too deep to allow them ever to join in the party. Uncle Joe, the greatest Georgian of them all, has cast a long shadow over his country.

16

Russia in the 1990s

The night before, I had been delayed for seven hours in an icy airport outside Moscow. The staff was on strike, the heating had broken down and the fuel for the planes was being rationed. Outside the departure lounge, a hundred pallid taxi divers hovered like vultures in black leather jackets, hoping that all flights would be cancelled. But we eventually took off, and I arrived in the Black Sea port town of Novorossiysk early on a cold Sunday morning in November.

My employers were cutting costs, so I had been billeted in a tiny flat, overlooking the windswept bay. The decor was West Hartlepool post war, in shades of dispiriting brown and beige, with plastic hanging plants and an ancient gas-fired water heater like a ticking bomb in the bathroom. The old lady who was renting it out in desperation for income had left all her cupboards stuffed with used clothes, tablecloths and bed linen. They were most of what she owned, I supposed. But the flat had a grandmotherly cosiness, and the few pictures on the walls were rather tasteful, particularly the portrait of the sad-eyed Russian poet, Anna Akhmatova. It was pasted above a lamp with a thick velvet shade under which the light from the 15-watt bulb was barely visible.

A gale was blowing outside, and I had not been out since I arrived. I sat at the window, with the rain drumming against the glass and watched the wind making skittering patterns in the puddles outside. The few old headscarved babushkas who had ventured out were losing their balance, and being blown sideways across the wide streets.

There were some eggs, bread and butter in the fridge, left by a previous occupant. Desperately hungry after my night flight without food, I boiled the eggs. They tasted like eggs had never tasted before, and reminded me once again of the luxury of poverty. Most of the others were scheduled to arrive the next day; so I settled down to a rare day to myself. I brought a wooden chair into the little kitchen, and sat close to the flames on the gas stove to keep warm, trying to read Russian, listening to the rain. I recalled doing homework on the end of the kitchen table in the 1940s: I was happy there.

At the end of the afternoon another of our group, a Dane, arrived unexpectedly. He had also been without food for a day, and, as the rain was subsiding to a drizzle and the wind had dropped, we decided to go out to see if any shops were open. On the way downstairs an elderly lady peered nervously out of the door to her apartment. She spoke some English, and told us that no shops would be open – only the street market a few miles away. Then she changed subject abruptly and began talking about Olga upstairs, as if we knew her. It emerged that Olga had been stabbed and killed a few days before, by visiting hoodlums to whom she owed money. They had broken the door down to get to her.

To find the market, our neighbour told us to follow the route of the town's heating pipe, which controlled all residential heating and was turned on, whether the temperature was cold or warm, on a preordained day in October. It was difficult to miss, being one of the ugliest scars on the urban landscape of many Russian towns – wrapped in peeling cladding, and supported by rusting metal brackets where it was raised to cross roads.

The route was littered with broken hinges and stank of seeping oil. We followed its path along potholed streets past tenement blocks and shops that looked like warehouses, neglected public buildings in damp brutalist concrete, desolate open spaces devoid of greenery and a few socialist realist sculptures surrounded by plastic litter.

The market, when we got there just after dark, was illuminated by bare light bulbs jiggling in the breeze on wires strung over the tops of the stalls. We picked our way through muddy puddles between trestle tables of pitted apples and root vegetables, gaudy clothes and kitschy pictures of crying children.

What they did well, though, was cheap leather; and my Danish colleague and I noticed some artificial leather jackets from Turkey that looked better than the real thing. We hovered over them for a few minutes, as the stallholder, a diminutive peasant lady bundled in thick layers of clothes like an old sepia photograph of Siberia, held back but eventually came forward and said, "$1500" (all prices had been dollarised as their currency was in freefall). We raised our eyebrows theatrically, but a lady at my elbow said in English, "She means $15." We were tempted but moved on to get food before the market closed. The tiny lady followed us, pleading, "How much you pay?"

"We'll come back."

"$12."

"Later."

"$10."

Half an hour later we returned to her stall. I tried on the leather jacket, and said, "Yes. Great. I'll have this one."

"How much?" she asked.

"Well, you said $15." She looked incredulous. A little crowd had gathered and she asked them if the foreigners were really going to pay $15. They nodded. The tiny grey-blue irises lit up like torches in her Siberian eyes and a smile exploded to the borders of her face. She gave a strange little squeal, opened her arms wide and threw them around me in a bear-like hug. Then she reached up and kissed me. The faces in the crowd warmed into the first smiles of the day; and my friend bought another.

The next day, my first at the office, I noticed a lot of whispering. I felt excluded at first, but they eventually told me that my predecessor in the flat, the owner of the eggs and bread, had been attacked and left for dead at the end of the last week. He was now back in Finland, having his jawbone and five ribs reset.

My job in Novorossiysk was to suggest how to privatise the port, the second biggest in Russia, according to internationally accepted guidelines. But I found that a few of the directors had already privatised it in the Russian style, by selling it to themselves. The port had an income of $150 million a year from the oil that passed through its pipes, and their costs were close to nothing. I went to see the directors in an office outside the port. They wore cashmere polo-necks, expensive jackets of the type Arabs buy at Aquascutum and highly shone shoes. I asked if I could see their contract to operate the port, and their accounts. They just laughed.

I saw some of them later in the best restaurants in Novorossiysk – best in the sense that they were at least heated. Most of the customers there were young, in more expensive black leather jackets with added features. Their faces, pale and inexpressive, had an air of menace. They reeked of hot money, dirty money – there was little clean money in Russia in those years; it would all have been to Cyprus in a suitcase at some time.

Their attractive girlfriends were dressed as gangsters' molls – mostly in black with little touches of rhinestone cowgirl. There are apparently many more words in Russian than in English to distinguish the more subtle refinements of the repertoire of flirtation – the lot of Russian women over the previous thousand years must have necessitated advanced survival mechanisms – and these girls laboured heroically through a lexicon of facial gymnastics to elicit reluctant smiles from the cold, dead barracuda eyes of their taciturn swains.

The food that brought them there was the badly butchered lumps of meat, but the menus were rescued by the wonderful warm soups – *borscht*, *ukha* and *okroshka*. Outside, the drivers, mostly older men who once had secure jobs, waited between the banks of Mercedes, their steamy breath like clouds under the street lights, clapping their hands together to keep warm.

Our last few days were spent in Moscow, for meetings with the government. We were taken round by our local representative, a capable lady in her late 30s. The women were surviving better than the men since the end of communism, she explained. She told us that one-fifth of all Russian income was spent on drink and the life expectancy of men had fallen to 59 while women still lived beyond 70. That year a thousand people were reported to have died by drowning in the seaside resort of Odessa in July alone, all presumed drunk. But despite the poverty and social breakdown, they didn't want communism back. I asked what she thought of Yeltsin. "The Russian people like him because, unlike Gorbachev, he drinks."

"Our men are hopeless," she told us. "They were told where to go and what to do all their lives, and they can't cope now."

I asked what her husband did, and she said without malice, "He's at home. I am the only one that works."

Sometimes the resourcefulness of the women went further. A survey around that time claimed that 60 per cent of Russian high-school girls would exchange sex for hard currency, although only for a time, to get the basics – a flat, a record player, a washing machine, etc. In fact, the hotel I was staying in had a little history. The friend who recommended it had, a few months before, come in late one night and decided to have a coffee in the foyer before going to bed. As he was sitting there a girl of absurdly good looks, dressed in fur and white leather boots came up and asked him if we was looking for company.

"Not really, I'm tired," but, impressed by her manner, he added, "just out of interest, how much would it be for the night?"

"$150."

"OK, then how much just to sit here and have a chat?"

"$150," she repeated.

"Come on," he argued, "it's too late for you to find anyone tonight. How about $30?" She agreed and they ended up talking for a couple of hours. She was a university teacher, and also worked one day a week for a Western management consultancy. But once a month she would come out to top up her income to the level she wanted. He told me that it was one of the most fascinating two hours of his life. The Russians are nothing if not well educated. But the night I stayed, there were only a few drunks in the foyer, and two beautiful but bad-tempered waitresses.

17

Bangladesh

There are 150 million people in Bangladesh, and most of them seem to be watching me. My priority this morning is modest – it is buying a battery for my electric shaver. But I expect trouble. I peer out of the hotel entrance cautiously. The coast seems to be clear, and I start to walk towards the Chittagong market. But he spots me before I reach the street. He had been waiting for me behind a pillar with his rickshaw, and his already crazed look turns incandescent at the prospect of a foreign customer. He is already on his third sentence by the time I see him coming.

"What you want, sir?... You change money?... You want shopping?..." The words come tumbling out.

He had attached himself to me like a leech on most of my previous forays out of the hotel. I turn my head away and raise the palm of my hand, miming, 'Please, no,' and walk on in silence. He rides alongside, clearing a way for me through the dense crowds. He is desperately thin and wiry and has a cancerous growth on his neck.

"No problem, sir, I get you good price. Because you are my friend. You want beer, bananas... shirt, photographs . Everything I get you..."

All the time his head waggles slightly from side to side, as if he is trying to dislodge a bee from his ear without infuriating it into stinging him. Or is he trying to hypnotise me?

"You like tea, sir. . . restaurant. . . no problem. I get you whisky, telephone, fax, TV. I take you everywhere, anything you want. . . I get. . . I will do the needful."

I look at his skinny chest and almost relent, but if I do he will be mine forever.

"No problem, no way, anything," he burbles on. (Strangely enough, no girls were offered.)

Defeated I turn back, without my battery.

Bangladesh is one of the world's poorest countries. It is the only country in the world where people have been shrinking, the next generation being smaller than their fathers. And women, who live six to seven years longer than men in most countries, die first in Bangladesh. It would be incorrect to say that it is a land of desperation; the people are too fatalistic. In contrast with the fierce warrior West Pakistanis who ruled them until recently, the Bangladeshis are a nation of poets and dreamers. But there is a hunger for crumbs and they are scarce. I am working here on a World Bank mission to get the ports and railways working better, but most of those who have been here before think the money will be wasted. It will be siphoned off by corrupt politicians and little will filter down.

Back in the hotel I return to my room and find the door open. Inside, a chambermaid is cleaning the bathroom. She is not unattractive, around 30, swaddled in thick clothes. She is startled to see me walk in, but I mime, 'It's OK, carry on', and go over to the desk to check emails. When I look up about ten minutes later I am surprised that she is still there. She notices me looking at her, leaning back in the chair with my hands behind my head.

"Are you resting, sir?"

"No, I'm just going for lunch."

"Are you a business man?"

"No."

"Who do you work for?"

"I'm working for the World Bank here."

"Oh. . . you are an important person," she said.

"I don't think so."

"All you foreign visitors are working too much; you should relax."

There is a barely detectable thrust of her chest beneath the swaddling clothes.

"You are probably right," I reply.

She stands at the end of the bed, her head tilted at a slightly odd angle. She seems to be showing me her best side. Then I notice that she has closed the door. Her eyes betray nothing but her mouth has just the tiniest whisper of a come-hither pout.

Ten minutes later I mention it over lunch to an Australian from Washington. He laughs and says, "Jees, it took me half a bladdy hour to get her out. She probably thinks we carry the Bank's dollars around with us and just hand them out for services rendered."

The next day we move on to Dhaka. It is said to have been ruined by congestion, but I find it surprisingly attractive, at least visually; many of its streets are wide and softened with greenery, and the congestion comes from hundreds of thousands of painted rickshaw bicycles rather than from cars. But it is best around sunrise, before the traffic starts, when the women can be seen striding to work along the roadsides, in their traditional, vividly coloured non-Western clothes of purples, oranges, greens and pinks, startlingly bright in the early morning light. They wear their Muslim faith lightly – many do not have their heads covered, and those who do make it a decoration, with hair visible beneath their scarves. But above all, their deportment is superb, due to the carrying of heavy loads on their heads. I have seen foreigners mesmerised by the sight of a team of Bangladesh women labourers on a building site, carrying loads of bricks on their heads up steep ramps. It was not the disconcerting spectacle of women doing such work that held their attention. It was the fact that they *looked* so beautiful.

Work back in Dhaka was slow, and slowed even further by the intricacies of the Bangladeshi class system. On my first day at the office I was walking over to the Xerox machine to copy a single page when a clerk rushed forward to intercept me.

"No, sir," he blurted in alarm, pulling the sheet from my hand. He turned to a junior. "Call the peon."

I had not heard the word since schooldays. Two minutes later the peon arrived, placed the sheet on the copier, pressed the copy button and submitted the copy for inspection to the junior who then passed it back to me, recording the event in a dog-eared ledger.

Their world of peons and sirs makes the English look like amateurs at class distinction. Every day, a very small man with a very straight back, a neat moustache and a bristling manner came up from downstairs and demanded, "When will the project director for the ports study arrive?" He made it clear that he did not want to speak to us. Every day we said, "Maybe soon"; and every day he turned and left without another word. The 'project director' was one of those people who rarely leave their home office in London, and he was never going to arrive. In the end we asked our visitor what he wanted.

"I wish to know how much cargo the port of Chittagong handles in a year."

"It was 30.6 million tonnes last year."

Hitler, which is what we had inevitably called him, looked surprised, thanked us curtly and left. He seemed disappointed.

The next day we visited the railway station at the end of the line on which we were working, and were transported back into England in the bleak years after the Second World War. The whitewashed walls, the dreary civic-buildings green of the ticket office, the cramped empty waiting rooms for first, second, third class and lady passengers, the hard wooden benches worn and buffed, the ticket punches, even the layout of the timetable – all were preserved in amber since the last advisor from British Railways left over 40 years ago. But the thing that made us laugh out aloud was the tickets. The little cardboard squares were identical in every detail – the colour and typefaces of the price, the destination and the date – to those we had in Sunderland in 1950.

The staff had been expecting us, and had well-shone shoes. Maps were spread over tables and operations were explained; then they escorted us out proudly to the waiting 'skate' – a scaled-down railway engine just large enough to carry two uncovered wooden benches on a square platform over four wheels. There was just room for four of us to sit perched up alongside the driver. We climbed aboard, a whistle was blown, and as we moved forward there was a little hooray from the crowd. We built up speed and clattered out into the countryside. All along the track, men lined the way, standing to attention and saluting as we passed. The elderly Indian railways expert who was with us was completely at ease; he had been used to this all his life. From time to time he waved his plump hand in acknowledgement of the people.

Only at the end of our stay did we get out of the city to see the real Bangladesh. The countryside, where most of the people live, is especially beautiful in spring – a mosaic of neat, lush green fields, rice paddies and rich vegetation; but above all it is a country of water. There is water everywhere, in streams, ponds, lakes, paddies and rivers; and here the vivid colours of the traditional clothes are even more intense against the pastoral background. I recall catching a glimpse of a woman with the deportment of a goddess as she glided along the narrow dyke between the rice paddies, her green-and-purple sari lit intermittently by the sun through the trees 'weaving the sunlight in her hair' – a life observed for a fleeting moment. And this was not an exception. There was a feeling of a timeless rural idyll in scenes from their daily life, in the fresh open faces of the schoolgirls, in their uniforms walking to school in the low sun – Kipling's 'sweeter, neater maidens in a cleaner greener land'. Out there, Bangladesh could sometimes seem one of the world's best-kept secrets.

But strong as this memory of the simple pastoral life of the countryside was, it was not the most lasting memory – which was of how the open, innocent faces harden and set rather grimly by the age of 25. The unpalatable truth is that the low expectations of those that have been here before were probably right. The money will be wasted. Corruption and corrosive social deference will ensure that little will trickle down. Long after India and China and other Asian countries have overtaken us, there will still be missions to Bangladesh, and my rickshaw man may still be waiting for me down at Chittagong.

18

Mexico

Rosalita's Cantina was more like an abandoned barn than a bar. Part of the corrugated-iron roof was missing, although this was not unwelcome on a night that was warm to the point of suffocation. In the corner a wheezy mariachi band, in their 50s and 60s, was playing the plangent laments and falling cadences so beloved of the Mexicans. Often the notes tailed off forlornly and the band stopped playing before the end of the song. I noticed that the guitarist was missing a finger. Around the bar the girls – thick-hipped, heavy-thighed and lazily sensual – lounged in PVC negligees on sofas, occasionally rising lethargically to dance together. From time to time they directed theatrical winks and listless come-hither pouts in our direction. Their livid make-up against their ashen skin was both repellent and alluring in the weak light.

Opposite us at the table sat Zertucchi and Ocampo, both in their 40s, sleek and prosperous. They were wearing tasteful T-shirts in different pastel colours, but with the same little crocodile labels. They were high up in the ministry in Mexico City, and had been recommended this place for the evening's entertainment.

"Have you got your eye on any of the girls?" asked Zertucchi, with a goatish smile. He was well educated and constantly aware that he had to speak

Spanish slowly for me. I started to dissemble. "Well... um..." I scanned the bar... But the two of them were already negotiating with a couple of girls, and suddenly they were gone.

I was left at the table with the young Mexican with whom I was working – Jesús García Gaitán. Thin-necked, serious and catholic, he was recently married. His stomach had been upset by the food since we left Mexico City.

"Are you going to go with one of the girls?" he asked, failing to conceal the tension in his voice. He was still dressed in his suit, although he had removed his tie. I affected to survey the girls again, and then said "No." Jesús looked as if he has been released from jail. His face lightened. "Oh... well... then we can have a beer together," he said, establishing a masculine bond.

We sat and chatted. His earlier reserve – I think he considered that I was not sufficiently well dressed for an Englishman – was forgotten. He was even able to enjoy some ponderous banter with the girls when they came to sit with us.

An hour later we were rejoined by a flushed and buoyant Ocampo, and we sat for 15 minutes over another beer. But when Zertucchi did not return, Ocampo started to look at his watch impatiently. A minute later, he stood up. "Right, he's had enough time. Let's go and get him." He paid for the drinks and we followed him through the saloon bar doors, out into a small square with swimming-pool style cubicles all around the perimeter. "Zertucchi!" he called. There was no reply; only murmurs and moans from inside the cubicles. A low rumble of distant thunder came from the hills outside. He raised his voice. "Zertucchi; where are you?" We stood silent for a minute or so. "Right, he's had quite enough time," said Ocampo, and started to hammer on each of the cubicles in turn, until he finally located Zertucchi. Five minutes later he emerged, his face a deep shade of crimson, and our long-suffering driver took us back to the hotel.

The next morning we sat over breakfast of chilli and beans on the veranda of the state governor's hacienda, high up in the fresh cool hills, looking down through the mist and low clouds to the plantations in the valley below. We were there to build a port to export his bananas. The governor was a heavily built grey-haired man, with a relaxed but menacing charm.

"Well, did you enjoy yourselves last night?"

"Yes. Most definitely," said Zertucchi, surreptitiously preening himself in a cut-glass mirror behind the table.

"I thought you would."

Their voices dropped to a lower conspiratorial register and they spoke much faster, no doubt to convey the fact that the young visitors had not fully participated. Mexico was the birthplace of machismo.

At the end of the table sat the governor's wife, She was fair-haired and pretty. She didn't join in the conversation. She was 14 years old.

Later that day we flew back to Mexico City – from the sticks to a temporary capital of the world.

Mexico City in 1970 was a sunburst. It may have been one of the most polluted places on earth and surrounded by a shanty town and a dust bowl, but the centre of the city was a jewel – with its weathered Spanish stone buildings, intimate dark timber interiors, Diego Rivera murals and unique blazes of vivid colour in its wall-hangings, blankets, serapes and ponchos. In that year it was also buzzing with the more adventurous of Americans. Less than ten per cent of them had passports then, but as the 1960s hit its stride many of those that did headed south, attracted by the legendary Acapulco Gold and hallucinatory peyote mushrooms. Ken Kesey was lying low in Mexico, to escape drug charges in the US, and Tom Wolfe had arrived in pursuit of his story; a pursuit that was to result in the *The Electric Kool-Aid Acid Test*. George Harrison had also passed through in the week I arrived. The city was filled with glitterati holding court in the Zona Rosa, with Mexico's plaintive, lilting music – dolorous, melancholy and morbid – echoing from the street cafés. In the second week I went to enlist in language classes, and sat on the university wall under cascades of red bougainvillea, watching as the American girls, all sun-blessed hair and perfect ice-blue teeth in their new ponchos, filed in to register. Warmed to the bones by the early morning sun in a cloudless cobalt blue sky, I recall feeling one of those rushes of almost ecstatic happiness that have recurred from time to time.

And there was more – the football World Cup was just about to start, and it was in Mexico. In my first week in the office Francis, our languidly aristocratic young director, wandered in and asked, "Do you like football?"

"Yes."

"Well, would you like to see some World Cup games?"

"Yes," I said, thrilled at the idea of seeing a game or two.

"Which ones?"

"Well, any England game, if possible," I replied.

He threw a block of tickets for every single game on to my desk. "Just take what you like."

There were still free lunches back then.

But... there was a problem in our foreigners' playground. The Mexicans detested the gringo. America's economic success had bored deep into the Mexican psyche, already damaged by the cruelty of the Spanish conquistadors. There was bad blood. In fact there had always been an almost formal dark savagery in the Mexican soul which goes even further back than the Americans and the Spanish. The gods of ancient civilisations of Mexico, the Aztecs and Mayas, demanded the sacrifice of human hearts, and they had an insatiable dark thirst for blood. The ceremonial centrepieces of the Aztecs' elegant cities were their pyramids, on the tops of which their high priests cut out the hearts of heroic warriors, fattened children and selected young virgins. The rituals included lighting a fire in the cavity left by the removal of the heart. Numbers mattered to their gods; so after battles they would offer up the hearts of up to 20,000 prisoners. Later, the Mayas used to roll the bodies of live men, trussed into balls, down the pyramid steps, smashing their bones into small fragments by the time they reached the bottom. Their great sport was the ball game. The penalty for losing was death; and the reward for winning was, sometimes, also death. Mexican art today still celebrates the macabre, their paintings filled with skulls, blood, skeletons and – a modern addition – soft-drink bottle tops.

Even before the football began, the Mexicans had the English in their sights. England had won the previous Cup in 1966, in a competition in which Brazil, the pride of the Latin Americans, had been fouled off the pitch. In fact, it was not England that had savaged the Brazilian team, but the Mexicans believed that England had cheated in other ways. Their official history of the World Cup had chapter headings like 'Italy's Glory', 'Brazil's Second Coming' and 'The Rise of West Germany'. The 1966 chapter was called 'The Robbery'. Then, before England arrived in Mexico, their captain, Bobby Moore, was accused of shoplifting in a neighbouring country. And when the England team finally arrived, the headlines screamed that they had brought their own water supply with them, a slap in the face for Mexican hospitality – although everyone knew that Montezuma's Revenge was a common affliction.

When the competition started, Mexico did unexpectedly well, and on the nights they won, almost a million people paraded through the city streets, banging the hub caps they had stolen from cars parked along the route, shouting "Up with Mexico, down with England". It was as important for them to see England lose as Mexico win. On the streets my English friend and I pretended to be German. For those few months the English were promoted above the American gringo in the league of public enemies. In the evenings, after a few drinks, I kept my mouth well closed.

Then a trivial incident intervened, and lay and festered for the rest of my time there. It was on a journey to the northern town of San Miguel de Allende, about 300 kilometres from Mexico City. I drove there with an American girl I had recently met.

It started badly. We covered 150 kilometres without seeing a petrol station. Eventually the tank ran dry and we free-wheeled to a halt. We had been told never to stop on the road; and an American car and a striking-looking girl made us unusually attractive targets. Scores of cars drove past, several of the drivers gloating theatrically at our plight. But eventually a high-cabbed ancient petrol wagon slowed down, and four smiling labourers in greasy overalls got down from the cab. We were nervous, but they were more than friendly and offered as much petrol as we wanted. They rigged up a pipe and filled up the tank. I gave them four times what the petrol was worth, and thanked them effusively, and they left waving back at us. So it was with great relief that we restarted the car, and drove off – for a quarter of a mile, after which we glided to a second halt. They had only put a cupful of petrol in the tank. This time, however, we were close to a farmhouse, where a farmer's wife helped us out.

An hour later we arrived at the outskirts of San Miguel. A town built on a hill, known for its unusual light throughout the year, it had been colonised by American and Mexican artists, who had conserved what was best and added to it. We knew that we wanted to head first for the Zócalo, but had no map; and after a few false starts we decided to ask the way.

On a street corner we saw a woman carrying a baby on her back in a coloured blanket. She was a Mexican Indian with a proud, handsome face, and an erect and dignified bearing. We wound down the window and the American girl asked her in passable but heavily accented Spanish, "¿Por favor, dónde es el Zócalo?" The Indian turned slowly and looked coldly past us into the distance for a few seconds, as if she did not understand.

Her face, immobile, seemed like a mask. Then she raised her head slightly as if composing herself to reply, and spat right between the American girl's eyes, turned her back on us and walked slowly away.

The town was entrancing, with its winding cobbled streets, ancient stone buildings, heavily studded wooden doors and art shops filled with stained glass and ceramics. That evening, in an old Spanish restaurant – the only lighting in the courtyard where we sat under canvas canopies came from candles flickering in heavy, antique glass holders – I began to fall for her. We said we should meet in ten years at the same café. I usually remember these sorts of trysts, even if they are only a quarter serious; and I have always been unusually free to travel, because of my work. In the event, I forgot. But I will remember that Indian girl forever.

I did not know it at the time, but the murder rate in the Mexican provinces was higher than in New York. Had I known this I would probably not have set out alone – the American girl had left – for a final weekend, driving to the last of the places I had wanted to see – Taxco. I started early. The interior of the car, borrowed from Francis, had a rich, luxuriant feeling; and the warmth of the morning sun had brought out the smell of the leather. It was a three-hour drive, and I arrived late in the morning.

Taxco is a maze of steep, narrow, cobbled streets lined with whitewashed houses, silver shops, potteries and weavers of ethnic textiles. Its narrow passages lead to enclosed courtyards overgrown with creepers and blossoms, with crooked timbered galleries and old stone cafés. I spent the late afternoon in one of them, furnished with dark wood panelling, heavy wood tables and Spanish lace.

I left Taxco just after dark. Driving out of the town centre, I felt conspicuous in a big, over-powered American car – a rich foreign brat, in T-shirt and flared jeans, worn only by the hated gringos. Mexico in 1970 was still a land of matrons and chaperones.

About half a mile out of the centre the lights were thinning out and an hour of sharp bends along the mountain roads lay ahead.

Without warning, a car materialised behind me, its lights flashing. It was an old and battered wreck, containing half a dozen Mexicans. They overtook and swerved in front of me to slow me down. My headlights picked out three faces grinning back from the open windows, two knives and a gun, which they banged on the doors of their car. They shouted, "Hey, Gringo, where you going?"

My first thought was – should I turn back? From what I knew of the Mexican police and stories of foreigners who had disappeared into Mexican jails, the answer was no. In any case, I should be able to get away from them easily, as their car was old and slow. So I put my foot on the brakes to make a little distance between us, and overtook fast. Within half a minute I was far ahead of them. But then came a series of bends, where I had to slow, allowing them to catch up, and swerve in front of me again, screeching with overexcited laughter. We were now several miles along the mountain road. I tried the same tactic again, but again they caught me up as soon as I slowed at the bends. I was now terrified. There was no moon and it was pitch black. There seemed to be only one possibility. When my headlights next picked out a stretch of straight road, I put my foot on the floor, pulling far ahead of them; and when the next bend came, still at speed but braking hard, I drove off the road and straight into the trees. I felt the car drop slightly, but hit nothing hard. It juddered to a stop and I turned off the lights. Ten seconds later the Mexicans drove past, still laughing and banging the sides of their car, and drove on up the road after me. Sitting there in the wood in the silence the thing I remember was my heartbeat. It was just a continuous roar. There were no spaces between the beats. About five minutes later, when their car passed by on the way back to Taxco, my heartbeat was at the same level.

19

Mumbai

Mumbai in the monsoon. It rains and rains without stopping. The city seems to be decaying, rotting like Venice. Buildings are stained with mildew, moss and damp. Gnarled ancient trees with dangling air roots shut out the sky from the pavements – creating dark and dripping corridors, overgrown by dank vegetation. The only birdsong is the ugly cawing of crows. The sky stays slate grey for days as the rain slants in from the sea.

The buildings are ornate and crumbling. The architecture is an odd mix of Gothic, old colonial and sui generis, with few modern buildings for a city with so much wealth. If they were people the buildings would be jolie laide, or Barbara Cartland. They are particularly evocative after sunset, when glimpses of Indian lives can be caught through a thousand shuttered windows in weakly lit rooms. Apartments in central Mumbai are more expensive than in London, but the interiors are neglected – with dusty chandeliers or neon strip-lights; slow, rickety fans; old net curtains, and drab paint.

In the city centre the damp air feels overused, as if it has already passed through ten pairs of lungs. It is impossible to walk in a straight line for five seconds without hitting a fellow human being.

But many Indians would live nowhere else. It is the home of the very, very rich and famous – stars from the Bollywood film industry which is the largest in the world; and the Parsees, the merchants of Iranian descent who are the captains of many of the industries that bring the wealth to Mumbai. They live on Malabar Hill in the centre of the city, where flats stained with mould in the constant rain cost a hundred times the annual wage of an Indian schoolteacher. Dominating the atmosphere of Malabar Hill are the vultures and crows wheeling over the Towers of Silence, where the Parsees have traditionally laid out the corpses of their deceased for the birds to pick the bones clean. The Parsees are considering ending this practice, as fragments of human flesh have been ending up on the verandas of the expensive high-rise flats nearby. The birds are said to be overfed.

And more and more thousands move in every day – not to live in Malabar hills, but to join the queue in the slums, which grow like mould along the coast. The stench is intolerable. Children and women are encrusted with dirt, their hair matted. They are huddled under shelters made of scraps of matting, wood, corrugated iron and cloth – the rain pouring in. They are like the trenches in the First World War.

But I am there with Dr Padamanaban, who had gone to university and worked in America, but then returned to India, whose way of life he preferred. I had travelled round the whole coast of India with him and he was a man to go into the jungle with as well as the slums. He was irritated by foreign criticism.

"Your journalists come here, and every one of them takes a taxi straight down to the slums, before they've bothered to find out anything at all about India," he said testily.

"Yes, I suppose it is an easy option."

"Isn't even that. Look, I challenge you; watch the faces in the shelters, and tell me if they look unhappy."

And he was right. Even under the low, grey skies in the ceaseless rain, the shanties are illuminated by the flashes of brilliant smiles; and sometimes there are glimpses of extraordinary beauty peering out from underneath the dark shelters. We watched a naked boy washing himself in the rain and mud, shrieking and wriggling like a silverfish, his white teeth glittering as he chased the other children through the maze of sodden cardboard shelters. It was difficult to deny that the faces looked more joyous than the washed-out pallor of the London or Paris undergrounds.

The dreams of escape from this poverty have spawned a film industry of extraordinary size and influence. There are hundreds of cinemas in Mumbai, playing reworks of *The Sound of Music*, with mountain landscapes filled by regiments of beautiful dancing girls with bright eyes and dazzling white smiles – rendered completely sexless by their bat-squeaky voices and pelvic thrusts like mechanical toys. The girls are pursued by plump, painted, perfumed puddings of men, with doggy eyes and sweet smiles. But hidden in the nonsense are some timeless truths about the boy-girl relationship.

I had arrived in Mumbai early in the weekend, and found a note in my hotel saying that the others had been delayed, leaving me a day all to myself to relax in the cultural capital of this most ancient of civilizations, with its strange elephant gods, its mysterious temple prostitutes, its peculiar mix of the spiritual and the materialistic – and its very different ways of doing things.

After a late breakfast I settled down to read the marriage advertisements in the Sunday papers. Most of their weddings are still arranged and the up-market papers have eight-page marriage market sections once a week. The eager parents seek handsome, fair (-skinned) men of 'high' or 'posh' status – specifying MBAs, dentists and computer engineers for their daughters; and 'wheatish' (i.e. light-skinned), 'very beautiful' brides of good moral character for their sons. Defects are admitted. That Sunday there were a few diabetics; one had 'had nervous breakdown, but now normal'; another had 'minor polio but able to drive scooter'. The top catch of the weekend advertised:

> Very handsome, world-travelled gentleman, seven-figure salary, owner of many posh flats and premier properties seeks extremely beautiful, tall, light-coloured, educated, cultured bride. Enquiries from beauty queens, top models and women from the World of Glamour will be considered.

Another was from a seaman requiring a quick marriage, as he would only be stopping in the port of Mumbai for a short time. Crucial to the decision on choice of partner is the compatibility of their horoscopes. It is, however, no longer an outdated procedure; the preparation and matching of the horoscopes is now done by computer.

Back in Hyderabad the month before, I had sat over long lunches with a young Indian who nervously invited me to accompany him after a couple of days in an office. He wanted to talk to someone from another world. He found a café he thought a Westerner would like, and as we sat down he asked tentatively if he could smoke.

"Yes, of course," I replied.

"That's good; my parents don't know I smoke, and even my friends disapprove."

Encouraged, he ordered half a pint of beer, and did so at our lunches for the rest of the week. He was getting married in six weeks. It was of course an arranged marriage, and he was happy to talk about their meeting and courtship. "All things considered," he said, "she is nice girl." It was clear that he wanted to say more, and he did.

"There is only one small problem."

"What's that?" I asked.

A pause.

"Well. . . She is. . . rather plain."

Later, there was another 'small problem'. He explained.

"She doesn't seem to want to go to the cinema so often now. . . And she spends a lot of time shopping. . . with her mother."

We went on to exchange every conceivable detail about life in India and life in the West. He was one of those I never met again.

Dr Padmanaban would have consoled him. He would have pointed out that Indian marriages last, and the children grow up with respect for their elders.

On the Monday morning I started on a round of visits to local shipping and law offices in the business district – an area of wider cobbled streets and fussily ornate Victorian buildings, not well maintained, but with a timeless charm as the sun filtered through the trees making dappled patterns on the stonework. It was already warm and humid at 9.30am. Arriving at the first office I climbed the rickety stairs, with the usual betel nut juice stains on the landings, to a floor with a brass plate bearing the shipping line's name. I opened the door and stepped into a different world – a vast open-plan office, halogen lit and tastefully furnished with the flat-screen monitors and leather armchairs of the more style-conscious offices of London's investment banks. Except that the staff were even better dressed.

The Indians I met were very bright – streets ahead of their European counterparts; and the majority worked until 9 or 10pm on most nights. Their wives or husbands rarely saw them.

"Why do you do it?" I asked.

"Simple," they reply. "If I don't they will find someone else who will."

"You're joking. It can't be as cut-throat as that."

"It's worse. You see, there is a vast oversupply of good graduates in India."

But they work cheerfully. One evening, about 9pm, an elegant young graduate started clearing her desk, and I asked, "Are you off home now?"

"Yes," she replied, with a nicely balanced blend of irony and cheerfulness. "Half day."

They were wonderful to talk to over lunch. Their knowledge of their traditional culture is deep, but they can be very flippant about it. I asked about the Indian spiritual leaders of the 1960s and their attraction for Westerners, such as the Beatles. They explained to me that, as his visitors sat cross-legged around him, the subject of the Maharishi's contemplation may well have been about the deeper meaning of balance sheets, revenues, expenditures, profit and loss. As we passed the slums they pointed to the mobile phones the inhabitants were carrying, and explained with sporty glee the complex economics of how it benefits the phone companies to distribute the handsets free.

The quest for money is relentless, from the top to the bottom of the social ladder. In my hotel, the foyer is staffed by sleek black-suited girls with shiny hair and '*ada*' (Urdu for 'elegant demeanor'), but the constant stream of attendants who knock at the door, bringing towels, fruit, turning down beds, come from a different world. They are the poor, the untouchables, the unemployed and the fakirs who have come into the city to find work – their poverty barely disguised by the uniforms draped over their bony, mostly elderly, bodies. All dawdle in the hope of a tip, competing in humility and self-abasement. There was one in particular I came to fear, making long unnecessary detours along the hotel corridors, to avoid him after a conversation in the first week:

"Is your room OK, sir?" His head waggled as if controlled by a puppeteer.
"Yes."
"What is your good name, sir?"
"Ted."

"No problems?"

"No problems."

"Are your towels OK, sir?"

"Yes."

He raised the stakes with a final gambit.

"You are sure that *everything* OK with you, sir?"

"Yes."

"It should be."

I looked blank.

"Why. . . should it be?"

"Because," he explained, "I have been praying for you, sir – every day."

20
Night Flight

The passengers for the last flight out of Hong Kong, the 23.55pm to London, were slumped listlessly around the departure gate. Many were sleeping, sprawled like dead weight over three seats; and I was sitting on the floor next to a vast air-conditioning machine, the only place I could find a socket for my computer. That night the flight was full of students, wearing the uniform of low-crotch baggy jeans and baseball caps. Nowadays even the respectful young Chinese pepper their conversation with impactless swear words; most things are 'crap'. But conversation around the departure gate was sparse; the waiting passengers were pale, tired and pink-eyed.

Two hours earlier I had dozed off for the last few minutes on the express train into the airport, and as I boarded the plane I was looking forward to sinking back in the seat and sleeping at last. But now, when I reach my place I find that I am wide-awake and the seat does not seem to fit the contours of my body.

The airline is modern and paperless. Its skymag boasts of its 'in-flight entertainment' – all electronic, with videos, sitcoms and computer games, and a wide choice of films starring Schwarzenegger, Stallone and Bruce Willis. Each of us has our own individual screen. The control panel for the screen has buttons in simple bright primary colours – red, green, blue and yellow – easy to understand.

Except that I can't understand it. I notice that the man next to me is reading a computer magazine about 'new software' so I ask him what to do. He accesses the programme I want in a millisecond, but like most computer people he neglects to show me how. He is wearing a blue blazer with gold buttons and grey flannels – safe clothes, of a type selected not to offend ten years ago. But, now out-dated, they suggest a fear of even being visible.

"How did you know which buttons to press?" I asked.

He seemed to think the question odd. He just did.

"Do you work in computers?" I asked

"No."

"So what were you doing in Hong Kong?"

"I work in change management."

He must have been used to people being at a loss for words, so I asked him, slightly mischievously, what change management meant.

"Well, they bring me in to find solutions to problems associated with change."

He seemed to skirt around the question, until the answer slowly became clear.

"Do you mean that you help companies sack people?"

"Well. . . er. . . yes. Big investment banks." He was a freelance management consultant, specialising in 'downsizing', and staff 'rationalisation'; a member of the grim high-priesthood of the new orthodoxy, cost cutting for competitiveness. He was an economist, practising a science that becomes more dismal with the passing of time. I recalled a newspaper report which had suggested that we now laugh for only six minutes per day, compared with 18 minutes in the supposedly drab 1950s; the reason, they claimed, was increasing obsession with economic gain.

"Tell me," I continued, "if the chairman of a company downsizing creates another $100 million of profit by cutting staff, does he usually get a percentage of this himself in his bonus – straight out of the pockets of the redundant staff into his?"

"That's not really my field," he replied.

I mentioned to him that I had been dismayed for many years that the financial services have sucked up most of the talent in Britain; anyone who got a first in geography or physics over the last 20 years has disappeared into investment banks and hedge funds.

He had no view on this. But he was not an unpleasant man, and when the food arrived he opened up a little about himself. He was proud of the fact that he was self-made. He had never been to a university. He had been downsized himself, after working for a management consultant for ten years. He was divorced and living in Swindon.

"Have you been to Hong Kong before?" I asked.

"Yes, many times."

" Do you like it?"

"Yes,... it's good to get out of London a little... and the food is wonderful of course."

"Ah, so can you recommend any really good restaurants?"

"Well... not any one in particular. I usually work 14-hour days when I'm in Hong Kong and don't get much time to get out."

He knew almost none of Hong Kong's bars, restaurants or sights, even Lan Kwai Fong, the matchless social centre for foreigners, electric with atmosphere on Friday and Saturday nights; and he seemed to regard this as a virtue.

As I settled to try to sleep, he took down the control panel for the computer games, and started to play Tetris. I dozed off from time to time, but rarely for long – and each time I awoke I saw his grey fish eyes, luminous in the reflected light of the screen as he concentrated hard, his thumb jerking as if in spasm.

Later in the flight I walked down the aisle. Most of the passengers were asleep, but a few of the women were watching films or reading, and some of the men had lurid purple faces, reflecting the screens they were facing. They were playing the same computer game as my change manager.

When the sun and breakfast woke us up a couple of hours from London I found that he was still playing. Maybe it improved the sharpness of his mind – encouragingly, as we would not want men of limited mental 'skills' to be playing god with our jobs and lives.

21

Hash House Harriers

"Well, see you all on Monday, at the Hash," said Geoff as we started to look around for taxis. We were standing outside Manila's Intercontinental Disco in the steamy tropical night air. It was 2am on a Sunday morning. No-one had been able to speak or hear for the last hour, as we stood packed together in the dense crowd holding our beers and watching the Filipino group and the girls and boys dancing to the pounding music. It was the last of the four clubs we had visited that evening, and we had all been relieved that this time nobody had said 'OK, where are we going next?'. The gang almost always moved in lockstep and nobody wanted to appear to be dipping out.

We were working together on a transport project; half of us were long stayers in the Philippines and half, including me, were there for a month or so.

"Yes, it should be a cracker on Monday," said Dave. The Hash House Harriers is an international running and drinking club.

But Monday was two nights away, and it was dawning on some of the gang that an empty Sunday was gaping in front of them.

"Hey, what about meeting at Nomads tomorrow morning – or at least *this* morning since it's Sunday already. We could meet at... how about 11 o'clock, and we can have a few beers – to get rid of our hangovers."

"No, too early. I think I had a few too many tonight. How about midday?

"Yeah."

In fact, they met at Nomads almost every Sunday morning, after the Saturday nights trawling the clubs. The Nomads is the expat sports club in a suburb of Manila, and the centre of the world for some of the British, Australians and Kiwis. When I arrived, around midday, there was a fierce sun directly overhead, and most of the gang from the night before were sitting up at the outside bar wearing dark glasses, looking pallid amongst the sunburnt young mothers and children. That morning the rugby pitch was grassless, dried-up and deserted and the squash courts and tennis courts were empty. Apart from the sound of the golden-limbed children splashing and shouting in the swimming pool, the only sign of life was in the little breeze-block restaurant underneath the corrugated-iron roof.

We had hamburgers for lunch, then dozed around the swimming pool. I lay staked out under the sun, oblivious to the trouble it would later cause me, and looked out under the peak of my baseball cap at the pale legs and baggy shorts, and the scattered computer and car magazines and Wilbur Smiths; and thought, I do not want to be here.

I considered the old days back in Manila ten years ago. We never came to the Nomads then. And we had what seemed a good life. The niggling concerns of home – good schools, washing machine breakdowns and insurance claims – were thousands of miles away. There was little talk of money, cars, politics, house prices and the climbing of rungs of ladders – the staples of London conversation.

Nothing was ours back then, neither the cars we drove nor the sprawling Manila houses we rented. When the car tyre went flat we just rang the office.

We travelled everywhere, visiting all but one of the 12 main islands of the Philippines. And we seemed to know everyone, with ten different nationalities coming to our parties. But the feeling slowly grew that we were wasting our lives out there, that everything we enjoyed was just a perfect imitation. A Sri Lankan friend used to talk of the gilded cage she lived in. And it ended in an unexpected disappointment. Back in England, the best friends we had made in Manila would ring to apologise that they could not come on the mornings of the reunions we arranged. We felt that we knew more about a couple after visiting them for a single afternoon in England than we had known in all our years in Manila. Perhaps Freud's narcissism of small differences is needed to give life a little bite.

My reverie was interrupted by a couple new to Manila who were being introduced around the pool. He was a bathroom equipment salesman from Birmingham and she was going to help at the British school. Someone was telling them that the Nomads is a great place to find new friends. Around 4pm the gang started to drift off one by one. Most were heading off to do some work.

"See you at Hash tomorrow," said Geoff as I left.

"I'm afraid not. I have something on," I lied. The truth was that I had never been to the Hash.

I had been avoiding it for ten years – ever since I felt myself being hoisted into the air from behind as my wife was talking to another young expat wife in a supermarket in our first month in Manila. I twisted round and saw a man who wore pink and primrose T-shirts but still looked manly, with his sunburned hair and decathlete build. It later turned out that he was the local squash champion. He was the young expat's husband. He lowered me to the ground.

"Well, you look in good shape," he said. "Just the sort we need to join our Hash."

I said I'd think about it.

"No argument. See you there. There's a great bunch of guys to hang out with."

I knew about the Hash, but had escaped it before, in Korea, Thailand and Pakistan. It advertises itself as a club for 'drinking people with running problems' and their Kennels, as they call their local groups, can be found in almost every country in the world.

They meet for runs and for fun, which is beer. The trail and the post-run fun is choreographed by the reigning grand master – or grand mattress in the unlikely event of a girl having broken though the glass ceiling to rise to that exalted position, through the ranks of the Hash House Harriets. Nobody there uses his or her real name. They are called No Name before their christening, and afterwards they use their 'Hash name' earned by an escapade (say, Richard the Lion Fart), a personality trait (zzzz), or the runner's appearance (Little Big Horn).

The run can be approached competitively or not, but most go for the fun that takes place at Circle, where they sing Hash songs ('beer beer beer beer beer beer beer beer beer beer, we all love beer'), call on virgins to step forward, relay news of absent members, and impose punishments of 'down downs' – drinking vast amounts of beer down in one – on offenders. The offences are usually fictional: Fred might have been suspected of drinking shandies after the last run; or leaving a girl gasping for it on a bed, while he fell asleep in the bath next door, having had just one too many beers. It is not quite my kettle of fish – no more than rugby club rituals, drinking eight pints of beer and then running round the square with no clothes on. My mental circuitry seem to fuse and misfire a little when inserted into ready-made groups – the rotary, the clubbable group around the bar, the men whose favourite drinks the barman knows.

My resolution to avoid the Hash was strengthened later by news of that month's Circle. The reigning grand master at the time was a tough little

Australian, and the runners that arrived back exhausted in the tropical heat found that they had to jump naked into a large hot tub full of girls bussed in from Del Pilar, the street of shame, to drink their beers. Later the grand master's baton was handed to an aristocratic German, who favoured serious running, but by that time I was a known non-Hasher.

For many years I thought little about the Hash. Once in Indonesia I came across an old friend, one blessed with good looks and an opening-batsman charm when I first knew him, but who had gone slowly to seed in Jakarta. He was still good company, although less so after lunch and his first drinks; but if there was a measure of his life's trajectory it was the declining levels of English spoken by his string of increasingly dull-eyed local girl friends. His only lifeline was the Hash. Peter's eyes would shine when he spoke of the cut and thrust of the banter and the heights of Socratic disputation scaled at the Circles in Jakarta. And it may have been true. The Hash had become his life.

I finally succumbed a few years later. I was passing through a city in India where a friend and his wife had been working for a year; and when I rang him to say let's get together.

"Why don't you come over for the Hash?" he said. "It's on Sunday afternoon."

I told him about my lifelong reservations, and he said he more than fully sympathised, but assured me that this one was a mild version of the real thing. Hyderabad was a family Hash with children (they call them Hash House Horrors), Coca-Cola as well as beer and drinking songs toned down.

When I arrived on the Sunday afternoon I found the whole of Hyderabad's expat community of under 50 assembled, along with locals from the aid agencies. They were dressed in the American clothes of the 1950s, baseball hats and baggy shorts, and the wives were handing round cup cakes. It could have been the Peace Corps of 40 years ago.

The 'run' was, as Michael had promised, walked by most of us. Nobody paid much attention to the 'On On' toots from the grand master's bugle.

And the Hashers seemed pleased to have a newcomer from the outside world to talk to.

After we had finished the trail I sat with my friends over a beer as the last laggards drifted in, until the bugle sounded for Circle time. As we got up my friend turned to me, and lowered his voice.

"Sorry about this," he said. "You're not going to like it. Just one word of advice – don't try to be too clever. Don't talk back."

The grand master was a pared-down-to-the bone Australian with long grey hair in a Willie Nelson ponytail, a broken nose and jutting jaw, bush shorts and a shirt cut away to show his taut shoulder muscles. The warrior look was rounded off by with his 'On On' bugle hanging at his belt.

He started to work up the crowd with a little banter and jokes, and soon they were baying for blood and beer and victims. They sang a song of borderline acceptability, although the children were now happily playing outside the Circle, and brought out two offenders for down-downs.

Then came the third item on the agenda.

"Roight, now... Can anyone see '*vir... gins*'." A virgin was a first-timer at Hash.

There was no chance of my keeping my head down, as fingers were already pointing in my direction. I was the only one, and I was frogmarched into the centre of the Circle in front of the grand master.

"Roight... here we have virgin. So... what do you think of him?" He spun me round. There were a few dismissive jeers.

"Okeye, would any of you... er... loidies... like to take him for a... er... test run?" Half a dozen of the girls in the front of the Circle made threatening noises, and a tall and savage-looking black girl with dazzling white teeth stepped forward. "I'll take him," she roared. When I spoke to her later I found she has a PhD in economics. And she was in fact the wife of the grand master. They affected to restrain her.

A question-and-answer session followed.

"Where are you from?"

"London."

"Aha, the poof. . . dah capital of the world."

Remembering Michael's advice I meekly assented.

"OK. A general knowledge question: which country has lost almost every test match against Australia for the last 30 years?"

I know little about cricket but rightly guessed the answer was England.

The interrogation went on for a few more minutes, and then:

"Roight, now let's get down to it." He looked at the crowd. "Let's see if he can take his beer." A Harrier came forward and filled a vast tankard with two or three pints of beer and handed it to the grand master. He held the holy sacrament above his head.

"All in one," he said. "Without stopping."

The Circle started to roar "down, down, down. . .," and the grand master handed me the tankard.

As he did so he turned his sculpted warrior face towards me, and away from the crowd. For my eyes only, his ferocious expression softened, he rolled his eyes to the sky as if to say 'Would you believe all this hokum?' Then he covered his mouth with his hand and said confidentially, almost sweetly, "It doesn't matter if you can't drink it. No probs at all. Just give them a little show of willing," and gave me a little wink.

22

The Philippines

It was a stiflingly hot summer evening in Manila in the candle-lit garden of our host, a wealthy Filipino. The sultry air seemed more enervating than in neighbouring tropical countries, as if sweat from the fetid jungle compressed beneath the city was seeping up into the warm night. During those evenings you could never touch your neck or forehead without feeling a layer of warm moisture.

The conversation, with the sugar-sweet young wife of the host, was on autopilot.

"How do you like our country?" she asked.

"Very much," we replied, as always, more or less truthfully. We had been there about two months.

"Ah, that's good, and do you like our food?"

"Yes," we replied, untruthfully. It is the only bad food in Asia.

We waited to be asked 'And have you been out of Manila yet?' But instead there was a slight pause.

"What do white people look like when they are dead?"

The Filipinos confound expectations. On first impressions, they are very Western. They speak fluent English, having been an American colony until 1945, and they are mostly Catholic, a legacy of the Spanish rule, from 1500 to 1898. After World War II the Philippines was the wealthiest country in Asia, ahead of Singapore, Japan and Hong Kong. But today Hong Kong is more than ten times as rich as the Philippines, and imports thousands of Filipinas as maids. Alone amongst the non-communist Asian economies, the Philippines has never quite made it. The other Asian Tigers are now all hi tech; but the Philippines has been left behind, a jarring mix of modernity and traditional superstition. It transpired later that the lady had been wrestling with the dilemma of whether to allow her young niece to see the body of her mother who had died the day before, and was concerned that the released spirit could harm her child.

The Philippines is a country not quite like any other – even more so than Japan or France. It takes only a few weeks to guess 80 per cent of what Filipinos are thinking, but the other 20 per cent will remain closed to the outsider forever. The spectacular car crash that is the Filipino psyche is patched together from a bran tub of spare parts, cast-offs, rejects and seconds from other cultures – garish jeepneys adapted from the army jeeps the Americans abandoned there after the war, a love of pork fat which the Spaniards threw them after taking all the meat from the roast pigs, the basketball for which their height rules them out of contention, the Christmas music and snow decorations that fill their shops from September onwards. And then there are the long self-improvement shelves in their bookstores, the Catholic prayer book, the Pepsi Cola and the ten-pin bowling.

The first wounds to the psyche of the sweet-natured Malays who make up most of the population were inflicted by the cruelty of the Spanish; and the second by the benevolence of the Americans. The second wound was more undermining. The Americans invited them to eat at their tables and to join them under the bonnets to mend their cars. The Filipinos found it difficult

to keep up; and emerged with their confidence ruined and love-hate feelings –
much more love than hate – for their old rulers. Watch a Thai girl cross a room –
confident and graceful. Now watch a Filipina; her eyes, like raw nerves screening
onlookers' reactions around a 360-degree arc, betray her self-consciousness.

And when they finally got their independence things got worse, under the
Marcos police state. The first couple controlled everything. A joke of the time had
it that the only real industry in the Philippines was mining. President Ferdinand
Marcos would point at the sugar industry and say 'that's mine', and then Imelda
would point at the top supermarkets and say 'they're mine', and then. . .

The extent of the Marcos's control was extraordinary. When we first arrived
we tried to order a few cane chairs from a small, roadside craftsman. He wasn't
able to do them for weeks, because Imelda had demanded that he produce an
impossible number of chairs at an impossibly low price for her. And at Manila's
cultural centre the audience would often wait for an hour for Imelda to arrive
before a ballet could start. Then at the interval she would hand out packets of
Maltesers in little red heart-shaped boxes to everyone. Sweet? Not really. It was
was a measure of her reputation that it was rumoured – Manila was a hotbed for
rumours in those days – that a few years after one of the president's girlfriends
had fallen from grace, Imelda drove to her house late one evening, knocked at the
door, asked her bodyguards to confirm that it was indeed the old girlfriend,
before stepping forward herself to throw acid in the woman's face. One of the
best pieces of advice I ever had in Manila is that if the attention of the audience
started to wander while you were giving a talk, just get to the end of a sentence,
pause and then say 'Imelda Marcos'. They would sit bolt upright, from pure fear.

Everyone wanted to leave. I once asked a girl who taught at the university
how many of her friends would do 'anything' to get out. "Maybe 70 per cent,"
she said.

So the Filipinos have learned to dream.

"We Filipinos are very roman-teek," said Innocentia, our chief statistician, a pretty but unalluring girl of 26 with a dolorous, enigmatic smile. She was already concerned about becoming an old maid. Her shelves were decorated with crucifixes, pink fluffy animals, pictures of The Carpenters and family photos, mostly with babies; and her desk was scattered with statistical yearbooks, much-fingered comic books of love stories, packets of dried fish and sticks of raw sugar cane. Sugar is the main product of their countryside; and, supporting the theory that you are what you eat, sugar, and a little spice, is what Philippine girls are made of. Plus all things nice, including purple and orange cream cakes, blue ice cream, pizzas with fruit and technicoloured junk food. Their veins bubble with warm, fizzy, soft drinks. Their books and folders are decorated with little red heart signs. Valentine's day, birthday and Christmas parties and their associated presents and decorations are planned months ahead – the men, seemingly endowed with an extra X chromosome, getting just as excited as the girls. There is at least one 'happy birthday' sung most nights in the restaurants, and all, including those who do not know the celebrant, join in; and everyone is pleased. Their music seems to have passed a compulsory sugar content test. The bars, clubs and restaurants are filled with a thousand Shirley Bassey imitators, pouring out their dramatic emotion and saccharine sentiment.

The sweetness goes right to the top, and is not restricted to the girls. When a violent coup to oust the new president, Corazon Aquino, failed, the punishment to which the leaders were sentenced by the army chief of staff was 50 push-ups. The leader, a handsome, swashbuckling right-winger universally known as Gringo, later went on to become a congressman.

But behind the sweet smiles there is a gloomy undercurrent – the gloom of the Iberian Catholic chapel, the world of rosaries and floor wax. Sad-eyed girls line the pews, devout and deferential, dreaming of love and escape. Their slender, hunched figures are often redeemed by beautiful hands, fragile but graceful. The influence of the Catholic Women's League lies deep in the bones of the Filipina. You see it even in the girlie bars, where the minds of the naive girls from the provinces, so conventional, and often so dull, are torn between the desires for material gain and the unforgotten teachings of the nuns.

And religion is a solace. Later in the evening of the conversation with the lady with the dead mother, I went wandering around her father's mansion (all Filipinos are wealthy except for those who are not members of the top 22 families) and found the inevitable luridly lit and coloured religious shrine, hinting at earlier and more primitive gods to appease. A good Filipino friend of ours, who is a highly intelligent MBA, once scolded a Western friend for not baptising his baby.

"Why?" we asked. He threw the question back at us.

"Well, what would happen if the baby died?"

We shrugged our shoulders and asked him, "Well, what would happen?"

"Its soul would have to live in the mango tree, forever."

We laughed – but then realised that we had offended him. He went bright red. He had been serious.

But they would be mortified to think they were seen as deeply religious.

"We pray a lot but play a lot," giggled Bong Bong, one of our economists, trying to blend his born-again Bambi smile with a hint of devil-may-care naughtiness. He was wearing a Donny Osmond T-shirt. We knew from the 'outside interests' section on his job application form that his main pastimes were 'smoking, bowling and shopping'. Ten-pin bowling is the only sport at which the Philippines have had world champions.

The top national sports, however, are basketball (in spite of Filipinos' limited stature) and beauty contests. Physical beauty has a special status in the Philippines; and beauty contests have the status of Nobel Prize competitions. The higher-level contests are called 'prestigious'. In fact, Imelda herself was a beauty queen, known as 'The Rose of Tacloban', and in 1974 the Philippines won the 'honour' of hosting the Miss Universe competition. As the great day approached bewildering sums of money were spent 'Potemkinising' the area around the venue, and painting the dried-out grass a lush green. But disaster threatened when, a few days before, heavy rains and a mild typhoon were forecast. They were due to hit Manila the day of the contest. Imelda consulted the weather bureau, and then brought in the military. The air force was told to go up and seed the huge approaching rain clouds. They did so, with spectacular success, unleashing a solid wall of water onto the main fish farming areas along the coast north of Manila. The fish escaped out to sea, and production was ruined for years. The Marcoses lost a lot of votes in the area. But the beauty contest was a resounding success.

Another escape is films. Like India and Nigeria, the Philippines has a vast low-budget film industry, and in the late 1970s Imelda decided to challenge Cannes as the venue of the world's top film festival. She invited a list of profoundly beautiful people, and drew up a programme of films which astutely combined potential Oscar winners, serious arty films and more run-of-the-mill films showing nudity, which had not been seen in the Catholic Philippines, and ensured high attendance. Then she had to build the film centre. It was started late and soon ran into trouble. Three weeks before the festival was due to begin they were two weeks behind. Imelda ordered 24-hour working, and they almost caught up – until, with a few days left, disaster struck. As they poured the concrete too fast a whole floor collapsed, and workers fell headlong into the quick-setting liquid. The authorities – that is to say, Imelda – were contacted, but the order came back – the work was to continue. They were permitted to try to rescue only the more accessible of the workers, and only as long as it did not delay the construction. Film smuggled out showed the agony of the dreadful last hours of the dying as the concrete slowly hardened around their bodies while the builders tried to offer comfort. Few survived; and most were entombed within the structure. Nobody knows how many bodies were there, haunting the glamorous proceedings; but even the government conceded that there had been a few casualties. The film festival was a modest success, although it did not last. A couple of years later it was abandoned. The film centre and its resident ghosts now lie empty in a curiously deserted area in the middle of Manila Bay.

23

Malaysia

"Wonderful to meet you at last. Was your flight OK?" asked Desmond effusively.

"Yes, no disasters. It got in right on time," I replied.

Desmond Braithwaite, the regional director for Malaysia, was social history – with his hound's-tooth sports jackets, thick cavalry twills worn throughout the year in the enervating heat, hair brilliantined flat off his forehead and sporty elocution He had left England in 1954 and had remained resolutely untouched by any event there ever since.

"Jolly good. . . Jolly good. . . So. . . um. . . how about an early lunch. What sort of food do you like?" Without waiting for an answer he announced, "I'll take you to where they serve the best food in Malaysia."

And so we went to the British Club, where they serve roast beef on Tuesdays, with Yorkshire pudding.

'A first-rate country for second-rate people.' This verdict on Malaysia was Noel Coward's. The people he referred to were not the Malaysians but the British who ran the country for almost two centuries. My first visit there, in the 1980s, came just before that era of British influence was finally swept away, as Malaysia reinvented itself as a Tiger economy, fuelled by investment from Japan, not Britain.

Malaysia is more than first-rate; it is high on the list of the world's tropical paradises, rich with orchids, cannas, hibiscus and heavy swollen breadfruit, papaya, mangosteens, rambutans and jackfruit; its lush vegetation nourished by torrential rains, and a humid heat on the coast which penetrates deep into the bones. The smell of the tropics – a sensual cocktail of the fragrance of orchids and frangipani; the rank stench of drains and rotting vegetation; the sickly sweet, decaying, cellulosic exhalations of durian; the everyday odours of sweat and sex; and the rich cooking smells of coriander and garlic – is at first mildly repulsive. Later it becomes addictive and deeply relaxing. For those who seek relief, however, there are the cool and fresh country hill stations of the Cameron Highlands and Frasers Hill. And even in the cities, the airy wooden homes with their ceiling fans, verandas and wide fresh lawns made it an attractive posting.

But it was always a posting for the third team. The businessmen of Kuala Lumpur were 'filth'; they had 'Failed In London, and Tried in Hong Kong'. And then failed in Singapore as well. Those who could not quite make it ended up in Malaysia.

There was a constant inflow of representatives, engineers and salesmen from Birmingham seeking better jobs, incomes and social standing in Malaysia than they would have had in England. They came for a year or two, then passed on, disappointed. Dressed in nylon shirts and grey trousers, they could be found on Saturday nights in The Ship, the 'only place in Kuala Lumpur you can get a decent steak'. (Surprisingly the Ship chain has not disappeared, but is now patronised by locals, especially Chinese.)

The long-staying expats were from a different background. Many had been NCOs in the British army in the 1950s, fighting the communists in the jungles of Borneo. Afterwards, loath to return to the drab routine of the UK, they stayed on to take jobs on the Sime Darby rubber plantations, the hardwood concessions, the tin mines and the palm oil estates. Big, brawny men, with rawboned faces, shorts, good leather shoes and long woollen socks ending just below the knee, they got things done, building this or that in nine months when it would have taken two years at home. They had been out of the UK for a generation, and were emphatic that they would never go back. Many of them were Scots – tough, practical exiles living out two-dimensional lives modelled on a Scottish template of hard work, hard drinking, the exercise of thrift, and the dispensing of no-nonsense common sense. They were much more traditionally Scottish than those left behind in the country to which they swore they would never return. The annual liquor-fuelled celebration of Burns Night, with bagpipes, kilts and food that had not been eaten in Edinburgh for 50 years had an importance for the Scots that had no equivalent for the English, Welsh or Irish; and experience taught me to be just a little careful in the bars late on Friday nights, when the expats had had a few beers and were looking for new people to talk to.

"Where are you from?" asked one, wearing a Rangers shirt.

"England."

"Hey, Jimmy, come and meet Ted. He's a Sassenach. . . but he's alright."

But although the banter was enjoyable nothing was more certain than that it was not going to be alright one hour and three pints from now.

Hamish, the engineer with whom I was working on the building of a new port, ran a small, tidy engineering office, staffed by an engaging group of young Scots. Pictures of them in kilts on Burns Night decorated the office walls. Hamish was a thin, quiet man, with a pale wife plagued by poor health. He had lived there for 12 years, was active in the Presbyterian church and highly regarded as a pillar of the local expat community; and he was corrupt. He bought his contracts. Deeply immersed in the local business community, he knew where some of the bodies were buried, and knew whom to pay. He fed off a government that existed to redistribute money from those who made it – the Chinese – to those who didn't – the Malay 'sons of the soil' – but mainly to the government officers themselves.

Hamish was good company, although he could suddenly 'turn' . One memorable afternoon we were walking along the beach, when a tiny Filipina lady approached us and said with a charming simplicity, "Hello, where are you from?"

"London," I replied.

"Oh, A lovely country," she said, with singsong emphasis on the 'try'. We didn't ask if she had been there, as she clearly had not.

We fell into a long conversation, about how she had come to live in Malaysia, the fact that her children did not speak the language of the Philippines and so on. Hamish dominated the conversation and seemed very relaxed. The lady was clearly delighted with the exchange and as we parted she said how lovely it had been to meet two such nice people from England. Hamish's face twisted into an expression of extraordinary cruelty. He rounded on the lady and spat out, "I am not English."

The lady was crestfallen.

"I am Scottish. Don't you know the difference?" And then proceeded to tell her.

It was so awful that five minutes later I pretended that I had left something on the beach and went back and apologised to the poor lady.

I came to like Hamish's long-suffering wife, who feared that she was going to, as she put it, 'die in a foreign land'. The expat wives lived a social life inherited from an earlier tribe – the colonial civil servants of the inter-war years. It revolved around bridge, mutual sympathy for servant problems, amateur dramatics, Scottish dancing, and high tea, which was still served in all the best hotels, especially on Sundays, and curry lunches. They enjoyed their curry lunches; but their assimilation went little further. What they really missed were their English sausages; but at least the supermarkets were full of Chivers marmalade, shortbread biscuits, Birds custard powder, Tate and Lyle syrup and Weetabix – with small sections with the novels of Tom Clancy and Wilbur Smith. The old colonial influence was also echoed in the 'teksis' the ladies took to their 'kelabs' – the Malay words for taxis and clubs mimicking the locution of the upper classes of the 1930s when black tie was still worn even for visits to the cinema. (The upper-class pronunciation is also reflected in the Malay words for 'customs', which is 'kastoms', and 'bus', which is 'bas'). The women were less stereotypical than their men. Some had a withering wit, sharpened on years of mediocrity. One feature united them. Underneath, there was an element of sadness; they wanted to go home.

I only encountered Desmond once more after that first day. He had called a meeting with some local civil servants. As we waited for the last arrivals he was in a pleasant mood, gossiping about local politics with his very old-fashioned charm. Time passed and he looked at his watch and saw that it was now ten minutes since the meeting should have started. He showed a little impatience, which turned quickly and inexplicably to anger. As soon as the last person was seated, he drew the meeting of quite senior civil servants to order with the words, "I would like to start the meeting by explaining something that people in this country clearly do not understand: it is punctuality. . ."

Meanwhile, the Chinese – industrious, intelligent, serious, and family-minded – went quietly about their business of making money. On my last afternoon there I visited two offices. The first was Harrison and Crosfield, an old established British trading company, with pleasant wood-panelled offices. Their manager was elderly, grey-haired and hospitable. He conceded that they were finding the competition tougher these days. He said of the Chinese, "Bright young fellows. Not completely sure about their methods sometimes. But they're learning the trade fast." Later I went to see a new Chinese company with whom they were competing. The manager was 25 years old, surrounded by computers and modern office furniture, and had an unusual grasp of both the detail of his business and the big picture. He was polite, extremely helpful and diplomatic. Only once did his diplomatic front slip, when I pressed on the question: "How do you see the future?"

He hesitated.

"If you would like my opinion," he said, "ten years from now, these old English companies will be finished here."

He was more or less right.

24

Turkmenistan

In the centre of Ashkhabad, the capital of Turkmenistan, a towering white tripod supports what looks like a giant spark plug soaring 60 metres towards the sky. At its apex is a 12-metre statue of President Niyazov, gleaming in the sun. His arms are outstretched as if he is blessing his people below. The statue rotates so that it always faces the sun. It is said to be made of pure gold, but it is probably only gold-plated, as even Niyazov could not have stolen enough from his wretched people to afford pure gold.

Turkmenistan is unchallenged as the most bizarre country in the world, run according to the whims of an increasingly deranged leader, the self-styled President 'Turkmenbashi'. It is a name he invented for himself, meaning 'the leader of the Turkmens'. Over the years he had banned the playing of recorded music at weddings, beards, car radios, long hair and lip-synching. He has closed all hospitals outside the capital, and replaced 15,000 nurses with soldiers; he has declared doctors' and lawyers' qualifications from outside Turkmenistan invalid; he has shut down rural libraries, claiming that people in villages did not read; and he has made fur hats, which he likes, mandatory for schoolgirls. Like Chairman Mao he has written his own spiritual guide, *The Ruhnama*, a 'vessel of knowledge, wisdom and sound thought', and incorporated it in the country's legal code; and he has let it be known that he has arranged with God that anybody who reads the book three times is guaranteed entry to heaven. He has also written an autobiography, and ruled that to get a driving licence the applicant must pass an exam on its contents. He has changed the Turkmen word for bread to the name of his mother, and renamed some of the months after members of his family. He also has strong views on teeth. Those with gold teeth have been told to have them extracted and to chew on bones. He has been watching dogs chewing since he was young and knows that they have strong teeth. Mr Niyazov also interrupts government meetings to read his poems aloud.

Under his rule the average wage in his country has settled at about $100 per month.

But it is not entirely Niyazov's fault; his country has never been much more than an empty desert which has been passed through, or more often overrun, since the beginning of time. Its only real claim to fame was being part of the Silk Road, along which silk, spices and jade were transported from China to Rome, and glass, cloth and pottery moved in the other direction 2,000 years ago. Later it was overrun by the Mongol hordes of Ghenghis Khan and Tamerlane who tore through Central Asia, living on horseback for days, and competing to cut off the greatest number of heads per day in the cities they overran. A witness of the time recalled the invaders:

> their stench was more horrible than their colour. Their heads were set on their
> bodies as if they had no necks, and their cheeks resembled leather bottles full
> of wrinkles and knots. Their noses extended from cheekbone to cheekbone.
> Their nostrils resembled rotting graves. Their chests in colour half-black,
> half-white, were covered with lice which looked like sesame growing in bad

soil. Their bodies were covered with these insects and their skins were rough-grained as shagreen leather, fit only to be converted into shoes. . .

Next came the Russians. They took over Turkmenistan 150 years ago, and held it until the early 1990s; and they did their worst there. The 'stans' (Turkmenistan, Kazakhstan, Tajikistan, Kyrgyzstan and Uzbekistan) were the outhouses where the Russians did their dirtier work. Kazakhstan, for example, was used to mine uranium and test nuclear bombs. But Turkmenistan didn't even get that.

My entry point to Turkmenistan was through the old port town of Krasnovodsk, which had been renamed. . . yes, Turkmenbashi, in honour of the president. It lies at the end of a 1,000-kilometre railway line from Ashgabat which crosses a hot featureless desert and comes to a dead end on the Caspian Sea. The town was built as a garrison town by the Russian army 140 years ago to defend the western terminus of their railway. It would not have been an attractive posting. To the west lies the tideless Caspian and to the east is the lunar landscape of the desert. There was nothing there then, and there is almost nothing there now – only an oil refinery and an empty port. Its only export is scrap. Like many of the ex-Soviet colonies it sits in the sun waiting for the construction of the pipelines needed to export the oil and gas that lie under the desert. But none of their neighbours will let the pipelines cross their land.

I sailed there in a lumbering old Russian rail ferry, a cast-iron hulk, from the relatively luxurious city of Baku on the other side of the Caspian. I took it after being challenged by a Russian girl in our group, when I asked about my air ticket to Turkmenistan.

"No, you're not going to fly. We're going to get you a ferry ticket."

"You must be joking," I replied. The ferries were known to be dangerous, in fact, only six weeks later one sank on a windy night, with all lives lost.

"Come on," she argued, "almost no foreigners are ever allowed into Turkmenistan, and you have the chance to be the first European *ever* to go there on the boat."

"Absolutely not."

"You have to. You're supposed to be the maritime expert."

I gradually weakened.

It was a joyless voyage. The ship sailed four hours late, when the crew had finished drinking, and it was almost empty apart from the oil wagons on the bottom decks. It had been designed to carry 600 passengers, and did so in Soviet times, but that night it was carrying only a dozen, and they stayed in their cabins drinking vodka, ignoring the 200-seat lounge, which had no doubt been the scene of happier times. I kept my head down, wary after my first exchange.

"Hello, what's your name?" said an unsteady shaven-headed man in a black leather jacket in Russian.

"Ted."

"Where are you from?"

"England."

He looked confused, then his eyes seemed to focus.

"England... Bobby Charlton?" he slurred, swaying slightly. "Ah, you will be my friend, my guest... we will drink vodka together."

"Sure, we'll find each other later."

I made sure we didn't: I retreated to my cabin, where I found no soap, no towel, a broken shower dribbling tepid rust-coloured water and no toilet paper. But it was almost clean and its bunk bed was almost cosy. I woke a hundred times during the night to feel the ship pitching, rolling and yawing as it heaved, engine throbbing and labouring, through the waves.

The journey was scheduled to take half a day. But the ship dropped anchor without explanation when it arrived in Turkmenbashi and lay in the blistering sun for another 17 hours. Only then did I get into conversation. It was with an old man standing on the rear deck with a black coat that was probably smart long ago, an Astrakhan hat and no teeth. He spoke, or declaimed, for almost an hour, in Russian, like an ancient mariner, seemingly oblivious to how little I understood. But I did understand a little when he ranted about The Dollar and the American Devils.

"Where are you from?" he asked eventually.

"London," I said, pleased to be able to let him know I wasn't American – although he must have known as I did not have the pig's snout and top hat that all Americans had in Soviet cartoons.

"Ah. London, USA. A capitalist. You have ruined our country."

"It was better when the Russians were here?" I asked sympathetically, to try to calm him down.

"*Konyeshna*. In Soviet times at least 'a man' could work. Now there is nothing."

I feared that he might rush at me and try to throw me overboard.

We finally docked at midnight. But that was not the end of the voyage. We shivered for another two hours on the cavernous, draughty ferry ramp, among the black rail wagons full of Uzbek crude oil, in the chilled early hours of the morning – waiting for the consul to arrive and grant us visas. He signed just before 2am.

The hotel in which I stayed – it was called. . . yes, The Turkmenbashi – was a five-star building with well-furnished rooms, beautiful Russian staff, tennis courts and a swimming pool outside. But the swimming pool had no water; in fact, the hotel had no water and there were only four guests apart from myself. On the top of the tenth floor was a huge picture of the fleshy features and raven-black hair of President Turkmenbashi. There was also a huge bust of His Excellency in the foyer.

The president's five-year plan included a promise that every Turkmen family would be given a Mercedes. But there in Turkmenbashi there were only Ladas – clunky, asthmatic Ladas, and almost all of them were part-time taxis.

I took one of these taxis. It already had a fellow passenger, a slender boyish girl, with short black hair, and some English.

"Where are you going?" she asked.

"To find a café. The restaurant at the hotel is closed."

"Why not come for a swim instead; with me?"

"Well. . . I have no swimming trunks."

"That's no problem." She smiled. "Maybe we could relax a little after."

She seemed very natural, and she did not sulk when I insisted that I had to eat, but she asked me for 20,000 manat, the local currency, for herself as I left the taxi and smiled happily when I gave it to her. In English money it was 60 pence – about twice the taxi fare, which was 30 pence for four miles.

After breakfast, my first meal for 36 hours, I found my way to the port. My local contact there was Gulnaza. I found her in a modest office on the second floor with a big bag of tomatoes on her desk. She seemed a quiet, pretty, unassuming girl, who, I found later, worried that she looked too Turkmen, with her slightly slanted eyes and sharp cheekbones. Unsurprisingly in this dirt-poor country, she had simple tastes. As I sat down, she offered me a tomato.

"I really love tomatoes," she said "and I've just got these from the market. . . Now, what sort of information will you be needing, and who would you like to meet?"

I told her, in some detail. She thought for moment, and then – rather than ask the specialists to come in – she started to answer each of my questions herself, sometimes with decimal-point accuracy. Halfway through, the phone rang and she said politely, "You'll have to excuse me for a few minutes."

Ten minutes later she returned. "It was the Minister of Transport, who's visiting the port," she explained. "He needed help on something." And then she continued with her replies to my questions.

The next interruption was from a heavily built Dutch engineer who burst in.

"Gulnaza," he sounded harassed, "sorry to bother you again, but the transistor on that machine I mentioned has broken. We'll have to stop work."

Gulnaza paused for a moment.

"Try a type B transistor," she replied. "It might work. If not call this number, and if you don't get anywhere, come back to me." It turned out that nobody moved without Gulnaza.

In the evenings I ate in the same place that I had breakfast on the first morning. It was the best café in town, serving well-cooked egg and chips. I usually walked there to fill in the time after work. On television, Turkmenistan was a technicolour country full of healthy young girls in swirling ethnic skirts and gold-thread embroidery, striding with heads held high through fields of swaying corn; but the reality I saw was a shabby ex-Soviet urban landscape. The homes I passed were like housings for electrical machinery, with metal window frames and broken hinges; and the shops were unchanged from Soviet times. They had no displays outside; and inside the crude steel doors the unappetising goods were laid out like spare car parts in a hangar. 'Magasin no 37' at the bottom of the main street was supervised by an attractive Russian matron of about forty, with hair hennaed a lurid shade of aubergine and a full set of gold front teeth. The people age early in Turkmenistan. But the president has helped them. He has decreed that no-one is old until they reach the age of 85 (although almost no Turkmens would ever reach this age). Up to 37 they are classified as 'youthful', from 37 to 49 they are 'mature' and from 49 to 85 they are in the years of 'inspiration'.

Halfway through my stay, we had to leave for a short visit to Kazakhstan, a few hundred miles to the north. The journey took 12 hours by car, mostly across trackless scrub – past concrete see-through skeletons of abandoned metallurgy plants, and chemical factories in the desert, one with a lurid beetroot-coloured lake, seeping toxic waste and a smell of gas chambers – and a few tortoises. There were also 'Mullah stops', where the driver was able to pray for a safe journey and make a contribution to a Mullah sitting beside a little shrine. It may have helped – because later we lost our way, and, with little guidance from the overhead sun, drove in circles through the desert for a couple of hours. Eventually we happened to find our way again, but I often wondered about the fate of a driver of a jeep we found abandoned in soft sand, far from anywhere. It seemed to have been abandoned recently. I asked the driver to detour to report it. But he said no; the driver may have been trying something illegal across the border and would not thank us for alerting the authorities.

Back in Turkmenbashi I worked for the last few days in Gulnaza's office in the port. At lunchtimes they locked the office doors, and I sat outside in the sun for an hour near a concrete tenement building, named after a local ammonia plant which closed years ago. A few pale, grey-eyed Russian children with the watchful faces of adults played in the dust; some head-scarfed old ladies in their 40s sat in front of makeshift stalls selling tiny bags of melon seeds; and old men on benches stared at empty horizons across the wasteland of their grassless park. Their blank looks saw no future; and they were more or less right. All the hopes of 1917 – the dreams, the idealism, the lofty speeches, the sacrifices, the promises, the five-year plans, the purges, the torture, the executions of millions, the uprooting of whole populations, the gulags and the secrecy – for this.

We were trying to help by persuading them to stop fleecing each other. In the offices we visited we explained the benefits of 'removing barriers to trade'.

"If you all stop charging other countries' containers $1,000 to pass over your territory," we said, "you'll all be better off." But the impact was like a nun selling catechisms around the campfires of Ghenghis Khan's hordes.

"You do not understand our country," I was told, once again.

I left no footprints, no memories; I might as well never have been there. With only one exception. On the ferry back to Baku (it sank soon afterwards, with 50 killed), I was trying to talk to some of the cadet sailors in Russian. They realised that I understood very little, but I did understand when one shouted to a friend on the deck below.

"Quick, you have to come up," he shouted. "You won't believe who we're talking to."

"Who is it?"

"It's Mr Bean."

Postscript: Two years later Mr Niyazov died and his dentist took over as president.

25

Java

There is a small island about fifty miles off the coast of Java. The engine on our boat has broken down and I am stranded here in a tiny beach hotel until tomorrow morning. The sun is starting to set over the sea, and the colours in the sky are the lurid pinks and pale blues which can sometimes seem tawdry – the colours of paintings sold in Woolworths. But they soften in the twilight as the sun dips towards the horizon. I recall that only a century ago the world's greatest volcanic eruption – at Krakatoa, just 100 miles away – left a legacy of memorable sunsets for many years afterwards

I am relieved to be away from the noise and fumes of Jakarta for an evening. The couple who own the little hotel are tiny, with bones like polished mahogany and embarrassed smiles. They fuss and worry and are ashamed, but the fish they serve is wonderful and the plain little beach shack I will sleep in is more than adequate.

Just before dark I go for a walk along the shore.

At the end of the beach I discover a small graveyard, close to the water. It is protected by a rockery which raises it a few feet above the level of high tide. The gravestones are simple, and the fading light is just sufficient to show that the dates are all from the 19th century. The inscriptions paint a picture of a small community, almost all Dutch. A few lived to a good age, but many died young. A young mother from Holland with a pretty name died in 1862, aged 27. The tablet records that she had three children, and two lie beneath a small stone next to hers. She presumably went abroad with her husband, maybe an engineer.

I sit on the beach and listen to the relentless whisper of the sea. I have no books with me; and the ubiquitous gamelan music, Java's haunting sound of moonlight and flowing water, is for once absent. There is nothing to fill the time this evening. There is only the company of the Dutch who were buried in this foreign land.

26

South Korea in 1972

"Wow, in like a tiger," said Murray, as I walked blearily into the breakfast room. It was 6.45am. Murray looked – as he might have put it – full of beans and ready to go in his crisp button-down blue shirt, Brookes Brothers tie and beige slacks. Still fit in his 60s, he was the only person I had ever met who looked like the American husband bringing their first refrigerator home to the adoring wife in the 1950s adverts. He was the most senior of the six people at breakfast – two of us from London, two American port engineers from the Deep South, and two advisors who were retired vice presidents of American shipping lines. A few minutes later Murray finished his coffee with a gulp and a flourish, smacked his lips together, observing, as he had done on the previous two mornings, "Well, that hit the spot," and stood up to meet the new day. Twenty minutes later a minivan arrived to take us in to work.

As we drove through the bleak empty streets, past early morning road sweepers and the dimly lit, grey concrete buildings of Seoul – it was still dark – one of our English group bore the brunt of the responsibility for conversation. He was Mark, a chartered accountant who had been brought in to help with the port's financial records. He was in his mid 30s, with an outdated opening-batsman hairstyle, tight waves cascading sideways across his forehead like Kenneth More's. He was perhaps not the brightest, but he had the infectious gaiety of a young army officer and was well liked. He chattered amiably to Murray about a letter he had just received from his wife at home in Epsom. She was due to visit soon.

Half an hour later we arrived at the Korean office of Jaguar Engineering Inc. They were military engineers who had already made a lot of money in the Vietnam War. But they knew that the war was going to end sometime and were diversifying into ports. They had somehow won a large contract to work on a national ports plan, but didn't really know how to do it, and had brought the rest of us in to help.

The first few days were spent in long internal meetings, trying to decide what to do, with the inevitable jockeying for position as each of us sought to establish credibility in uncharted territory. There was one clear natural chairman, Murray, and it was assumed that he would take on that role. But he turned out to be more modest than his manner had at first suggested; in fact, he was a thoughtful and considerate man, helping me out when he sensed that I was already having trouble with the project's manager, Hank Bull. Hank, an ex-US army engineer, had a boxer's physique, a fleshy face and heavy black eyebrows, and he had decided on the first day that I was a communist, probably because my longish hair was not out of the American template with which he was familiar. My standing was not helped when we all went downstairs to a bar at lunchtime on the second day to watch Muhammad Ali fighting the latest of the 'great white hopes'. Hank was noisily supporting the white boxer and was visibly irked at my seeming to favour Ali, and when Ali won he stormed out without a word. Murray, noticing the friction, was generous at the early meetings, listening courteously to my new-boy's views in areas which he knew well.

The meetings were long and tedious. But out of them a natural leader did emerge. It was Chuck, one of Jaguar's engineers. About medium height, in his mid 30s, he had a passing resemblance to Steve McQueen. With a steady stare and slow smile, his strong sense of identity was rooted solidly in the Old South, with a backdrop of humour about grits, good old boys and country and western. But when he spoke, in his deep laconic voice with his gentlemanly Southern manners – he called everyone sir – everyone deferred.

To save money and make Jaguar profits we ate evening meals together at the apartment. It was cheaper than giving us a per diem allowance. So we lived in lockstep, an arrangement that is rarely to my liking. But in this case the company was good, and I enjoyed listening to the Americans banter.

After dinner Chuck sat over a beer, talking to Rod, the other Jaguar engineer.

"Ada had another fit in the office today," said Chuck.

Rod was silent for a few seconds, then asked,

"Has she found something?"

Ada was Jaguar's office administration manager. Loud and cheerful, she would have been pretty if she had not been so plump. She had a photograph of herself on her desk, with her hair in an Alice band, selling cupcakes at a Daughters of the American Revolution garden party. She was responsible for the apartment, and she thought some of the men were bringing girls back there at night.

"No, but she says she can tell. She burst into tears in front of Bull this morning. She told him that she knows what's going on, and if it doesn't stop, she's leaving. So make sure you leave nothing around. She comes here in the daytime. Hide everything."

"Where?"

"Where she won't look. In the grits carton, inside football magazines. . . or in your poetry books, you know, high culture. . . if you have any." He pronounced 'high' slowly in three syllables.

There was another silence. Rod was smiling.

"Chuck I've been thinking, couldn't we. . . kinda. . . get someone pay her a little attention from time to time. If she was looked after by someone, maybe she would stop coming down on the rest of us."

Chuck sipped at his beer, saw what Rod was getting at and cocked his head to one side. "Well I'd go into the jungle with you, Rod, but. . . not that. Beyond the call of duty. . . Anyway, not sure I could handle her. Have you ever seen that look in her eyes when she sings in church on the army base? There's some pent-up passion deep down there." Again three syllables in the 'there'.

They sat quietly, savouring the thought.

"Anyway, she's family in Jaguar."

He noticed the clock.

"Well, who's for Itaewon?"

Itaewon was the sprawl of bars and clubs outside the Yongsan army base where most of Korea's 40,000 GIs were stationed. We arrived around 9pm and opened the door of the Rodeo Saloon to a gale of Credence Clearwater at full volume and a dance floor full of bodies flickering under the strobe lights. The club was packed, but one of the most attractive girls came up to Chuck, whom she obviously knew, and led us to a table. There were six of us – the two American engineers, three of us from England and Hank Bull. This was one of the best of times for music and clothes. The blacks and whites had only been integrated in the army for a few years; and from time to time black soldiers came up and stared at me.

"Hey man, are you from the world?"

"From London."

"Man, where's that?" I smiled but couldn't understand much of what they were saying against the music.

Chuck and Rod were in the habit of inviting a stream of girls over to our table to tease Mark, who enjoyed the atmosphere but was there for the beer, the company and the music, not the girls. The Korean girls, unlike other Asian girls, were sturdily built and often tough-looking; and although some were strikingly beautiful, most spoke little English. There may have been a *Teach Yourself English* book circulating amongst the girls with a first chapter that recommended a sweet smile followed by "Me your number-one fuck. She number ten. I give good time mister."

Mark was always gallant; he chatted happily with the girls and would often get up to dance with them. But at the ends of the evenings, when Rod or Chuck asked him what he thought, he would always say "She's very charming, but I think. . . not tonight."

Until the night he met Miss O. It was an evening on which he had had a little more to drink. "Hey, Mark," Chuck drawled. "Come over here. We'd like to introduce you to Miss O. Miss O is class act. Believe me." She was tall and thin with bones like sword blades, and narrow eyes cut into a face of sculpted planes, but what really made her stand out was the Kennedy clan hair – thick, shiny, straight, no nonsense and aristocratic. Her English, although brutally direct, was much better than most of the girls' and she was very assertive. She homed in on Mark, applied her fierce charms, and soon they went off to dance together. At the end of the evening Mark was not to be seen.

We spent much of the next few weeks travelling round Korea – a country which still had a timeless natural beauty in those last years before industrialisation, a land of craggy hills, mountain streams, waterfalls, misty valleys and forests. We also found deep sadness in a country that had been a colony of the

Japanese and then torn apart in the Korean War. They were in their last years of being poor. There was little apart from dried fish, rice and *kimchi* to eat, and we drank in cold bars in the evenings, still wearing our anoraks. From time to time we were joined by Mark. He had been seeing Miss O, and, although discreet, he could be drawn on the subject. He shook his head in wonder as he said, "It's opened up a new world to me. . . I had no idea."

One night, back in Seoul, I got to the club a little late and found the others convulsed with laughter around Mark, looking sheepishly pleased at being the centre of attention.

"What's happened?"

"Go on, Mark, repeat it for Ted."

Mark at first demurred, but was talked into it.

"OK. Well, I wouldn't normally talk about this sort of thing, but I was telling them about my first evening with Miss O. If you recall I'd had a little to drink, and we ended up later in a hotel. And there I was lying in bed covered only with a sheet as Miss O came out of the shower. She asked if I could see an electric kettle, and I said yes, it's over there. She put it on, and I said, 'I think there are tea bags there as well'. She busied herself drying her hair for a couple of minutes and then went into the bathroom for another towel. But when she came back, instead of making tea, she poured the boiling water over the towel. I remember thinking that's odd, but before I had time to focus she darted towards me, pulled off the sheet, lunged at my expectant JT, and wrapped the boiling towel round it, squeezing it tight, and then tighter and tighter. It was pure agony for a moment, but she smiled at me reassuringly. The girls apparently believed that a scalding poultice will bring out the evidence of any social disease. I passed the test, and after this she made it up to me. . . in a lot ways I had no experience of. . ." He grinned sheepishly and shook his head disbelievingly.

The next week we all went down to Pusan, Korea's main port, 300 miles to the south. Mark now had a liking for the bars and the girls. But he had become impatient, and we were surprised at the girl he was dancing with that night.

Back in the apartment in Seoul a few days later, we noticed that Mark was no longer the life and soul of the party. He was evasive, but eventually confessed that he had been feeling some pain in his nether regions and it was getting worse. At first he refused to go to the doctor, as he had heard bad reports of how they treat foreigners. But Chuck and Rod marched him onto the base, where the army doctor confirmed that he had a very bad infection and gave him a cocktail of antibiotics and medicines, and told him it should be gone in ten days. More precisely it should be clear on the day his wife arrived. That is, as long as he kept off alcohol and rested sensibly.

I doubt if any group of people have ever shared pain so fully with another human being. We cringed as he minced across the apartment with crossed legs to visit the toilet. We stopped going to Itaewon in the evenings, out of sympathy, and in case we met Miss O, whom he was clearly missing. And we even limited our consumption of beer to make him feel better. But Mark was not a good patient. He kept taking beers out of the fridge when nobody was looking, arguing that one wouldn't matter.

Murray had returned to Seoul for a few days, and we got him to take Mark aside and give him some fatherly advice. He told Mark, "Look, these pills may seem not to be working but in the end they always do. Just relax. And no alcohol."

"Are you sure of that they always work?" we asked Murray afterwards. His look said – you must be joking.

"No. At least I have no idea. But I think if he believes that, he might get better just a little quicker. "

After five days the pain was getting worse, and Mark was still sneaking into the refrigerator. So Chuck took over. He decided that there was to be no alcohol in the apartment. We protested, and he said nothing. But that night he removed all the bottles and put them in a safe place.

"Don't worry. It's not been put down the sink. It'll be back the day his wife arrives."

With two days to go there were signs of recovery, and on the night before his wife was due we asked:

"How are you?"

"Not sure." He crossed his fingers as he said it.

Mark's wife Jennifer was from a world unfamiliar to me – an English rose who might have been seen on the arm of Trevor Howard in an old black-and-white film. London was ruled by Biba that year, while Jennifer was dressed beautifully and expensively in beige cashmere. But she was quick to join in banter with Chuck and they had a long debate about the provenance of the antebellum Southern belle in the evening. Next morning she and Mark were in good spirits, and after breakfast they set off for two days in a log cabin up in the mountains.

A few weeks later I left Seoul, on the same day as Rod. We didn't go to Itaewon on our last night. It was Rod's decision. "No, not tonight," he said, "I'm still thinking of Mark. And in any case I'll be home tomorrow and I'll have to pass the pressure test." (Again, 'test' in three syllables.) Chuck nodded.

I came across Chuck only once again, many years later. He had stayed with Jaguar. He was heavier and had lost some of his understated charisma; the gothic South was reclaiming a free spirit. And later I bumped into Hank Bull from time to time in odd bars around Manila and Jakarta where he was also still working for Jaguar. I had ended up on better terms with him, as he had once done me a good turn when I was in trouble, and I had also done him a good turn in a roundabout way. He told me that Ada had married a 'Chinaman' whom she had started seeing late during our time in Seoul. Apparently she used to meet him in her apartment in the daytime, claiming she was out buying office stationery. They lived in Hawaii. I never saw Miss O again, although in that last week in Seoul I had caught sight of her coming out of a room in the basement of the city's top five-star hotel, and, by enquiring at the desk, found she was living there. Apparently she was not just one of the girls at Itaewon – she was a 'mamasan'. There had always been something about her. Murray I never saw again, nor Mark nor his wife. I often wondered. . .

27

The Real India

Goa, the port guesthouse, Wednesday 15 July, 6am. It is still dark when the servants come to wake us for the long drive south. We are ushered out to the car in the chilled morning air by the bearers, who present us with little, brown-paper parcels of samosas for our breakfast. The paper is folded into neat triangles at the back and meticulously tied with twine, doubtless in exactly the same way as they had been since the Raj began. I am surprised to see no sealing wax. The bearers' faces are leathery and lined, although they are probably ten years younger than us. They seem almost incandescent with excitement at the brief visit of the foreigners, and they wave us goodbye as if we are their own relatives going on a journey. As we turn out of the compound into the city streets, the first light is filtering through over the hills in the east, the rooks are cawing, men in lungis are setting out on their morning walks and the wood smoke is rising as the women start to cook.

I am already starting to doze in the back of the van. It has been two days since we had left the big cities behind. "You haven't seen the real India until you get out into the villages," they told me in Mumbai, where the beginnings of India's economic miracle were being hatched in a maze of

Victorian baroque buildings in narrow streets. There, the stale air had felt as if it had been recycled a dozen times by different pairs of weary lungs; the sunlight was filtered out by the dense canopies of overhanging branches of the timeworn trees that line the cobbled streets, and you could not walk ten metres through the crowds without bumping into someone scurrying, head down, between the rabbit warrens of offices. They have a big-city disdain for the provincial, but they still have a romantic attachment to the simple villages they have left to seek their fortunes. . . And they said it again in the other great city, Delhi, the government capital where the civil servants – tired, once-clever men – yawn under the slowly revolving fans on the high ceilings of their cold empty offices. There is a timeless beauty in Lutyens' imperial government buildings, especially around sunset, but, inside, every stairwell is stained with betel juice spit and the air of listlessness is tangible. They grumble about Delhi, maybe because they have mortgaged their lives for power and money; and, as in Mumbai, their eyes light up when they talk about their home villages. So it came as a welcome suggestion when they said, "We'd like you to travel down the coast to look at the small ports."

9am. I awoke in bright sunlight, to my first sight of the other India I had been promised. On our right was the Indian Ocean, like a motionless pond stretching to the horizon, and on our left was the beginning of 500 miles of flatlands, rice fields and inland lakes, like glassy mirrors reflecting the few wispy clouds high in the blue sky – a tranquil pastoral landscape with farmers, bony limbs burned like mahogany, planting crops knee-deep in water, and buffaloes hauling ancient ploughs through the waterlogged fields. There was a spareness everywhere, in the scattered palm trees, in the angular wading birds silhouetted like sculptures in the rice paddies, and even in the buildings – flimsy, skeletal, more like shelters than homes and shops.

Around 10.30am, the coast road started to fill with school children. The boys were smart and seemed well-behaved, and the girls had the straight-backed deportment that came from helping their mothers carrying loads on their heads. Their crisp white blouses were dazzling against skin burned almost black, and their skirts of dark green blended with the emerald and apple greens of the countryside. With their long plaited hair, glossy with coconut oil, and wholesome faces they might have been the model Baden Powell had in mind when, after returning from India, he set up his girl scouts. They were, it turned out, coming back from, not going to, school. They had started around dawn and were making way for another set of children arriving in mid-morning.

We – two Indians and three Europeans – stopped for a drink, stretching and yawning as we hauled ourselves out of the van. It was already warm. A sun shower had coloured the wet laterite soil a deeper red and was drawing a rich humid smell from the vegetation. A man behind a stall cut coconuts open with a brutal-looking machete, and the schoolchildren clustered round and stared, quiet and uncertain, as we drank. For a few seconds the only sound in the stillness was of insects buzzing in the shimmering heat. But when we said hello to the children they burst into a hundred wide-open smiles, with glittering white teeth and bright credulous eyes. Tell us, please, about the world outside, they seemed to say.

But the appearance of a pastoral idyll could be misleading. Further down the coast we passed groups of women breaking stones for aggregates at the roadside, their dark muscular limbs only partly protected from the sun by black umbrellas lodged between the stones. Again, their bearing and boniness had a sculptural beauty, but the work was of grinding misery.

Thursday, 6pm. We arrived at the Tuticorin port guesthouse. The bearers and the cook had been waiting for us outside, standing to attention as we drove up. They grabbed our bags and led us up to our rooms, vast but sparsely furnished, with mosquito nets under torpidly rotating fans. My helper pointed at my case. "I will take your clothes to wash, sahib." It sounded like an order. In India even the servants sound bossy when they speak English. I hesitated but handed my shirts to him.

Downstairs, the cook presented himself. He was in his 70s, and was excited by our arrival.

"I have worked here for many years and cooked for many foreigners. What would you be liking, sahib?"

"How about a nice chicken curry and some vegetables?" said our German tugboat captain.

The cook seemed a little disappointed. Maybe it was too simple a meal to allow him to show off his abilities. But he waggled his head in agreement.

"Acha, sahib. It will be to your satisfaction." He turned to berate his assistant and they withdrew to the dark concrete bunker that was the scullery. We sat and drank a beer and then two and then three. Time passed. Long babbling exchanges were audible from the scullery. After about two hours we went to ask how the food was going.

"Only a few minutes it will being ready. All is tickety-boo, sahib."

Another hour later he called us in, for our meal of pork chops in gravy with potatoes and peas.

"This was the favourite of Captain Higginbottom, harbour master in the wartime, before the Partition," the cook told us. "A very fine English sahib. You will know him, of course."

I thought. . . he would probably be over a hundred by now.

Dessert was bread-and-butter pudding with custard.

"And your drinks, sahibs." Dark brown tea with condensed milk.

"Did it fit the bill, sahib?" he inquired eagerly afterwards.

We exchanged glances and told him that it was wonderful, just like food back home.

Friday, 8am. I was due to leave this afternoon, so I walked round behind the guesthouse with the German to ask how our shirts were going.

"It is all in order. I am drying them now," said the dhobi. There was a pile of shirts lying beside a sink at the other end of the room. They were not mine – mine were all white and these were tie-dyed blue and pink. He noticed me looking at them.

"You like?" he asked with an eager smile.

"Oh. . . um, yes."

"They are better now."

I turned and saw the German's pale-blue eyes blazing with what seemed like suppressed ecstasy. He was struggling to keep quiet. It may have been the happiest moment of his life. He had twigged before it slowly dawned on me.

"But. . . why. . . er. . . have you dyed them?" I faltered, lost for words.

"They look better now, sahib," he explained. "They will be dry by this afternoon."

10am. Into the meeting with the port director. Most of India's port directors are high achievers on three-year postings on their way to the top of the formidable Indian Civil Service. Often they are austere intellectuals. In Cochin, the port director had looked at my card and said, "Ah hah, are you related to the psychologist R D Laing?" And although disappointed that I was not he went on to give well-informed views on the psychologist's writing. But in this distant town at the southern tip of India, the director was a local politician, who interpreted his remit to manage the port to mean imposing strict discipline on his staff. A plump angry man who seemed to be wearing some sort of makeup, he brought about forty of his staff to the meeting, announcing that he always involved his top men; but then spoke for three hours without a pause. The only two minor interruptions were swatted mercilessly aside. We were there to find out how they wanted their port to grow and what money they needed for investment, but he kept diverting to stories of how inappropriate behaviour was given short shrift. "Blooming cheek. I gave him a most severe dressing-down. Then I sacked the damned blighter on the spot," he bellowed.

All through the meeting a young man crept up silently behind my chair and whispered questions.

"Your good name Sir?"

"Sorry?"

"Your good name is needed to arrange your train ticket on to Madras, first-class, sahib."

A few minutes later he was back for my title, and then my passport number, my religion, caste age, village of birth, name of my father, and maiden name of my mother. All were necessary to buy a ticket for the train, first-class.

At the end of the meeting, we, the visitors, were asked to step forward one by one. A young lady placed a scarlet sash decorated with plastic orange flowers over our heads, and five photographers appeared unexpectedly from behind a screen in the corner of the room where they had been crouching to record the event.

We had to be at the train station well before seven o'clock, but at five pm the car had not arrived to take us so I asked a receptionist to telephone to check if it was on its way. She rang and reported back.

"Yes it will be coming soon."

Another 20 minutes passed.

She rang to check again.

"Yes, it is coming," she assured me.

Another ten minutes and it looked as if we might miss the train.

"I think we had better find another car."

"Oh, no, sir, he is coming already."

"Yes, but when will he get here?"

"He is waiting downstairs. He is coming half an hour ago."

We sped off to the station. My only companion on this leg of the journey was Mr Krishnamurti. He was sleek, plump, a little epicene and immensely pleased with himself, but very useful as he had been a port chairman himself before retiring. I told him about the long list of information needed to get the ticket. He nodded and confirmed that these details were most important. One mistake would mean that you would be 'removed from the train forthwith'. I scrutinised my ticket, to check that all was in order, and was disturbed to find an error. It showed my age as being 20 years older than I was.

"What do you think?" I asked Mr Krishnamurti. "Might they throw me off the train?" He took out his reading spectacles, perused the ticket, and smiled as if to himself.

"There will be no problem. They will not suspect that you are not of the age shown." Outraged, I turned to him to protest, but he was already looking out the window, chin raised, with a little hint of the smile still on his face.

We arrived just in time and found the way to our carriage. But when we got to our seats, one was occupied by a prosperous-looking Sikh. We looked at our tickets and checked, and he did the same. Yes, we had both been given the same seat. The conductor was summoned and arrived with a look of a master of all that surrounded him. He took the little cardboard tickets – copied from the English train tickets of the 1940s and with the dates smudged in purple ink – raised his chin and scrutinised them with the air of a high court judge. I feared that we might be removed forthwith because of my incorrectly recorded age. He nodded gravely, paused and delivered his verdict. Oh, how the Indian public servant loves his authority.

"Gentlemen," he addressed us. "Your tickets are indeed for these seats on the 7 o'clock train. That is to say, for this evening's 7pm train, due to leave in one minute. The train in which we are standing, however, is the 7am train which is 12 hours late. The gentleman here is sitting in the correct seat for this morning's train. You must detrain speedily; your train will be arriving in a jiffy."

I had a story to tell about the real India.

28

Another Tropical Paradise

It is Sunday morning, and the local director has invited me to meet him and his family at the swimming pool at the Intercontinental Hotel. The weather is perfect: the sky is sapphire blue, the sun is already high, there is not a cloud to be seen and the air is warming. We sit outside to take a late breakfast of pineapple, papaya and watermelon under the massed bougainvillaea which covers the hotel garden walls. Most of the guests breakfasting are businessmen or aid programme consultants. At the next table a group of pale, balding engineers are wearing coloured shirts for the weekend. I notice with some surprise that the only non-white man there is the local representative of the African Development Bank.

At about 11am the young mothers start to arrive, dropped at the hotel by their drivers. They settle down together around the pool, watching their sunburnt children swimming as if they had been born in the water. Although they are mainly Portuguese, most of the women are blonde. The wives prefer this hotel for Sunday mornings partly because it does manicures and has the best hairdresser in the city.

Two of the young mothers, smartly dressed in blue denim and seersucker shirts, leave for an hour for a session in the gym, joking about the need to remove the cellulite on their sunburnt legs. Another group leaves to shop at the local commissary, where prices are far below local levels. They return with sun lotion and band aids for one of the children who cut his foot. The most attractive of them mentions that there is a new book section at the commissary and pulls a thick new Wilbur Smith novel out of her shopping bag. Two of the ladies laugh, as they both have the same book there on their poolside tables.

The husbands arrive together before lunch at the patio restaurant. They are wearing smart casual clothes and sunglasses. There are cheery greetings, and beer and cigarettes. We sit for a while, and conversation subsides. The only sounds are of the children as they splash into the pool. I watch the moving patterns of the sun's reflection glittering under the water, and wonder how many artists have changed the way we see things as much as David Hockney.

The man next to me seems slightly edgy: his feet tap incessantly under the table. Another husband arrives. He has just bought a new four-wheel-drive, and the men walk out to the car park to check it out. The wives call for the bill for the morning's pina coladas and cokes, and scour it with laser eyes as they move over to the restaurant.

I join the queue for the Mongolian barbecue, which they have every Sunday. As we wait I am introduced to a British engineer. He has a small grey beard and is smartly dressed in a slightly old-fashioned manner, with meticulously shone shoes. I asked him what he was doing.

"Well, a few months ago the World Bank approached me to ask if I would be willing to coordinate the cross-cutting policy issues on transport infrastructure maintenance in the land-locked countries of the region. So for my sins here I am."

"So you are here long term?"

"Well, I'm here for a couple of years at least."

"With your family?"

"Not yet, but my wife will be joining me soon."

"And how do you think she's going to find it – living in a small African country."

"Oh, she's used to it. We have spent most of the last 27 years in different African countries. In fact we've hardly been back to the UK since the 1980s, after McAlpines made their big staff cuts."

"She's still in England now?"

"Oh, my god, no. We moved to Spain years ago. I could never live in England again, what with the weather and the cost of living. We have a nice villa in Spain in a wonderful development; there are lots of English neighbours."

He joins our table, where we speak in English, the only language we all share. It emerges that we know a lot of people in common, mostly working in other African countries; consultancy is a small world. Later, conversation turns to plans for the Christmas break.

After lunch, my host has to leave early; his brother-in-law's car has been stolen, and he has to help with a problem over the insurance. Soon after, the other men leave to pick up bulk orders of food for next week's carnival party from the bright new shopping complex that has just opened on the edge of town. They suggest that I might go with them to change money as the exchange rate is very good there, but I decline. They leave the largest of the Range Rovers with the women to bring the children back.

The families all arrange to meet later, in the evening, to watch videos and for drinks and a barbecue.

Most of the women decide to stay on until the late afternoon, while their children swim until the sun dips behind the bougainvillaea and the air cools.

They are very friendly and invite me round later, to join them for the barbecue. I think quickly but cannot come up with a plausible excuse. I accept with a cheerful smile. Another evening in paradise.

29
South Korea in 1985

Our client was Mr Cho of the Korean Port Planning Bureau. He was a Young Turk, recently promoted, and anxious to win his spurs. He was whippet thin, with cheekbones like blades threatening to pierce his skin; and his face was a flat hard plane, with a sharp chin and eyes like razor cuts. His approach was direct. He entered the room and said, in front of 20 onlookers, "Your report is full of demerits; it is worthless." He insisted on an immediate inquest, in front of the local and foreign staff. He picked up our report as if it were a long-dead fish, and opened it at the first page.

He started: "First sentence: 'The ports of Korea handled 106 million tonnes in 1972.' It is wrong."

"Well," replied our director, on safe ground, "we know your annual report says it was 120 million, but in fact there was a mistake in the addition."

Mr Cho looked at us with withering disdain, and turned questioningly to the statistical assistant, Mr Lee.

Mr Lee squirmed, torn between the highest Korean virtues of loyalty and truthfulness. He bowed his head and stuttered, "Sorrowfully, small error was made in statistics." Mr Cho remained impassive, but blinked.

"Point number two," he intoned. He lost that one as well; and so it went on for an hour. The score was approximately 25 to 1 in our favour. After the last page, he stood and left, proud and straight, conceding his shame.

We felt sorry for Mr Cho. "Why did he do it?" I asked my American colleague, who had been to Korea before.

"Because he feels they can do it themselves without our assistance. He thinks it's demeaning to take 'American charity'." We were funded by the World Bank.

"OK, but why didn't he stop when he saw he was losing?"

"Aw, they love to suffer."

Korea has always been a country of melancholy, suffering and cruel self-imposed honour codes. A hundred years ago it was conquered by the Japanese, who took away their rice and their best women, addressed them as 'dirt' and often buried them alive. But the Japanese days were not the worst. Five years after they left, the brutal Korean War dragged the country down to new depths. An eye witness recorded the degradation of a group of several hundred prisoners of war he stumbled on in the rain in 1953:

> [dressed in] filthy, indescribably ragged kimonos... manacled with chains or bound to each other with ropes. They were skeletons, puppets of skin with sinews for strings... Their faces were a translucent grey and they cringed like dogs, compelled to crouch in the classic oriental attitude of subjection, the squatting foetal position, in heaps of garbage. Sometimes they moved enough to scoop a handful of water to drink from the black puddles around them. They shuffled forwards with the numb air of men facing their deaths; and most of them were.

These were not North Korean prisoners. They were South Korea's own political prisoners.

Thirty years later in the 1980s, when I first worked for Mr Cho's group, violence was still a part of the routine of everyday life – strangely so for a scholarly and respectful people. On the streets men slugged it out, Western-film style, with bare-knuckled punches to chin and stomach, blood everywhere, in circles of perhaps a hundred onlookers. While they did not cheer, nobody intervened. Late in the evenings drunken men kicked their wives and girlfriends in the gutters, while the world walked past; and early in the mornings women knelt in arctic temperatures on the icy streets, their foreheads touching the ground in the formal position of total self-abasement, alongside their babies, swaddled in thick clothes, and little boxes for coins.

Endurance is the quality on which they pride themselves. The day before our meeting with Mr Cho we had visited a new car factory where the temperature was minus five. Their great luxury was mugs of warm water on tap. The staff had voted to work without heating until the year they made their first profit.

And they did make a profit that year. Everything was changing. Korea had been a land of low hills and misty clouds, and the countryside had been achingly beautiful, suited to melancholia. Then the economy took off; the thatched roofs in the countryside were replaced by government decree with modern corrugated iron, and the population moved from the fields and the fishing villages to the cities and the shipyards.

As the weeks passed, a few chinks in the Koreans' armour-plated reserve appeared. Perhaps it started the day the office staff challenged us to a competition between our electronic calculators and their abacus champion, a shy 18-year-old girl. She always won. Then the men invited us out – to drink beer and play poker in icy, draughty, noisy, cowboy-style bars that stank of boiled cabbage, garlic and urine, and where at closing time the red-faced drunks sang their national songs ('Danny Boy' with Korean words was the favourite!) in their haunting bass voices, tears running down their anguished faces.

Slowly their suspicion of us started to melt. Mr Kim was our interpreter, gofer, translator, typist and defender, and gradually emerged as a man to go into the jungle with. He was very concerned with honour. He often worked through the night to type our overdue reports, and we found out later that he had almost lost his job over his refusal to submit reports about our out-of-work movements, particularly anything to do with girls. One afternoon, about six weeks after we arrived, he approached me cautiously and said "Mr Laing, I would like to speak to you in private." We went out to the lifts where there was nobody within hearing distance. He told me that he had worried for days, but had to speak to me. Then he seemed to panic. . . But I encouraged him and he started, falteringly.

"I am ashamed, and find it painful to raise this subject." He faltered again, then bracing himself, blurted out the whole story. "I am sorry to say that some of the Korean staff, behind your back, are calling you not Mr Laing but. . . E. T.!"

He could also be cruel to be kind, if my honour was at stake. Later he drew me aside again and said:

"Mr Laing, you may think that you make a good impression by doing your work well. But you are mistaken! Why? You behave pleasantly to the staff, you work hard, your clothes are reasonable if not good. But then we look at your shoes and know that you are a man of no importance, almost dirt."

My shoes were of soft suede and rubber-soled. All Koreans wear black leather shoes with little holes in them, highly polished. I found out later that further damage to my standing was caused by my turning to look at junior people when they spoke to me. A senior person looks straight ahead, and inclines his ear barely perceptibly to one side, to allow the supplicant to make his case. The most senior sat like statues, backs rigidly straight with hands on knees, knees locked together, and a fixed, passive stare, like Buddha.

Another Mr Kim – almost all Koreans are Mr Kim, Mr Lee or Mr Cho – was a retired minister of construction. He was part of our team because of his contacts.

In his late 60s, he was ramrod straight, thin and ascetic, with a still-handsome face, a wintry charm and the bearing of a very senior man. His demeanour was that of a scholarly and thoughtful civil servant, but in his twilight years he was a businessman; and he had decided that he wanted to enlist the 'skills' of myself and my elderly American colleague, Dan, in developing his 'projects'. For this purpose, he arranged an evening meeting. It took place in an expensive Japanese restaurant at which we ate but, more importantly, drank large volumes of sake. The intention was for us to get drunk together, and to reach a deal, which would stand when sober. This is how it is done in Korea (applicants for jobs sometimes have to submit their beer-drinking capacity). The food was superb and Mr Kim piled on the charm, but the evening did not go according to plan. While the sake seemed to have relatively little effect on me or Dan, Mr Kim's face soon had the familiar Asian Glow*, and he slowly succumbed to the drink. By the end of the evening his voice was slurred, but he insisted on taking us back to his house, where his elderly wife plied us with more food and drink. Half an hour later Mr Kim lay on his sitting room floor, fast asleep, dead drunk. We sat around for a while not knowing what to do. Eventually his wife came in and mother-henned; and then shook him until he woke. Mr Kim sat bolt upright, realised what had happened and apologised, shamefully. He then ordered a car for us, and escorted us unsteadily to the gate. At the last moment he must have realised that the objective of the evening had not been achieved, but wanted to finish on a positive note. If he had been more sober it is unlikely that he would have done what he did next. He lurched towards me, lunged quickly, kissed me full on the lips and said "I love you." The beatific joy that radiated from Dan's face as he witnessed the kiss, and, presumably, my face, will be imprinted in my memory forever.

In the taxi back he mused, "You know, I think they're starting to like us a little."

---

* Many Asians have a low tolerance for alcohol that shows itself in a deeply flushed face after a few drinks.

30

Pakistan After The 2008 Election

In 2007 *Newsweek* ran an eight-page story informing us that Pakistan is *'the* most dangerous country in the world'. It painted an ominous picture of single-minded Islamic militants training secretly in camps along Pakistan's northwest borders – aided and abetted by the cream of Pakistan's intelligence services who had originally created the Taleban to fight the Russian invaders. Other journals warned of the dangers posed by Islamist elements in the highest ranks of the military, dedicated to the destruction of the West, the great Satan, and the dream of the victory over India. It is also well known that at least one of the country's top scientists will sell the bomb to anyone who will pay, including the Taleban. The combination was a powder keg.

And three months later Benazir Bhutto was duly murdered, seemingly confirming the worst fears.

Then came the elections. . . and, unexpectedly, everyone was pleased. The polls appeared to have been moderately fair and Musharraf accepted his defeat. But they had yet to form a new government. Which way were the chips going to fall in this enigmatic country?

I visited Islamabad a week after the elections, and found a Pakistan which bore little similarity to *Newsweek*'s portrayal.

I had arrived a day early and, with a Sunday free to relax, I sat in the lobby of my favourite hotel, the Serena, reading the papers and looking at the day, when my attention was caught by a modern Pakistani memsahib gliding across the marble floor, in floating black traditional dress – a model of haughty, straight-backed, no-nonsense elegance. She probably rode horses in the cool mountains that surround Islamabad; you could almost see the whip hanging from the waistband of her loose-fitting trousers; and she may have gone to a Catholic school, like Benazir who had never really been at ease in Urdu, the main language of Pakistan. In all but dress, she could have been from the English shires.

On the plane I had talked for most of the flight to an elderly Pakistani air force pilot with a white handlebar moustache and a blue blazer. He had fond memories of the English school he had attended in the hills of the North West Frontier, in what was still India, in the late 1930s.

"Anyone who said there was any racial discrimination there was talking through his hat," he declared.

He gleefully recalled the school dances.

"We got more dances with the British girls than the British fellows," he said ". . . and, gracious me, that last year, there was a bumper crop of young ladies."

His eyebrows arched mischievously, in the manner of the sports-car cad.

Because his school had been in the North West Frontier, he had strong views about its warrior tribes. He spoke romantically about the mountain-dwelling Pathans – the amber-eyed warriors, with their Caucasian, snow-leopard beauty – two centuries ago. The Pathans were later to dominate world squash, hitting the ball so hard that it threatened to perforate the tin.

"Yes, of course, they are tribal, ungovernable, untameable and lawless. And yes, their mediaeval honour codes and vendettas – over money, women and land in that order – are primitive. And yes, they score very low on the acid test of female literacy, which, as far as anyone knows, is below ten per cent."

But he also spoke about the mutual respect that has sprung up between the British officers and the Pathans two centuries ago and had lasted until his own time.

The untameability of the northwest is one of the reasons that it is the army that has governed Pakistan for half of the 60 years since independence, allowing democracy a few interludes before their next intervention. Their tentacles spread far beyond military affairs; and it has only recently been discovered how much of the economy the 600,000-man army controls. A recent book estimated the military's net worth at over £10 billion. Instead of chasing bin Laden they are building golf courses and running the country's trucks. They are in it for the money. *The Economist* described them as a 'selfish gene of an institution'. Unlike the People's Liberation Army of China, the Pakistani army is not seen as a protector of the people.

But there are other reasons why the army has often taken over. The civilians do not like it, but they can see sense in the military's role in politics. I listened to one view at lunch in the Karachi Boat Club. It is often observed that the only Englishmen left in the world are in India, but Pakistanis are two steps ahead. The speaker could have been from a London gentleman's club in the 1940s – parchment-white skin, long swept-back grey hair and a manner so languidly arrogant as to be unacceptable in England today. He explained why, regrettably, the military may be necessary.

"You see, democracy in Pakistan is nothing like democracy in the West. The votes are for the tribe, not the policies; and the politicians are all from the powerful families. All are corrupt, including Benazir's PPP. Some even pay handouts to buy their votes; to be specific it cost one of our top politicians $24 per head to buy his votes."

I asked him what he thought about Musharraf.

"He's a decent man. He is not considered corrupt... It's a pity he sacked the chief justice, though," he added.

"Do you think he killed Mrs Bhutto?" I asked.

He replied, "Many people believe that she was bumped off by the CIA – with a laser gun."

So much for the views of the high-born and the wealthy. Most of the votes, however, are cast by the poor; and over 90 per cent of Pakistanis are dirt-poor. Most marry their cousins. For them, life can be worse than primitive, particularly if they are women. Two years ago a woman was sentenced by a tribal council for a 'crime' committed by her 12-year-old brother. His crime was that *he* had been seduced by an older woman. The punishment – for the sister, not the boy – was to be raped by four of the villagers. This outrage, unlike many, became public knowledge, and the rapists were eventually arrested. But their prosecution was blocked by the law that if a rape victim fails to present four male witnesses to the crime, then she herself could face prosecution for adultery. Islamic pressure groups opposed attempts to reform the law.

A better insight into ordinary Pakistani lives, however, can probably be drawn from a little book called the *Muslim Marriage Guide* which I picked up at a mosque. There were a few unexpected surprises. It tells us that a wife does not *always* have to obey her husband. There is one exception. If the wife believes that the husband's orders are inconsistent with the teachings of the Prophet, she must bring this to his attention, and a discussion must then take place. And even more surprising was the advice to husbands, that 'whenever any one of you comes across an attractive woman, and his heart is inclined towards her, he should go straight to his wife and have sexual intercourse with her, so that he may keep himself away from evil thoughts'. But these were exceptions; the overall impression was that the book was sensible and thoughtful, and even quite modern.

Even the tragedies seem rather British in many ways, although definitely not in others. The newspapers reported the sad story of a young Pakistani who went to a neighbouring village for a party to celebrate his forthcoming marriage. There was 'very, very great rejoicing'. His friend got so very, very excited that he started to fire his pistol in the air. Then he got even more excited and 'forgot not to aim at his friend'. There was 'deep sadness' when they brought the poor bridegroom's body back to his village for burial.

Decent, sensible people, most ordinary Pakistanis cannot stand the fundamentalists. They are outsiders, beyond the law and, damningly, they hate cricket, the game that binds together ordinary Pakistanis from high to low. The Islamic fundamentalists regard it as decadent and Western – a game that the British colonists used to emasculate their credulous subject peoples.

On my last day, a work colleague invited me to high tea at the Marriott. The restaurant was already full, mostly with little groups of women. About half of them arrived with their hair partly covered, although all but a few had removed the scarves by the time they left. My colleague introduced me to one of the women, who was bantering waspishly with her friends. The conversation moved to politics, and I mentioned the *Newsweek* article about Pakistan being the most dangerous country in the world. She turned on me with that wonderfully snooty charm of the ladies who take tea. She said, "You foreigners all think we are crazy fundamentalists. Do you know how many seats the Islamist parties had before the recent elections?"

"No," I replied.

"Well they had 59 of the 268 seats, and they also had full control of the North West Frontier Province. And do you know how many they won this time?"

"Again, no."

"They have three. That's what we, the Pakistanis, think of them."

31

Azerbaijan

One of the devices Stalin used for intimidating his people was the concrete monolith. Take the forbidding Azadlyg Square in Baku, Azerbaijan. At the top of its windy ceremonial parade ground, facing the sea, stands the massive Dom Soviet, or Government House, built on Stalin's orders by German prisoners of war, and from which Moscow ruled the Republic of Azerbaijan. Twenty years ago a huge statue of Lenin stood on a pedestal outside, in classic pose, pointing the way forward. But it was torn down after the Russians left, and now the square is empty, except for two louring concrete identical-twin buildings at opposite ends of the parade ground, confronting each other like Soviet tanks. The buildings are the hotels where the apparatchiks used to stay in the old days. One of them is still state-owned and lies more or less empty, while the other has privatised itself in an unusual way, leasing out different floors to different managers. A few of the old guard still stay there, but there is an air of abandonment, and the only people in the square when I was arrived were a few babushkas in black headscarves and threadbare overcoats selling Snickers bars and well-thumbed Russian pornography outside the hotels in the chilly wind.

I had been billeted in the 14th floor of the semi-privatised hotel, at least for a few days, as the newer hotels in the centre of Baku were full. It had no reception area, just a long concrete-walled foyer without furniture or desks, like a pedestrian tunnel under a busy road. I asked a man with a suitcase how to check in, and a few minutes later a shabby man in a grey suit and a black polo-neck came out from an unmarked door and walked towards me. I introduced myself.

"I have a room booked for..." But he interrupted me as if he was expecting me.

"You pay."

"For tonight?"

"Da... Yes."

I paid him, and he turned to go.

"Where do I go?"

"14th... floor."

I took the lift and was met by a morose *dezhurnaya*, who showed me, without speaking, to my room. It was clean enough, with grey walls, furniture which would have been modern in the 1950s, and a plastic lamp with a cracked shade and a 25-watt bulb. There was no sign of a restaurant in the building and the streets were dark outside, so I had an early night.

The next morning I asked the *dezhurnaya* where I would find breakfast. She sent me to the main restaurant, which was on the top floor; but when I opened the door a group of unsmiling men and women turned to stare at me. Standing there with their coffees, they were a throwback to the old days of hard-faced functionaries; a poster in Russian suggested that they were social development experts. Their stares made it clear that I was not one of them.

One of the waitresses suggested that I might go down to the third floor where they sometimes served breakfast. But the small café I found there was boarded up and the chairs stacked in the corridor, and I was on the point of giving up when I passed a bedroom with an open door and saw that it was set up for breakfast. Probably run by an entrepreneurial outsider, it was a little oasis of 1940s cosiness. It had three tables with plastic chequered tablecloths and was warmed by an oil heater. They had tried to make it just a little welcoming with small table lamps with orange shades, which were unnecessary that morning as a weak sun was shining through the windows. The table was pre-set with slices of thick white bread and some jam. After a couple of minutes a stern-faced, careworn lady brought a heavy mug of thick tea, and said something that may in retrospect have been "Dobriy dyen, yaichnitsa?"

I mimed apologetic incomprehension.

"Yakes?" she seemed to say. Still nothing.

"Yakes... yeggs." Then it connected. The Russians put a 'y' before an 'e'.

"Da, dva," I said and started to laugh at myself, at my modest achievement. It elicited just a glimmer of a smile from the lady, just for a second, as she struggled to recover the stern composure that was the face she presented to the world. Then a couple of uncertain emotions flickered across her face like a dim light short-circuiting, and she surrendered to a broad smile.

She retired to the other end of the room to fry the eggs on a Belling-style cooker and returned with them, seeming apologetic and asking if they were OK. They tasted like heaven after 20 hours with no food. She would not have believed me if I had been able to tell her.

"See you... tomorrow," she said in Russian, then tentatively in English, as I left.

But my stay was short. On the second night, at about 11pm, a man in a black leather jacket knocked at my door, stared coldly at me, and muttered, "Dyengi" (money). He had the air of a petty gangster, and it was only when the *dezhurnaya* arrived behind him that I realised it was just a request for the nightly room charge. Then on the third night, when I was fast asleep around

3am, someone burst noisily into my room. I sat up, rigid, to see a heavy man in an overcoat illuminated by the striplights in the hallway. He looked at me as if I had offended him, grunted and walked out. He had arrived late and wanted to see a room so the *dezhurnaya* had sent him to look at mine. I left the next morning, and that was the last I saw of the old Baku.

The centre of the new Baku is only a mile away. A hundred years ago the city had been the oil capital of the world, accounting for half of the world's production. Its reign was short, as a lot more oil was soon found in the Middle East; but during its brief heyday the oil money and the arrival of the Rothschilds and Nobel brothers had brought fine civic buildings, solid homes, theatres and concert halls to Baku. They had fallen into disrepair and been in hibernation for 100 years, during the Soviet times and for ten years after. But now the hard bone structure that lay beneath the neglected exterior of the city has been stripped down and given a face-lift – most of all in the tree-lined Fountain Square with its pretty terrace cafés and its nightly *passeggiata* of meticulously groomed girls in tight white jeans and bare midriffs, and their entourages of chaperones, aunts, matrons and 'blue men' (the local and Russian word for gays). The boys stand in separate little clusters. Their main sport is weightlifting.

It is oil that has revived Baku. But the city has two other industries. It is still the caviar capital of the western Caspian, and, being an attractive city, it is now a home for the international economic development industry.

I was there with one of the economic development agencies – to work on its pet project, the revival of the Silk Road, the trade route from China to Europe that was used 800 years ago by Marco Polo to bring silk, satins, spices and jade from China to Venice, and send back glass, cloth and pottery.

The revival of the Silk Road was the mother of all castles in the air. It could have been the winner of an international competition to devise the most implausible transport route ever conceived. In Marco Polo's days it meant an 8,000-mile trek stopping at 100 caravansaries along the way. But today it would mean entrusting your goods to a succession of sclerotic and unreformed Soviet-style railways – Kazakhstan Railways, Turkmenistan Railways, Azeri Railways, Georgian Railways – and along the way passing half a dozen borders manned by bribe-hungry customs staff.

As if this didn't go far enough, the plan for the New Silk Road included the diversion of the traffic to the shores of the seas along the way (the Caspian and Black Seas) and the transfer of the cargo from railway to ship and then back to railway at the other end. Their only concession to common sense was bypassing the remains of the Aral Sea, or at least the dusty bowl which is all that is left after the Russians drained it to irrigate a now defunct cotton industry.

This grand design has been packaged and promoted by international development agencies for about 15 years. They had spent almost 200 million dollars on it at the last time of counting. But the route has not yet attracted any significant cargo, and probably never will. Even if it did get going it would not be long before it would grind to a halt again, as the cash-strapped governments spotted the chance to impose transit fees. It is possible that if even if you charged nothing, there would be few customers.

But this has not deterred the band of international experts who have come to specialise in the new Silk Road. Planning it and promoting it is now a multi-million-dollar industry – with a prodigious output of reports, PowerPoint presentations, buzz words, international protocols, cost comparisons and colourful promotional blurb. To the experts, these products have become more real than the trains and trucks and ships that actually carry the cargo.

The curricula vitae of the experts grow longer and more apparently impressive with each investigation of why the new Silk Road is not working, their long experience guaranteeing them work on further studies of how to make it work in the future. And so the circus moves on, with its freight of studies, international travel budgets, training programmes, conferences and banquets. It has become a self-sustaining parallel universe – a fact-free zone disconnected from the real world, a practice pitch for abstract theory unhindered by ugly facts, for pure rather than applied research.

The industry even has its celebrities. One afternoon, Yuri, a Silk Road expert, took me to one side and said, in awe, "See that man on the stairs. He is the man that actually signed the second protocol on trade facilitation initiatives."

Later we arranged meetings with one of the top men. And one of my first questions, after a few pleasantries, was:

"Why do you think that, after ten years of promotional effort, nobody uses the new Silk Road?"

Yuri, who had to translate, lowered his voice and muttered through clenched teeth, "You. . . can't. . . ask. . . him. . . that."

Why not?"

"He is the director."

"I know. Maybe he has some useful things to tell us."

Yuri avoided our eyes and translated, or pretended to translate, the question. The director replied at length – about the history of the Silk Road, the international agreements signed so far, and the conferences planned for the rest of the year.

The compensation for this dispiriting work was that we worked in an elegant mansion in the centre of a pretty, bustling city with excellent restaurants and the pick of the English-speaking Azeris to work with. Our main translator, Ulviya, a lovely woman, had been a teacher of English literature at the university. She would have been paid a miserly salary if she had stayed there, and she had, like many local women, to support a well-qualified husband who could find no work. Her English was immaculate, and refined by that aristocratic pronunciation that comes from having Russian as a first language. "Would you like some core-fay?" she would say. Even her occasional lapses were endearing. She referred to 'vegetarianians' and was embarrassed by our insistence that she should keep saying it. She also asked questions which gave little insights into what the Soviets had told their schoolchildren about the West but made palpable hits.

"Tell me," asked Ulviya, "it is true that the English send their children away to boarding schools and sleep with their dogs?"

"Well. . . maybe that's partly true. . . at least, amongst the upper classes."

"What a country," she said, shaking her head.

Our only outside chance of making the Silk Road work was to persuade the shipping line that held a monopoly on the Caspian to cut its prices and run a half decent service. But prospects were poor, as the shipping line, despite being owned by the government, was run not just as a tight ship but as a personal fiefdom of the much feared Captain Baghirov. I asked for a meeting with him, and after two months – and the intercession of one of the well-connected secretaries – I was granted half an hour. On the appointed day I was met downstairs by a man like a barge, with no neck and amphibian eyes, clearly a minder. But it emerged that he was the second-ranked officer in the company. He, like most of the staff, wore a white naval uniform with gold trimmings, immaculate from a distance, but slightly grubby at close quarters. As we trooped upstairs a welcoming party, all in the same naval uniform, stood rigidly to attention. The captain, however, was surprisingly hospitable, and answered all questions openly, until, in the last five minutes, I came to the only one that mattered:

"Could we have a copy of your accounts?"

He smiled, hesitated for about ten long seconds, and said in a theatrically quiet voice, "Our company had been operating for over a hundred years. What you are asking for is our crown jewels... Out of the question." He had clearly been waiting for the request, and had probably used the same set of words many times before.

Decision times came when the delegates – the representatives of the railways and ports of the 13 Silk Road countries – came to Baku for the progress meetings. They didn't like us much. They didn't like being told what to do; and they didn't like being told about new ways of doing things. "You don't understand our countries," they said. When we passed them in the corridors or met them in the bathrooms they blanked us. And they didn't seem to like each other either. At coffee breaks, lunches or dinners the national groups didn't mix; they just stood and talked amongst themselves.

I asked a French woman who had worked in the region for years and spoke fluent Russian, "Why are they like this? The ordinary people are so warm. But these professional people are cold as ice."

"Well, you have to understand that for most of their working lives they had to keep their mouths shut, especially to anyone outside the family, or their enemies would... do you say 'snitch'?... on them, and, take their jobs. At least; they could end up in prison, or worse."

"You think it's as simple as that."

"Yes. Really. The communists built it in right from the start, back in the 1920s. Stalin encouraged denunciations, and rewards for reports on anyone heard saying anything against the rulers. They even encouraged children to sneak on their parents."

"But I thought the family was very strong in Russia."

"It was, and the Bolsheviks didn't like it. They thought the bourgeois family was the enemy of socialism, because it brought the children up to love their parents, not the state, and it made them selfish, not socialist. So the new citizens had to be reprogrammed to love the social family, not the bourgeois family. In fact, the Bolsheviks wanted the family to disappear in the end: the state would provide the apartments, canteens and the nurseries; and private life would be replaced by the communist brotherhood... So if they couldn't trust their own children how could they trust anyone else?"

On the last day of my last visit, the delegates reluctantly hammered out a draft protocol, which was a bit of a compromise, but it was something. There was unanimous agreement, a toast, and then we adjourned to a banquet – leaving the translators to produce the Russian text from the English original. The key sentence of our protocol, drafted in English, read:

'The delegates have agreed on reforms to...'

When I saw the translation into Russian the next day I found that they had inserted a 'not' between 'the delegates have' and 'agreed'.

32
Sierra Leone

When we met Jim nine years before in Freetown, he was thinking seriously about leaving. He had been working on a two-year contract in the port and he was enjoying life there. But the news coming through from the south was not good. A rebel army was on the march and had already taken control of many of the villages. It was led by a living Satan called Foday Sankoh. He purported to be fighting for the poor against the rich, but in reality he was fighting for Sierra Leone's diamonds. And it was not only Jim who was uneasy. We had noticed that the waiters in the hotel were often clustered around tinny radios. They were listening to the BBC World Service, but when we asked them what was happening they looked evasive and dispersed. One evening in the bar we asked Jim if he knew what they were listening to.

"The radio reports are telling them that the rebels are meeting no resistance and that they are pioneering macabre new ways of terrorising the locals. When they come into the villages in the south, they line up the pregnant women in the square and cut off their arms, so that they'll never be able to hold their babies. Then they take away their children."

"And the government troops can't stop them?"

"No, the rebels have been winning all the skirmishes. But they aren't having it all their way. There was a story last month that when the managers at one of the big diamond mines heard the rebel army was heading towards them, they knew they couldn't resist. So they abandoned the mine, leaving tables full of food – all poisoned. Half an hour after the raiding party arrived, most of them were dead. So now they are after revenge."

"And you're nervous that they may eventually get to Freetown?"

"Yes, very nervous."

He left soon after that.

Nine years later* we had just touched down in Freetown's Lungi airport on our second visit, and had been herded into a shed outside the arrivals hall. We were not sure why. An airport official had said "Just wait." A tropical rainstorm was drumming on the metal roof, the humidity was close to 100 per cent, and there was a smell of rotting vegetation and wet clothes.

After about 20 minutes there was a distant clacking noise, which became louder and louder until we had to put our hands over our ears. Then two helicopters dipped into view under the awning of the shed, slowly touched down, and as the propellers chattered to a stop the passengers clambered out and sprinted to the shelter of our shed. A few minutes later the pilots ambled over, their faces flushed in the rain, their yellow clothing garish in the flashing lights of the helicopters. They were tough, brawny men, speaking Russian. Then something was shouted and our fellow passengers rushed for the helicopters. The Danish engineers I was travelling with were quick off the mark and clambered in, keeping me a place to sit, on the floor between two metal trunks. Rain was streaming in through the holes in the fuselage as we clattered off over the jungle into the night and to the centre of Freetown.

---

* In 2004

There can be few places where rain is theatre, but that night after dinner we sat out on the hotel veranda and watched it driving in from the sea. Sierra Leone is the wettest country in Africa and it is also the hottest, on one criterion at least – having the highest average night-time temperature. The rain, illuminated every few seconds by violent sheets of lightning and carried in on a gale force wind, was like no other I had seen. Sometimes the gusts were of such cataclysmic power that we ducked as the deluge thundered down on the canopy above us. But later the storm subsided, leaving the rain drumming steadily but relentlessly, as it always had. Sixty years before, it had been a fitting sound track to the loneliness, disappointments and regrets of Graham Greene's lost British colonials in Freetown, as they drowned themselves in gin and heard – that haunting image – the vultures clanging down on the corrugated-iron roofs.

But that was not how Freetown seemed the next day. Poor it was, but depressed it was not – at least on first impressions. Much of Freetown is a sprawl of sodden shacks on gentle rolling hills, with little electricity or piped water, but as we drove in fitfully through the puddles and the traffic jams, the constant stops gave us little glimpses into the intimate details of daily lives in the shadowy unlit rooms seen through the open windows of the tiny ochre-painted houses along the way. Women in bright colours cooked and washed and waved goodbyes to their children, well dressed in white shirts and ties, as they left for school. Sierra Leone had been repopulated two centuries ago by repatriated slaves, originally from many countries, but they mix surprisingly well. They are a smiling people. It was good to see as we drove through the centre of the city that the huge cotton tree with its fruit bats has not been touched, and Siaka Stevens street still had its little shops and restaurants and the travel agency.

We started our work that morning with a visit to the port directors' meeting. The chairman was a tiny man with a Muslim *kufi*. We started with prayers, written to be acceptable to both Muslims and the Christians who were a majority in the room. All bowed their heads, observed a minute's silence and then the meeting started. There was bright well-informed discussion, with robust views presented politely. We asked for information we needed to help them get a bank loan and they went out and brought it back. It is not always like that. Later we had a tour of the port. At the end of the day, Gunnar said, " Well, I think that was a good start." It is always a relief at the end of the first day of a new project to know that it is going to go well.

That night when we got back to the hotel we found the hotel staff dancing jubilantly on the second floor in front of a football match on a big television. They were watching the European Cup, 2004.

"We've scored. We are winning," they told us, their smiles almost wider than their faces.

"*Who* is winning?" I asked. Sierra Leone could hardly have been playing in the European Cup.

"We are. Our team. England!"

We are not used to England being so popular. But in this case there was a good reason.

Jim had been right to leave. Because the rebels *did* come to Freetown; and when they finally fought their way through to the outskirts of the city their plan of attack was code named 'No Living Thing'. It was icily self-explanatory. But it turned out to be almost a euphemism. The reality was much worse – a descent into a new dimension of hellish savagery. The rebels, the Revolutionary United Front, had recruited much of their army from the children they had taken away from the villages. One of the first tests for the children was to shoot prisoners or be shot themselves. Next, the rebels made them eat the livers of other prisoners while they were still alive, to instil bloodlust. One forced recruit described how a commander called Savage asked his soldiers to go to look for human hearts and they brought back a sackful to eat. Girls were recruited as well as men and regularly raped; so to stop themselves getting pregnant they swallowed gunpowder, which they believed was a contraceptive, and would also make them fierce in battle. They said it gave them red eyes to frighten the enemy. From the first days they were fed a regular diet of cocaine and heroin, inserted in incisions cut in the skin.

When they came to Freetown a few of the rebels worked with surgical precision. They had done their reconnaissance and knew where the most attractive girls worked. So within an hour or so of breaking through the defences of the city they went down to the offices of the airlines and the government where they raped the girls for hours. We remembered the airline girls from our first visit, with their crisp cotton shirts and those dazzling African smiles. One had been particularly helpful over a change of a flight date.

But much of the terror was random and of sickening barbarity. The low point eventually came in January 1999, when the rebels made a surprise attack assisted by infiltrators inside the city. The RUF had commanders with names like Dr Blood, Captain Two Hands and Betty Cut Hands, and they set about a programme of cutting off arms, lips, hands and ears with machetes, and forcing children to kill their parents. One witness saw a man offer all his money to the rebels not to take his daughter, but they took his money and then squirted mosquito spray down his throat before taking his daughter anyway. They were joined by independent terror squads with names like the West Side Boys who roamed the city like mad dogs. If the RUF was organised crime, with objectives rooted in the diamond industry, the West Side Boys were disorganised crime. They saw themselves as gothic American gangsters, and wore voodoo devil uniforms of women's wigs and flip-flops and the bloodstained clothes of their victims. They were almost always drunk.

Thousands were killed that month, but the terror lasted for a mercifully short time. In 2000, Tony Blair sent in British soldiers and a year later there were almost 20,000 of the blue hats of the UN to be seen around Freetown.

The civil war was over, and Blair's contribution was seen as crucial. Later they made him an honorary chief.

Our work was going well. The old type of foreigner, Graham Greene's sad, lost colonial, had been replaced by a more can-do set that mixed easily and were not dreaming of return to their countries. Information was not difficult to come by, and much of our best advice came from the local agent of the top shipping line. A long-haired and laconic American, possibly ex-Peace Corps, had to be highly intelligent to be employed by that line, which usually favours the Germanic rather than the English type of Dane, well-groomed and good-looking. The American had another style of presence.

"So, what do you think of the port?" we asked. We were there to arrange a loan to expand it in the expectation of an upturn in the economy now that the war had finished.

He smiled, and his smile grew broader; and he said nothing.

"Well, do you think it improved a lot when they got the German manager in to run it?" He had left a few years before.

He still smiled, and kept smiling. Eventually he said:

"Well, they say he was a *moderately* competent farmer before he came here. Anyway, he came and he went. And in the end the police didn't press charges."

The American had been in Freetown for many years, and he liked it. He ran a small oasis of north European efficiency. He gave us all the information we needed, but when we asked the most important question of all – "Now the war's over, do you think the country will grow fast?" – he smiled once again, and eventually said, "Come back another time, for at least an hour, and we'll talk more about it."

In the evenings we sat in the open-air restaurants around the bay – run, as all over West Africa, by the Lebanese. We were aware that we spent more in an evening there than most locals earned in a month, *if* they earned anything. It was 2004, around the time that poverty in Africa became *the* fashionable concern of the year, until the media tired of it and turned to global warming, then oil and food prices, and then the banking crisis. So the competing theories about why Africa remained poor had been well aired. Now, here we were in Sierra Leone. Out of 177 countries covered in the UNDP Human Development Index it was ranked 177. What better place to take out our notebooks?

We certainly knew that the government didn't work very well. We had to liaise with them, but most meetings were no-shows, and there was only one man worth talking to in our ministry. Clever, extremely good-looking and the darling of the international agencies, he was friendly and charming; but when we tried to get meetings with him he was always busy. Often we found his room locked. Sometimes we saw one or other of the secretaries leave his office and re-lock the room as she came out. One was extraordinarily beautiful and sometimes looked flushed as she passed us at the end of the corridor.

There is often an expat in the poorer countries of whom you are told, "If you do nothing else there, you just *have* to talk to Buffy: he's been there for years; he knows everything about the place and he'll put you in the picture." Sometimes they add, "But. . . just. . . don't go to see him too much after 11am, as he does like a little drink." The meetings can take time to arrange and when you eventually get there they can be disappointing. You come hoping for nuggets of wisdom polished by long experience, but you often get, in answer to the key question – say, "How fast do you think coffee exports will rise in the next five years?" – a reply. . . "Well, I always say that life is like a golf swing. . ."

But one of our last meetings in Freetown was with a better kind of the man who knew it all. He was an elderly Englishman, neatly dressed in a grey tweed Dunn's sport jacket when he met us in his unassuming office; he had been in Freetown for over ten years. He was expanding his factory, but only modestly.

"So you don't think it is really going to take off now?" I asked.

"No, I think modest growth is more likely."

"But why?" I asked, "looking at Freetown as an outsider, there really does seems to be a buzz about the place, and the war is ended. What's going to stop them?"

Here I had a chance to get the views of a grounded local on all the usual candidates for the 'real' reason for poverty in Africa and Sierra Leone in particular. So I asked first about climate.

"Drought, you mean? Well, certainly not here!" he said with a laugh. Of course, I recalled, Sierra Leone is the wettest country in West Africa.

"How about the import duties and quotas Europe and the US put on your exports?"

"Well, it would help a lot if they were removed. But it is not as bad as you'd think."

"And the writing off of your debts?"

"That would help as well."

"And civil wars?"

"Well, of course. So many African countries have them, and ours was one of the worst; but it's over now."

"So you don't think these are the main things that are going to hold you back... Let's see... how about the African mentality? Do you think they are wired to seek economic success?"

"Well you've spent two weeks here. What do you think of the people you've met?"

"I've been pretty impressed."

"Agreed."

" So then why is it such a basket case?" I asked.

"Well... in the end it's all to do with politics and corruption, which are the same thing in our case. Here it's not a matter of power corrupting: they go into politics already corrupt. I don't know if you read the local papers here, but if you do you'll see they're full every day of gossip about frauds and scams and accusations. That's life here. It's what gives them a buzz. And it percolates down to everyone. . . I was out at a restaurant the other night, with a really interesting group and we had a great evening. What did we talk about? Graft, corruption, gossip about who is doing what to whom. You see, they all hustle each other, even the nicest. Did you know that Sierra Leone is now down to 160th out of 180 countries in the 'Ease of Doing Business' rankings? No, in a nutshell, it's the government and the rich, and their baleful influence on how even the good people think. . . that's life here."

"Isn't there any chance of a new grouping coming in to clear things up?" I asked.

"There have been attempts."

"Oh, there has been such a movement?"

"Yes. There was a group that set out to bring about 'equality and the end of corruption'. It attracted a lot of people. It was called the Revolutionary United Front."

33
Kazakhstan 1

Something strange had been happening to the Caspian Sea. The water level had been rising – not by a few centimetres, but by over seven feet in the 20 years since the mid 1970s. Coastal villages had been drowned while inland villages had become coastal villages. And even the Russian scientists, formidable as they are, could not work out why. It might have been because the Caspian is really an enclosed lake, not a sea, albeit one of 143,000 square miles – so that there was no way out for the water that flowed into it from the River Volga, carrying much of the waste disgorged from Russia's heavy industry. But that would not explain why the water level had actually *fallen* by nine feet in the 50 years before the recent rise. The mystery remained unsolved.

For the port at Aktau, the only town on the northwest coast of the Caspian, it was not just a mystery – it was a death sentence. It was in danger of becoming the world's first underwater port; in fact the waves had already started coming over the top of the breakwater. But Kazakhstan had no money, and it was for that reason we were there – to rebuild the breakwater.

If a photographer had wanted to capture the desolation of the former Soviet Union in spare, grainy black-and-white, Aktau in 1997 would have been a first stop. Before the Soviet Union collapsed the town had been thought of as a good posting. It had assets much valued during the Cold War – uranium mines and a nuclear power plant – and it was paid to be the dumping ground for much of the dirty work the Russians did not want to do in their own back yard, such as the testing of their nuclear bombs. Anything military brought high salaries. But by 1997 the brains and the bombs had gone – and with them had gone the salaries, leaving Aktau run down, without work and unhealthy. Being on the edge of the desert, it had always suffered from dust storms which blotted out the landscape for days, and now the abandonment of the mines had added uranium particles to the dust.

But the day we drove into Aktau there was no dust storm, only wind and sleet. Our windscreen wipers were not working properly and it was hard to see, but as we approached the port we spotted faint lights high up in the air in a control tower and then out of the swirling sleet came a sign with missing letters announcing Aktau Port. We drove in through muddy puddles and potholes, past dimly lit ramshackle grey buildings and rusting steel coils. John, the port engineer who I was accompanying, was at home in muddy boots and rain, and had worked in some dreadful places. He looked out and said, "Jesus."

Our destination was the operations department, where we found half a dozen staff in thick sweaters and anoraks huddled round a two-bar electric fire. They were just finishing pouring tea from an enormous old kettle, and were warming their rawboned hands on the cups. They were Russian-speaking, as almost all the staff were still Russian; but had enough English to tell us that we would have to wait for Grusha, who was to be our helper and interpreter for the week. They gave us tea, and were friendly enough, but they seemed uneasy in the presence of foreigners.

After 20 minutes a slight figure burst in from the sleet outside, bringing a cold draught in her wake. She was not at first sight prepossessing, with raven-black hair against a pale face. Her black clothes were more stylish than the others', but she was wearing some heavy overshoes, like galoshes. She started to take off her wet anorak, but changed her mind.

Then she reached into her bag and raised her hand triumphantly. She was holding a single Mars Bar. We knew just enough Russian to guess correctly.

"Look what I've got," she said. She counted out that there were eight people there and carefully cut it into eight pieces.

"This is Grusha, she will be looking after you," said the director.

It was immediately clear that the others deferred to her. Her bearing amongst the weary group in the room, who clearly saw life as a cross to be borne, was that of a young Cleopatra – whom she resembled with her proud aquiline nose and black hooded eyes. It was not entirely clear what her position was. She had no visiting card and it was uncertain which department she belonged to.

She asked us what we wanted to do for the rest of the week, and then took us out to trudge around the port. By evening we seemed to know her well.

"Where are you eating tonight?" she asked.

"We have nothing arranged. Have you any recommendations?"

" I'll take you out and show you a good place."

The restaurant Grusha took us to was one of the best in town. It had white strip lights in the entrance, a cold smell of fish and toilets, and a stone floor that remained wet throughout the evening from the slush brought in on shoes from outside. It had been a government office but had been converted to a restaurant by the simple devices of painting the walls dark red and then covering the tables with a red gingham-check fabric.

At the beginning of the evening only a few tables were occupied, mostly with men still wearing thick outdoor clothes with the collars up, their faces flushed from the cold and vodka. A mix of engineers, mechanics and fishermen, they talked in low voices, occasionally looking around furtively as if to check for eavesdroppers. They knew Grusha and exchanged banter with her from time to time.

Grusha had brought along one of the more interesting engineers from the port, although he spoke only a little English. She asked if we knew much about Russian and Kazakh food, and when we said very little she said, "Right, let's start with our traditional *zakuski*" – the cold starters of pickled vegetables, salted fish, sour cream and salads. It was still slightly chilly, and we chatted about the project. But by the time the soup came the room was starting to warm up. The soups are usually the best course in Kazakhstan, and this one – *ukha*, a fish soup with a bonnet of pastry – was the best of the soups. It had to be taken with vodka, and with the arrival of the vodka, Grusha changed gear. No more shop was to be talked. She leaned back, sank her third vodka, flashed her eyes archly at John and said:

"Well, John, tell us about yourself. What do you like most in the world? What are your passions?" and sat back to listen.

John smiled sheepishly, hesitated for a few seconds and replied, "Well... I'd say... maybe, computers... and history and... one of my ambitions is to climb every mountain in Scotland by the time I retire. I'm halfway through at the moment."

"Computers!" Grusha sat upright, affecting a theatrical incredulity. "How can anyone be passionate about computers?"

John looked defensive and started to dig his way out.

"That's maybe what most people think. But they really are changing the world now," he said ingenuously. "We have a saying in the West that 'knowledge is power'."

Grusha's companion looked amused. He emptied another glass of vodka, grimaced as if in pain, raised one eyebrow and said in deep, droll voice, "That would not apply here. We have a saying here that 'Knowledge can get you sent to prison. . . or worse'."

"Yes, come on, John," continued Grusha impishly, "tell us about what is really important to you. . . um. . . let's see. . . tell us about the loves in your life. Tell us how many times you have been in love."

John was a rabbit caught in the headlights. I thought, he's not going to say it, after Prince Charles had made a fool of himself a few years before. But he did.

"It depends on what you mean by love."

Grusha's eyes shone. She pounced. "You English. You have no souls. Come on, come on. . . don't you love your wife for a start?"

"Well. . . um. . . yes. . . I suppose so. . ."

"You are *so* British."

She turned to me and said playfully, "What do you think? Do you 'believe in' love?"

John was not taking this too badly, so I had no compunction about fuelling Grusha's tirade.

"I'd say that falling in love is far and away the most wonderful thing in the world," I replied, only partly mischievously.

"Good; well, John, you are with us for a week here so we will have to work on you." She played him like a fish on a line, teasing him without mercy. She asked him to tell us who his favourite poet was and then to quote some lines. He was able to summon up a few lines of 'I wandered lonely as a cloud', but spoke like an unwilling schoolboy, sending Grusha into a harangue about how our nation of shopkeepers is not interested in the culture we have inherited. Then she launched with fierce national pride into the subject of the beauty of the Russian language and started to quote from their beloved Pushkin. She spoke wonderfully, and loudly, causing others to turn to listen as she declaimed, first in Russian and then in English:

> "Tatiana – deeply Russian being
> herself not knowing how or why –
> in Russian winters thrilled to seeing
> the cold perfection of the sky,
> hoarfrost and sun in freezing weather,
> sledges and tardy dawns together
> with the pink glow the snows assume
> and festal evenings in the gloom."[1]

By this time she was more than a little excited by the drink and went on to regale us about the Russian soul, the sacred earth of mother Russia, the romantic emptiness of their snow-covered landscapes and the beauty of the Russian women. Nobody, it seemed, can love like a Russian.

I asked her about her recall of so much literature.

"Ah, well, all of us had to learn the lines by heart at school. And not just our poetry." It was true. Many Russians can quote pages of foreign writers such as Bernard Shaw, Jack London, Dickens – approved Western writers with good socialist sympathies.

Eventually she let John off the hook and she entertained us with more gossip than is normal in the former Soviet Union.

"That was a good evening," said John slightly ruefully as we walked back.

We were staying at a flat, rented from one of the port directors for the week.

---

1. From *Eugene Onegin: A Novel in Verse* by Alexander Pushkin, trans. Charles Johnston (Harmondworth: Penguin, 1977)

John was fascinated. He said it was the worst-built flat he had ever seen. None of the angles was straight; it was overbuilt as if by a bomb shelter engineer; and neither the electricity nor the water were working. But we managed to create a little home in it for the week. We had found a packet of Scott's Porridge Oats in a converted warehouse that was being used as a shop, and cooked them with exaggerated ceremony each morning.

The weather improved and the drawings and information we needed were slowly coming through. We seemed to be doing well until the last day, when it dawned that we were still missing a lot. We explained this to Grusha, and she said, "Right let's go." At 4pm she marched into the operations room, made a few calls to assemble some more staff, told them what was needed and that they had to stay until it was finished. They didn't argue or even look unhappy. They just settled down and wrote it all out in longhand. They finished about 7pm.

Ten years later I went back to Aktau. By that time the water level in the Caspian was falling again. In fact it started falling the year of our visit to rebuild the breakwater. In the meantime the port had been transformed, from an empty, desolate ruin to a busy modern seaport. And it was not only the port that had changed: Aktau and Kazakhstan had been transformed – by oil. The world's biggest oil discovery in the last 30 years has been made just north of Aktau. People had a spring in their steps and there were new restaurants, supermarkets and pubs everywhere.

Grusha had left the town a few years before.

One evening on that second visit the port staff took us out to a traditional restaurant. At first conversation was kept under tight control by the discipline of formal toasts. But in the course of the toasts they had decided that the foreigners had a sense of humour, and started to loosen up. The atmosphere was warming, and I started to talk about how gloomy Aktau used to be and how far it had come up over the last ten years. They all looked proud. As they now seemed relaxed I said, without thinking too hard about it first:

"By the way, was Grusha KGB?"

There was a silence and glances were exchanged. I don't know if Grusha was KGB. But the port directors, who would almost all have been in the Party, would certainly have known.

34

Egypt

Dawn is breaking and the muezzin is calling the faithful to prayer. From my hotel room looking down through a milky mist over the Nile, I can see the vendors in the stalls starting to stir, and the tiny wooden feluccas gliding silently away from the riverbanks like swans, their sails billowing listlessly in the early morning breeze. It could have been a scene from 2,000 years ago – the design of these simple craft has not changed much since the time of Cleopatra. In fact, much of what is most memorable about Egypt – the feluccas, the pyramids, the Nile at sunrise, the impenetrable mysteries of the Pharaohs and the Sphinx – is old and unchanging, including the people that make the rules and call the shots. I recall a man in the next seat on my last flight back from Cairo giving me some advice I wished I'd had on the way in.

"It's never worth talking to the number two in Egypt," he said, "only see the top man. The Egyptians keep their cards close to their chests. It's not a country for young men on the way up. Stick with the old men, the men who dye their hair."

Five thousand years ago Egypt was the world's greatest civilisation, and while the British Empire lasted three centuries the Egyptians' lasted for 30. For most of that time it remained mired in a steady state – with the same gods with dogs' heads, the same statues, the same rigid hierarchies and the same institutionalized incest. Only towards the end did it take off intellectually – and not under Egyptians: it was when Alexander the Great conquered them in 327BC and, magnanimous in victory, built them the glittering new city of Alexandria. It became the home of the greatest library in the world, the repository for the manuscripts of Greek literature, and attracted the world's great thinkers. It was where Euclid thought, and it was one of the Seven Wonders of the Ancient World.

But Alexander's reign was short-lived, and after he left the Egyptian empire died a slow death – effete and decadent and overrun by foreign powers. Its last stand was staged by Cleopatra. First, she murdered her rival teenage sister and married both of her two young brothers; and then, increasingly desperate to hang on to power, she married the leaders of two invading armies – Julius Caesar and Mark Anthony – before killing herself when all escape routes were at last closed. After her death Egypt was relegated to being a province of Rome, and spent the next 2,000 years in the shadows. Like other great powers that once ruled the world – the Persians, the Greeks, the Romans, the Vikings, the Mongol Hordes, the Ottoman Turks and the Spanish – the Egyptians never rose again.

We were in Egypt to advise on whether it was worth buying up an old shipyard in Alexandria and making it into a container terminal. Our contract, I was told by our engineer, was with a doctor.

"A doctor of what?" I asked. "Engineering, physics?"

"No, I think he does obstetrics."

"So. . . what's his connection with ports?"

"I don't know. I've been told that he has good contacts."

We met Dr Hatem in his department in a hospital in the centre of Cairo, in a tiny room with a grey plastic desk and two chairs. He was a friendly unassuming man who was speaking respectfully to the nurses he had around him when we arrived. After quarter of an hour they left and he said, "OK, I think I have an hour free now. Well, who would you like to see while you are here?"

We ran through the shipping lines and ministries on our list.

"Yes, I'll get on to this. In fact, I'll take you to see the ministries this afternoon. You don't really need to see the president, do you?"

"Well, I think, yes, it's his shipyard, so I think we should talk to him."

"No, I meant President Mubarak."

"What?!. . . Oh. . . well. . . no, I don't think that will be necessary."

"Ok, but I might try to arrange a meeting with his son. By the way, which hotel are you staying at?"

"The Pyramids."

"Ah, you should change. You need a better address than that. I'll fix up a good place."

He made a short telephone call.

"That's OK. It's fixed. I'll get a car to take you over there. Then the same car will pick you up after lunch at your hotel."

We took the lift down to the basement where we found a chauffeur with a stretched Mercedes. He spoke almost perfect English.

That afternoon and for the next two days we were whisked around the shipping agencies and ministries, mostly to meet retired admirals. I have never met an admiral in England, but in Egypt I must have met one a day. They were welcoming, polite and helpful, but knew almost nothing.

They had no statistics; they seemed unsure about which shipping lines called at their ports; and the man who knew it all was always away, in London or New York. There seemed to have been some awful mistake – they had staffed the commercial shipping industry with retirees from the navy, perhaps the least commercially minded people in the world. Meetings were always attended by four times the number of staff needed. They seemed excited to have someone to talk to. The most specific thing I was given was a map.

"Look at this," said the man at the ministry of transport, proudly. It was a map of the world with a big heart painted in the centre, in Egypt.

"Yes," he declaimed, "Egypt is where West meets East and North meets South and a quarter of the world's trade passes our door."

It was almost the same as the maps I had seen in Turkey and Greece and the Lebanon, each with the heart painted over *their* main port. All we were accumulating was a growing list of the most important men to talk to, if they ever came back from London or New York.

The pace of life in Cairo was slow. Work finished around 4pm, and we then took tea in the hotel. The Egyptians are supposed to have invented cake, and it is still part of their traditions. On the first afternoon we sat under the hanging plants in the palm-court atmosphere of the hotel's patisserie with the doctor. He had very grounded political antennae, and he agreed that the admirals lacked the right mindset.

"One of our problems," he said, "is that, unlike Turkey, Egypt has never had an Atatürk to drag us into the modern world. Nasser was a strong man, but not as far-seeing as Atatürk, and he chose to follow the Russian way, with the government running the economy. So, now we are a country of civil servants. Look at the people in here."

It was true; they walked less than briskly and they dressed like schoolteachers, in English tweed sports jackets, often in brown, a colour no longer favoured in Britain. Their faces were resigned and philosophical – with the notable exception of some younger men behind us in black leather jackets, one sitting with a sour Russian girl with silver hair.

Later we sat for an hour and watched the guests arriving for a wedding in one of the function rooms. Behind the bride – in frothy white lace, lit up by 1,000-watt floodlights for the cameras – stood the paterfamilias at the head of the welcoming party. With his grizzled lived-in face, he might have been a rough diamond who had built a construction empire, or a well-connected man with a monopoly of imports of something or other. I asked Dr Hatem what he might be. He smiled at us.

"Ah, you English, you always want to know what tier of society, what class, everyone comes from."

"Well. . . Maybe that's right. . . It's just that he doesn't look wealthy and he doesn't look poor."

"OK. But it's not like that here. He could be anything, but if you ask me to guess, I'd say there was a debt of gratitude for a small service rendered somewhere in the past and he was given contracts by the government. Egypt is a country of patronage. . . But he doesn't have any tell-tale accent or manner that I think you're looking for."

Around him stood his sons and sons-in-law, well groomed and angerless young men, waiting patiently for middle age, when they might be handed some of the reins of power. Deferential, with unlived-in faces and anxious eyes, it was not their world yet. Nor their day. They looked unsure of their role there, as the women – dutiful, dark-eyed dried flowers – chattered amongst themselves or danced with their children and grandchildren, the little girls in sugary-pink frills and the boys in white shirts, bow ties, scrubbed faces and oiled hair.

Not having found out much in Cairo, our hopes were pinned on Alexandria, and I set off with a young Egyptian economist to drive north through a long bleak industrial landscape to the city that was once the centre of learning of the world's greatest civilisation. Two thousand years later the city had continued to entrance a string of literary heavyweights in its last years of cosmopolitan decadence when a polyglot mix of upper-class British expatriates, Greeks, Lebanese, Jews, Italians and Arabs took refuge there during the Second World War. The city had been many things to these writers – the 'city of the soul' to E M Foster; and the 'capital of memory', the 'princess and whore', the 'city of more than five sexes', and 'the great wine press of love: those who emerged were the sick men, the solitaries, the prophets; all those who have been deeply wounded…' to Lawrence Durrell. So when we drove into the famed corniche of Alexandria late in the afternoon just before sunset, my eyes and senses were open to impressions and my expectations were high.

It was not a complete surprise that Alexandria turned out to be the capital of disappointment. It was a dud, dreary and dead. Or, at least, whatever there had been there is now invisible. The famed corniche was lined with drab cement buildings and traffic jams of smoke-belching buses. The city is supposedly renowned for its antique shops, but I could not tell if shops were antique shops or just ordinary shops with out-of-date goods – except for those selling pink dolls. On the second day I walked for an hour to find a bookshop, but in vain. The only signs of nightlife were in seedy discos with Arab pop music. The library and all traces of the Pharos Lighthouse are buried deep below the sea level, and little had been done to bring the rich history of the city to life.

The guidebook told us that Alexandria is not as well known as Cairo for good restaurants, so I asked Ayman, the young Egyptian who was accompanying me, if he could recommend one. He had spent a few months there doing a course, so he knew the city. He looked unhappy at the responsibility, but then his eyes lit up.

"I am not sure," he said, "but I have heard that they have just opened a branch of my favourite Cairo restaurant in Alexandria. It's not high-class food, but it's simple and good."

He asked a man on the street who nodded and five minutes later we arrived at a fresh modern café. It was small, bright and very clean. As we sat down Ayman's face was beatific.

"Have you been to a restaurant like this before?" he asked.

"No, I don't think so."

"Well I'll order for you. I know what's really good."

He was wreathed in smiles as he sat at the white Formica table.

"My favourite food and my favourite place," he breathed. It was a Kentucky Fried Chicken.

Work picked up a little. We started to piece together information from the port and a few shipping agents, and at the end of the week the only meeting left was with the grand old man of shipping in the city, whom the admirals had told us was *the* man to see. After a couple of postponements we arrived at his office in a rambling rococo town house, and took an iron-caged lift to a landing with huge plants in terracotta pots, blue tiles and faded carpets. There was no staff: just the great man and his secretary, a woman in her late 40s, with a deeply lined face and an engagingly sad smile – she had probably been a great beauty in her time. She ushered us into a drawing room cluttered with models of the great steamers of the 1930s, Louis XV furniture and lush oil paintings of old sloops, cutters and feluccas in full sail under red-streaked sunsets. There was a smell, rich but faint – it could have been sandalwood. But there were no computers, only a few ring-binders. Our host when he arrived was a vast shambling man in his late 70s, with the handsome lived-in face of a once great actor, immaculate manners and high-voltage charm. He talked at length about what he thought should be done with the shipyard.

It all sounded sensible and thoughtful. But it was all wrong. It had been tried in other countries and it hadn't worked.

Walking back to the hotel Ayman remarked on the strong smell of the drains.

"Everything is old here," he said. He was right, but it wasn't just the infrastructure that was crumbling and sclerotic. Egypt's crippling mix of Russian-style planning, Muslim religion and deference to all forms of authority were hardly a recipe for success. But by far their worst fault was their gerontocracy. The future had to lie with the young, the Aymans; or, if not, the future was bleak.

As we drove back to Cairo later in the evening, Ayman opened up a little about his ambitions. He thought of himself as being modern in his outlook, and hoped to join a large trading company. But although his parents were reasonably well-off, he didn't have family connections. He was going to do a computer course to strengthen his CV. He was 28 and unmarried.

"Do you have a girlfriend?" I asked. I watched his face in profile in the oncoming headlights to make sure that he was not embarrassed. But he was relaxed enough.

"No."

There was short silence and then he said tentatively, "But I have a secret. . . would you mind if I confided in you?"

"Not at all."

His secret was that he spent much of his time in the evenings poring over pictures and stories of Princess Diana, whom he thought had outshone Cleopatra as the most beautiful woman the world had ever known. She had died that year.

"Did you ever see her in London?" he asked.

"No. . . but my wife did. She talked to her at an international women's group dinner."

Ayman was awestruck. He seemed almost too nervous to ask, but he did. "What was she like?"

"My wife thought she was very beautiful and very natural. She said that close up you could see what wonderful skin she had. They talked mostly about their children."

Ayman smiled rapturously, and he kept smiling as we drove on towards Cairo.

35

The People's Power
Revolution, Manila

A black stretched Mercedes glided up to the entrance of the Manila Cultural Centre, and the crowd stood back. Out jumped four athletic and well-groomed Westerners in immaculate dark suits, white shirts and ties. They moved fast and purposefully. We took them to be stars of the film whose premiere we were going to see. But one of them, after screening the crowd and nodding to the others, returned to the car and opened the rear door.

It was the first time I had seen Imelda Marcos. She graciously accepted the assistance of the hand of her bodyguard and rose to her full height. Tall, statuesque with powerful legs and dressed in scarlet, she had a star quality that was heightened by the glare of the camera lights. There was a touch of steel about her. She swept into the foyer, an hour late; but they had delayed the start of the film for her.

President Ferdinand Marcos, on the other hand, I never saw during my five years in Manila. But many times during my stay I waited at the side of the road with the others until the convoy of cars, all with black-tinted windows and all with his lucky numbers – 77, 777 or 7777 – sped past, with a motorcade flashing its lights in front and behind. I never knew which of the cars Marcos was in, if any. My failure to see him in five years is evidence of my peripherality. Nothing important happened without Marcos.

In those days, the 1970s, the jury was still out on the Marcoses. Most of our fellow expats disapproved, but with reservations. An American who had been there for 20 years argued, on balance, in his favour.

"At least he got the crime organised."

"So you regard him as a criminal?"

"No, not at all. He stopped more crime than he started. Before he brought in martial law in 1972 most Filipinos carried guns, and the first thing you saw at an entrance to a club, bar or restaurant was a sign saying 'Please leave your firearms here'. But Marcos came down hard on the gangsters, and soon life was less complicated. The warlords and protection gangs disappeared, and now you just pay your 15 per cent to the top, to the Marcoses. And that's the end of the matter. Clear and simple."

To the ordinary Filipinos they were the royal family. He was extravagantly rich, and that is what Filipinos wanted to be; and she, Imelda, was a queen.

"She is very byoo-tee-fool," said one on the secretaries in our office, her eyes shining. "She was already a beauty queen when she was 18. She was The Rose of Tacloban."

They were proud of Imelda's riches, even if they were really theirs, taken from their own pockets. Of course they would vote for her; she handed out little treats when she appeared in public, often decorated with little red hearts.

What the more educated Filipinos thought, however, we never got to know, at least until much later. They smiled nervously and said nothing. There was a lot of fear in those days. Nor did we have access to international opinion. No foreign newspapers or magazines were on sale in Manila, apart from *Time* and *Newsweek*, and even they had columns blacked out – especially when they called her 'the steel butterfly'.

But by the time we left in 1982, the country was drifting into freefall. Less than 40 years before, the Philippines and Burma had been the richest countries in Asia, far ahead of China, Hong Kong or Singapore. Now they were at the bottom of the pile. The Marcos kleptocracy had bled the country dry. But in his last years of power, Marcos was ailing. A tiny man with built-up shoes and watchful simian features, he was now suffering from lupus erythematosus, a disease that needed regular dialysis. And Imelda, once a formidable imperial presence, was starting to lose her bearings. That year she had addressed the foreign women's association at a memorable meeting where she told them what made the Philippines special.

"We are God's chosen race," she said. "There is a hole in the atmosphere above the Philippines and only the Philippines, through which God lets special rays shine on our blessed people."

And then she sang a little song.

There was no serious opposition. The Filipinos were not a warrior race and were easily cowed. The only significant opposition leader had been Ninoy Aquino, a lawyer and journalist from a wealthy family, who had spent the last three years in exile in the USA, and before that had served seven years in a jail in the Philippines for supposedly being a communist. He conceded that he had been treated moderately well, being allowed books and some comforts, so when he decided to return to Manila he may have thought that he had little to fear. He observed that 'assassination is part of public service in the Philippines', but it was meant as a joke.

Ninoy was due to return in August 1986, and would provide a rallying point at last for the opposition. What was to be done? The Marcos inner circle ran though all the options, but failed to find one that was foolish enough. So they thought of *one* more. And they did it. They shot him dead at the top of the staircase as he walked out of the plane bringing him home. And then the guards shot the gunman.

"What?" we said, in unison. We were back in the UK by then, but still knew a lot of people from Manila after our five years there. It was barely credible.

"But who did it?"

"Marcos?"

"Impossible. Whatever you think of him, everyone concedes that he's always been a brilliant politician."

"The army?"

"No, they would never do it without Marcos' blessing."

"The killer on his own, a loner with a grudge?"

"Unlikely, the guards shot him straightaway, while they could have arrested him. They wanted to make sure he never spoke. Like Lee Harvey Oswald."

It is a country where rumours spread like wildfire, but the Filipinos looked embarrassed, giggled and said nothing. Perhaps in this case they really didn't know. But a few weeks later some friends reported that a local colleague had taken them aside, lowered his voice, looked left and right and told them what people were saying.

"It was Imelda and Ver." General Fabian Ver was the lantern-jawed army chief, a man of little refinement who had risen to the top as a crony of Marcos.

"What? They did it without telling him? What happened when he found out?"

"They say that when she told Marcos – he was in bed and quite ill – he threw a glass ashtray at her head."

But it was never confirmed.

Whoever did it, the Marcos regime was dead from that moment. But it took a long time to die. We arrived back there two years later in 1985, and were shocked at the decline. The country was more or less bankrupt, and it showed as the taxi bringing us in from the airport drove through the seedy back streets lining Manila Bay, with their pay-by-the-hour hotels and the sickly smell of vinegar, sugar and garlic rising from the broken drains. With the taxi windows wide open in the sweltering humidity and the pall cast in the sky by the sulphurous yellow street-lights we didn't feel as relaxed to be back as we had hoped.

Marcos' health was deteriorating fast by this time, and his palace at Malacañang had an abandoned air. A friend reported that when she took an official tour there was a smell of mould, and dog droppings on the carpets.

The president was now an embarrassment to his American allies, and they pressured him into holding a snap election to legitimise his control over the country. He complied – confidently, as he was surrounded only by people who told him he would win, and anyway he had rigged elections before. Money was the key to victory and his wealth was spectacular.

The opposition was led by Cory Aquino, the unassuming and until now apolitical widow of the murdered Ninoy.

The election was held and Marcos announced that he had won. It is just possible that he did, and won it fairly. To the voters in the provinces he was still the great man and Imelda was still the queen; and they had the money to give the people the best presents at the rallies. In Mindanao they handed out two Coca-Colas and a T-shirt to everyone, outbidding the opposition.

But in Manila nobody believed that he had won fairly, and the simmering discontent at last boiled over, not so much amongst the dirt-poor who lived under the shadow of the putrid mountain of refuse in the slums of Tondo but amongst the young professionals in the modern business centre of Makati. Suddenly I was hearing – for the first time in the ten years I had been in and out of Manila – strong political views. Their badge was a yellow ribbon, the same ribbon that was worn at the arrival of Ninoy three years before. Most people in our office were wearing one.

Events speeded up. Both Marcos and Cory Aquino claimed victory and both took the oath of office in different parts of the city, with Cory attracting much more support. Then, for the very first time, two top figures in the government broke with Marcos. The minister for national defence, the handsome Juan Ponce Enrile and the deputy chief of the armed forces, Fidel Ramos, declared their support for Cory and holed up in the police headquarters on the EDSA highway. They would have been arrested easily by the army which gathered outside, but the leader of the Church – the man with the never-to-be-forgotten name, Cardinal Sin – broadcast a radio message urging all patriotic citizens to go up to EDSA and block the oncoming tanks. They came in their thousands, and eventually, their millions. Young office workers, nuns and priests, with guitars, food and ice cream. Nuns knelt in front of the tanks and men and women linked arms to block the troops. It was a standoff.

The expats were nervous. We lived in villages with guards at the gates, and in houses that were provocative in their affluence. The locals – angular, bony and getting poorer every year – walked past and looked in. They were always smiling, but they kept things inside and were known to snap, and run amok. We had no feeling for how they would react if law and order broke down. They might move into the wealthy villages and take revenge. There was no precedent in the Philippines, but the closest foreign precedent did not bode well. In Indonesia, the next country to the south, and with similar Malay people, the threat of a coup 20 years before had led to half a million deaths in a frenzy of violence unleashed by the government. At its climax the top generals were cornered one dark night in a swamp outside Jakarta and left to the mercy of the women's wing of the Communist Party's army, who were said to have cut off their private parts and stuffed them in their mouths in their dying moments.

We had to make arrangements for leaving in a hurry. A rumour was circulating that the British embassy had not even made plans for getting us out. It was said that we would be looked after by the Americans, but, if so, we could see ourselves being well down the queue for the helicopters out. And we had a problem, a big problem. We had just adopted our daughter, a Filipina, and none of the papers were ready yet. So we made arrangements with the maids that if we had to leave quickly they would take her to their village and keep her there, and we would get back somehow to reclaim her when it was safe again. But the maids were not entirely to be trusted. They were deeply envious of a Filipina being adopted by 'rich foreigners'. Only a few weeks before, a pretty and well-educated girl at work had burst into tears when she heard we had adopted. Then she turned on me with eyes like raw nerves and said, "Why didn't you adopt me?" They were desperate to get out.

On the second day the bombers swooped in over the air base just a mile from our house, and we ran out to bring the children in from the garden. They were ecstatic, there eyes shining, as they heard the bombs drop. They made their fingers into gun shapes and shouted 'bang, bang'.

We didn't even know who was bombing whom. There were reports that the air force had changed sides, and then the radio announced that Marcos had left the country in a helicopter; but he broadcast his own message from the palace, assuring us that he had not. He was still in the palace giving the orders, while Imelda, they say, was kneeling in her private chapel, looking bewildered, and praying from time to time.

Then suddenly it was over. It was inevitable after a radio communication that was intercepted and reported:

Marcos: My order is not to attack.

Gen Ver: They are massing civilians near our troops and we cannot keep on withdrawing. . .

Marcos: My order is to disperse them without shooting them.

Gen Ver: We cannot withdraw all the time. . .

Marcos: No, no, no!. . . You disperse the crowds without shooting them.

So Marcos, in the end, was not all bad. He wouldn't turn the guns on the people. There were rushed negotiations with the Americans, safe passage out was guaranteed, and a helicopter took Marcos and his family away to Hawaii, leaving the palace empty. The crowds, denied entry for all those years, wandered in. There was no rage or revenge. There was a little looting, but mostly they just walked around, looking curious.

"We did it!" they repeated again and again in the office the next day. "We did it." They *had* done it themselves, with no guns and no deaths, no settling of scores; just two million office workers, priests and nuns with yellow ribbons. It was the first-ever bloodless people's revolution. There was a heady feeling of 'bliss was it to be alive on that dawn', of seedy streets sluiced clean. A day's holiday was announced, but everyone stayed in the office and we ordered ice cream.

Postscripts

• The year after the People's Power Revolution in the Philippines, the Estonians staged their 'singing revolution' against Moscow. They started by singing national songs forbidden by the Russians at a stadium in Tallinn and went on to organise a 600-kilometre human chain across Estonia,

Latvia and Lithuania by getting two million people to link hands. It lead to a wave of more or less bloodless revolutions and the collapse of the Soviet empire.

• Marcos died in Hawaii in 1989. Cory Aquino's government refused Imelda permission to bring him back to the Philippines for burial, fearing that his grave might become a rallying point. So Imelda kept his unburied corpse on display in a plastic capsule for years until they allowed her to bring it back.

• Imelda still lives in Manila. In April 2009 her glamorous daughter, Imee, once the rebel of the family, was promoting Imelda's new range of designer clothes, the Imelda Collection: a 'funky, streetwise line of jewellery, clothing and shoes'. They hoped the fashion line would attract a younger generation. They are both back in politics now: in 2010 Imelda became a member of the House of Representatives and Imee became the governor of her home province.

36
Another Twenty-Hour Night

I wake to find a head resting on my shoulder. It is my neighbour in the next seat on the plane and he is fast asleep. He is wearing a bow tie. He moves his hand over, grips my arm and snuggles up. I shift in my seat to try to dislodge him. But he doesn't move. We are both drugged with tiredness.

It seems to have been an age since I left the bar in Hong Kong, but my watch shows that it was only six hours ago. I had arrived at the airport for the Friday evening flight, drained after a week of immersion in people and talk and meetings. At last the tap of incessant input and output had been turned off, and I sat sprawled in the departure lounge watching a tropical storm outside lashing against the high glass windows. An announcement told us that we would be delayed for an hour, and we went through the motions of grumbling, but there was an air of togetherness; we were all in limbo, in dead time. When I at last got to my seat on the plane it was less comfortable than I'd hoped. My brain in neutral, I tried to relax, but despite being exhausted I found at first that I could not sleep. . . But that was a couple of hours ago, and it was the last thing I remember.

The man next to me starts to stir. He looks confused, then disturbed and removes his arm from mine. He is probably over seventy – with fluffy white hair, pink skin, and a Dunn's sports jacket. He might be a retired doctor.

"Oh... Where? Um... Sorry... I really am awfully sorry." He mutters, trying to pull his thoughts together. His accent is Scottish.

"That's OK, I think we are all tired," I say, adding, to divert the subject away from his embarrassment. "Where are you travelling to?"

"London, then Edinburgh. And where do you live?"

"London."

He seems unexpectedly excited by this information. His thoughts seemed to be coming slightly into focus, but he is still disoriented.

"You know, I'll soon be travelling to London for the marriage of my daughter. It'll be in Kensington. And my wife and I have a particular reason for looking forward to it, because we will be able to use, for the first time, our new tea-making machine."

"Your what?"

"What happened was that we found when we booked a few months ago that the hotel where we will be staying does not have any tea-making equipment in the room."

"Really?"

"But this disappointment has proved a boon," he continued, "as it led me to purchase this wonderful little machine, very compact (he illustrated its measurements with his hands). Although it is a little slow, it can make two good cups of tea, for myself and my wife. Yes, it is a VERY handy little item. Both my wife and I are very enthusiastic about it."

He sat there smiling, at peace with the world.

A small meal of indeterminate association with any time of day arrived. It was neither breakfast, nor lunch nor dinner. It was a type of bread with an Italian name and a filling, and a shortbread biscuit in tartan wrapping.

We started to chat in a more coherent manner. He told me that he had started his career in Africa in the 1950s, in the colonial civil service, in a small town in Malawi.

"They used to dress for dinner then," he said. "In fact we even wore evening dress for a visit to the local cinema."

"By the way," he added unexpectedly, "Edinburgh is a good place to live." He was a pathologist.

I eventually fell into a deep sleep about fifteen minutes before we landed in Dubai to change planes.

It was 1.30am in Dubai when we were decanted out into the airport. My intention was to find a seat to doze for the three hours in transit. But the much awaited new Terminal Three in the early hours was not a place to sleep. Strolling past me were wide-awake Stepford wives and their spouses – chatting, browsing in tasteful boutiques, eating at elegant little cafés, surrounded by greenery and Japanese ponds. It was a shopping heaven. The travellers were rainbow-coloured, nocturnal mutants with watches showing 12 different times, but speaking mainly English. A five-year-old girl with blonde hair ran away from her mother, across the floor in front of a café, in shoes that seemed too big for her, then stopped and glided like a ballet dancer on concealed wheels while the watchers clapped. If this is the future – Stepford wives or not – it seems to work.

I thought of the end of *The Truman Show*, when a tear appears in the sky, to be penetrated by a brilliant eyeball-piecing light, revealing that the whole of Truman's life had been lived in an artificial theatrical set of an ideal world. Except that in the case of Dubai it would be dark outside, and everyone in the city would be sleeping.

Only the locals looked ill at ease. A Middle Eastern businessman in an almost smart, ill-fitting black suit, a white shirt and a silver tie walked self-consciously around the shops with his two small children, both in ill-fitting black suits and silver ties – and his wife, in black robes, with only her glittery eyes and gold bangles visible. All four reeked of perfume.

We boarded the plane again; 3am – or 7am if we had left our watches unchanged at Hong Kong, or 11pm if we had already set them for the destination – to fly on through what was adding up to a 20-hour night* towards London, chasing the dawn across the world.

This time I was sitting beside a man with a black jacket, blue jeans and expensive casual shoes. His hair was thick and shiny like a healthy animal, and he was holding a crumpled copy of *The Economist*.

He settled down in his seat, and said with a rueful smile, "If they come with food, *don't* wake me."

The light went out and he slept. But I didn't. I tried to catch my tiredness at its peak, but missed it and dozed restlessly. From time to time I strolled down the aisles to watch the video screens flickering across 200 faces, also still awake, with earphones clamped on their heads, feeding 'in-flight entertainment' directly into their brains in the mother of all distractions from reality – that they were five miles up in the air in an aluminium tube, it was black outside, the temperature was minus 52° Celsius and the roar of four giant engines would be unremitting.

We came down into London on a cold grey morning just before dawn, into a mosaic of weak street lamps, with their poisonous sulphur-yellow light; and filed from the plane into chilly metal corridors. The early morning staff was a mix of pretty young matrons in dark-blue uniforms, and pallid short-haired security bullies.

---

* Three hours in Hong Kong airport, three in transit in Dubai, 13 in the air and one in London after landing, all in the dark

The luggage was late to arrive in the baggage reclaim area and mine was almost last. The only people waiting for the last few cases included my neighbour in the next seat.

"Do you live in London?" I asked.

"In a way. I have a flat in London and one in Hong Kong. Between the two of them I can work in the busiest markets when they are open – in Tokyo, London and New York." He seemed weary.

It turned out that he had been born in Switzerland and educated in America.

"Where do you feel most at home?"

"Maybe nowhere. Maybe everywhere. I sometimes do a million air miles a year," he said with another rueful smile. He had just broken up with his girlfriend.

His luggage did not arrive.

"Third time this year," he said. He did not seem upset.

The plane had been early and I didn't want to wake my wife, so I sat in one of Heathrow's cafés with 18 types of coffee. I asked for an ordinary filter coffee, and had to explain the order to the young Syrian who was serving.

As I sat over my drink, I watched the early morning arrivals. There is an irony in airports, those most commercial and impersonal of places, being the setting for such intense emotions. Of all the tears and raw unselfconscious public emotion I have seen, a large part must have been at airports. That morning I watched a man in late middle-age, about seventeen stone, with a grizzled grey beard, wearing a T-shirt despite the early morning cold. I guessed that he might have been an oil contract worker. He was waiting with his wife for his son who eventually emerged at the exit door – tall, in his early 20s, a rough but good-looking kid. There were big smiles, bear hugs, a fond reunion. Both the father and son had masculine, gravelly voices. The mother said how wonderful he looked. The tough old grey-beard turned away. I caught sight of his face. It crumpled; he was crying. Next to them a grey-haired lady in a Laura Ashley dress, with the last traces of prettiness just fading from her pale face, greeted her husband – neatly casual in a linen jacket and slacks – with a shy kiss on the cheek.

Surly chauffeurs, uncomfortable in smart suits and short hair, scowled as they waited to meet their less formally dressed passengers. Young Middle Eastern boys with doggy eyes and soft skin were met by their older brothers. Whole Indian families had turned out to celebrate the return of a relative. And an American girl with a dazzling smile spotted her boyfriend as she came through the gate, abandoned her trolley, ran and threw herself at him, yelling with excitement, her legs wrapped round his waist. Many of them, however, spoil the surprise with their mobiles: "Where are you now... I've just arrived in the baggage hall... I'll be out in a minute... I'll ring again when I get though customs... shouldn't be too long... is Doris with you?"

I took a taxi back. We entered London just as dawn was breaking. The roads were slate-grey, shiny in the dew. London looked monumental, leafy and full of substance in the first light. We passed lone figures walking home, pale and hunched against the chill in the morning air. Those alone are always more interesting than the couples. The green and red of the traffic lights are strangely intense at this hour.

My 20 hours had been like a night of disturbed dreams – a series of unconnected fragments which would be forgotten if not recorded soon afterwards. I was almost home myself, but there are people who never quite get home. I thought back to my neighbour on the plane and his lost luggage – still in his conditioned air and windowless artificial light, waiting for his overnight bag, as a few abandoned cases circled round and round on the carousel.

37

Sri Lanka

The croaking of the frogs in the drains around the bar was rising in a crescendo. It told us that the storm was coming soon. Through a gap in the bougainvilleas massed around the hotel garden wall we could see a hot red swollen sun dipping towards the sea out of a vast stricken sky of angry blackening clouds lined with gold. A hundred little candles floating in tiny containers in the pond alongside the bar were starting to flicker. The humidity was around 100 per cent and there was sweat on the back of my neck.

When the rain came it came in a torrent, pounding on the thatched roof and sluicing down the canopies, bringing a sudden freshness to the air. We sat over our drinks in silence, watching the lightning forking through the clouds out at sea. Someone mentioned that Marco Polo had called Sri Lanka the best of all small islands; blessed by nature, it has always been a land of lush greenery and squeaky white-sand beaches, with the fragrance of cinnamon on the breeze. He was being ironic, trading on the unexamined English convention that all rain is bad. But I have always loved rain – from the misty veil that covered Ireland when I was young to the violent cyclones of the tropics. The more eventful the weather, the better. Sitting there, with a short respite from the intolerable heat, the rain hissing on the leaves, and the air cleansed and cool, I thought of the 'soft refreshing rain' we used to sing about at Sunday school.

"Well, I don't think we are going to be able to eat outside tonight," said one of our group. We had intended to go to an open-air Sri Lankan restaurant next door.

"So where?"

"The Cricket Club?"

There was a unanimous "Yes".

We waited for the rain to ease up a little and the nine of us piled into three tuk-tuks, the dangerous little auto rickshaws powered by snarling lawn-mower engines.

"How much?" we asked. It was disastrous not to ask first. The driver, in shorts, flip-flops and a T-Shirt and already soaked, eyed us, assessing what the market might bear.

"Two hundred."

"No *way*," we said, feigning incredulity and starting to get out.

"No. No. You stay. What you pay?"

"One hundred. . . but three hundred if you get us there before the other two tuk-tuks with our friends over there."

"OK," and we shot off down the black shiny wet streets, veering from side to side.

The rain was starting to spatter again just as we arrived, and we scurried into the restaurant – for the Cricket Club was not a cricket pitch but a restaurant. It was housed in a wooden bungalow surrounded by an overgrown garden and a veranda; and for Sri Lankans it was a cameo of heaven. Every wall in the two dining rooms was cluttered with illuminated autographed cricket bats, pads, balls, flannels, sweaters, scores of photos and cricket memorabilia;

and around each room soundless screens played different games of cricket of historical importance. As we came in through the door in our damp clothes, happy Sri Lankan faces turned to nod hello, despite never having seen us before. They were the open, sporty faces of young men who still clapped good play by the other team. We even heard an occasional 'jolly good' that evening. As we ordered from a menu combining colonial curries with steak and chips and sausage and mash, an Australian who had joined us for the evening fell into a bantering session with the young Sri Lankans. He was revealing an encyclopaedic knowledge of cricket and they soon squared off for a battle of wits – the Australian fielding every barb thrown at him with a sidelong crooked smile, like a dog with its tongue lolling out, panting, anxious for acceptance as one of the gang; and the young Sri Lankans responding as if from English private schools, which they may well have been.

"You certainly love your cricket," I said to him later.

He looked at me, leaned closer and said, "I can't stand the bladdy gime."

His manner had changed. He had dropped the one-of-the-gang expression, and was speaking in a more dispassionate way that hinted at a steely intelligence.

"Look, I'm an Australian, and I travel all over the world in my work. If they meet an Australian who doesn't know about cricket then I'm a big disappointment. Second: I've been working in and out of Colombo for years and if you work here you've got to be able to talk about cricket. It's half the battle. So I swot it up."

The next morning was Saturday, and a wonderful sunny day. It was my second weekend in Colombo, and I walked over to Odel's. It had been recommended for buying clothes, which had displaced tea as Sri Lanka's main export. Odel's was an old folly, like a toy castle painted white; but, inside, the light flooding in through its glass ceilings fell on a bright air-conditioned temple of boutiques and craft shops, selling soap scented with cinnamon, paper processed from elephant dung, and picture frames made from chillies. Many of the shoppers – if they were shoppers, some of them may have just liked being there – were Europeans, mainly mothers and children like models for healthy living, with their light golden skin and sun-bleached hair and the international expat uniform of sky blue and white cottons, seersuckers, calicos and linens. They mingled with smiling Sri Lankan families whose teenagers were still happy to exchange cheerful banter with their parents. They seemed a reminder of a kinder and nicer age; and although it came as a surprise, I thought 'Well, that fits' when I found the display at the record store full of remastered CDs of Alma Cogan, Frankie Vaughan, Frankie Lane, Cliff Richard and Aker Bilk, with a selection of country and western for cooler tastes. Later, in Odel's French delicatessen I found the Australian from the night before.

"Well, this is the first shop I've been to in Colombo," I said, "what a coincidence." It wasn't: *all* expats went to Odel's sometime or other on a Saturday morning.

Just as they all went at sunset to the Galle Face, the grandest of the old hotels, with a long list of past guests scrolled on what looked like an honours board in the entrance – Winston Churchill, Gregory Peck, General Patton and Ingrid Bergman amongst them. There the expats sat over drinks at tables scattered over a vast lawn rolling down to the sea, the evening breeze cooling the air and sunburned skin glowing in the last of the sun. Conversation would lapse as we looked up at the stars and listened to the sound of the waves breaking on the rocks at the end of the lawn, knowing that we were at the centre of a small universe.

. . . and just as everyone went to the cultural events. They are rarer than in London, so a string quartet will attract half of the culturati of Colombo into old halls packed with fold-up seats. They used to say that the only English left in the world are the Indians, but the Sri Lankans are more English even than the Indians, who in the end are too excitable, too feverish to be truly English. And as in Odel's there was no generation divide; the young were at ease with their elders, and the concert halls were full of polite young women with lustrous wavy black hair, so different from the flattened coconut-oiled hair of southern India. As at the Cricket Club, they would turn in their seats to give a lovely smile to a foreign visitor.

That was my first fortnight in Colombo. I have never much liked small towns. I have always preferred big cities where, like icebergs, much is hidden, invisible and unknown beneath the surface, and there is much to learn; but Colombo seemed as good as a small town gets.

So my first meeting came as a shock. As part of my work on the port I had to talk to all the exporters, and my first encounter was with Mr Tea, the much-quoted chairman of the tea planters association. He had his office in an unexpectedly dreary building, old-fashioned in the worst sense, with drab dark-brown wood and plywood panelling; it had probably been their headquarters since the 1940s. It might have been a difficult meeting anyway, but I certainly got off on the wrong foot. I just happened to have noticed on the way there that their main export markets were the Middle East and Russia. This was highly unusual – most countries sold their exports to the US and Europe.

I asked him why as we settled down in the meeting room with his marketing manager. He exploded.

"The reason," he hesitated, "is that you English – you are English, aren't you; but the rest of you Europeans and the Americans are just as bad – are happy to drink muck. Muck."

He was a stocky man with a small moustache dyed black, balding in an unhealthy way, and lacking the relaxed elegance that a captain of a traditional industry would have in most countries. But I was assuming that this was an elaborate joke that he had played out with visitors many times.

"You mean that it's only the Russians and Arabs that can afford good tea now?" I said.

"Not at all, it's just that you don't have any taste. Your taste is so poor that you'll buy any rubbish supermarkets sell you."

I was still waiting for a smile. But no; he was very annoyed.

"Clippings and fannings and dust, the leftovers, that's what you drink."

"Here," he shouted, "bring him some tea, some real tea."

A fearful tea boy came in and deposited a plain white cup of a 1950s design in front of me.

"Drink that; proper tea. And tell me what you think." They watched me drink.

"Doesn't it taste like the tea you drank when you were a child?"

"Yes, definitely." He was preaching to the converted.

"Well go back to your country and tell them about our tea."

"OK, I will. Tell me which of all your teas you would recommend."

Seeming a little vindicated, he then settled down to answer some of my questions.

The textiles people were the same. In another gloomy building the assembled bosses told me their goods were threatened by unfair foreign competition. But it was not their fault. Nobody appreciates quality and quality is what Sri Lanka does best. They were all running scared of the Chinese, who were taking over everywhere. "So why do the Chinese do so well," I asked.

"Because they are cheap"

"How about your prices? Could you meet theirs?"

"We are not going to reduce our prices."

"So you think it's all downhill from now?"

"No not necessarily. It depends on the government. They need a plan to support us."

I heard this again and again, in the rubber plants and on the coconut plantations. They were not at peace with themselves. The government was letting them down, they complained.

It was, however, questionable whether 'The Government of the Democratic Socialist Republic of Sri Lanka' could help anyone much. The name tells a story. The government was designed for purposes 40 years out of date. Even North Korea is only a Democratic People's Republic, Vietnam is only a Democratic Republic and China is only a People's Republic. One afternoon I went to see the manager in the department responsible for attracting foreign investment (we were trying to attract a foreign operator into the port). He brought 12 people to the meeting. They seemed pleased to see a foreigner; in fact they seemed pleased to have something to do for an afternoon. They gave a presentation in PowerPoint. It showed beautiful pictures of Sri Lanka and listed hundreds of 'projects' for which they were trying to get foreign money.

"How many of your projects that depend on foreign investments are going ahead?" I asked.

They gave a long answer, but it was 'none'.

"So what's going wrong?"

"Well, the war."

They thought it would all change when peace returned.

There is something I have omitted to mention. It is that as you walked the quiet streets of Colombo, with their worthy institutions from an earlier generation – the Sri Lankan Housewives Association, the Girls Friendly Society, the Young Women's Christian Association – you would pass, every few hundred yards, a pile of sandbags, a checkpoint and a group of soldiers in full battledress brandishing guns; because despite the placid surface of Colombo on a quiet weekend there, the country had been at war for 25 years.

The golden period of stability following independence after the Second World War had hardly lasted ten years. It ended when the Singhalese, who are the majority in the population, and Buddhist, won an election in the late 1950s. The Singhalese were not as bright as the Tamils when it came to exam results, so the new government curried favour with the voters by letting the Singhalese into universities on lower marks. Then they made their religion, Buddhism, the national religion and Singhalese the national language.

The next step by the government, like those of India and Pakistan, was to opt for the socialist path – the great illusion of that period that governments can run things better than the citizens they represent. They nationalised the tea industry, the oil industry, the bus industry and other industries, and although they recanted by the late 1970s, the corrupt bureaucracy that grew to manage the economy of Sri Lanka remains in the centre of the web. While the Indians dismantled the 'licence raj' that had been strangling their economy, Sri Lanka's government remains as self-serving as it was 40 years ago; only a few years ago the prime minister had five relatives in his government.

The first civil war came from the fashion book of the time. Its leader, Rohana Wijeweera, was a photogenic dropout from Moscow's Lumumba University, who returned to Colombo to start a Marxist revolution in 1971. He affected the appearance and dress of Che Guevara, with the same beret, spectacles and wispy beard. His revolution petered out in a few months, but in that short period it had killed 25,000 young men and women. Rohana went underground, but, undeterred, he returned in the 1980s, this time inspired by the work of the Khmer Rouge in Cambodia. He favoured a population of simple peasants in the fields. His second revolution saw 60,000 deaths before he was captured in 1989. He was executed, like his hero Che, immediately after his capture, but postcards of him in fashionista poses can still be found around Colombo 20 years later.

Meanwhile the resentment of the Tamils had come to the boil, and given birth to the Liberation Tigers of Tamil Eelam, the Tamil Tigers, possibly the largest and most efficient terrorist group of their time. Their cause – the ending of discrimination against them at universities and the relegation of their language – would normally attract sympathisers. But their brutal methods did the reverse. Their leader's first public act at the age of 21 was shooting a mayor at point-blank range as he was going into church, and that set the pattern. They invented the suicide bomber, and sent out a young girl to kill Rajiv Ghandi, the prime minister of India. The grisly photograph of her blackened incinerated head lying in the dust remains an iconic reminder of the spirit of the Tigers. They tortured Tamils they considered too moderate and they recruited women and children to do their fighting. All had to carry a cyanide capsule, in case they were captured. Their leader, a plump little man with a bushy moustache – he might have been a cleaning contractor – presided over the killing of around 80,000 and eventually took thousands with him in his last stand.

Marco Polo may be turning in his grave. His most blessed of small islands has ended up one of the most cursed. It may never have suffered the horrors of the Cambodia, Rwanda, or Russia in the 1930s; but it has surely been less fortunate than most in the baleful influence of its politics and politicians, its leaders elected and unelected, and Che Guevara wannabees – exploitative, bullying, posturing, uncompromising, deluded, psychotic.

The conversation often turned to the war as we sat out well after dark at the Galle Face listening to the waves, the sea breeze in our hair, and the women in shawls as the evening cooled. None of us had ever been able to take sides. In fact we had always been disturbed to be unable to work out who, if anyone, was right. It is conventional wisdom that the gun can't solve anything, that all settlements must be political in the end. But there had been many cease-fires, brokered by intermediaries, and all had lapsed. One night the British military attaché was with us out on the lawn. The military attaches in the past were not always the brightest, but he was one of the new breed of analytical, articulate soldiers and he was working closely with the Norwegian intermediaries. It was at a time when there were great hopes of a permanent peace. We asked him how he saw the future. It was important for us in the planning of the port. Was the optimism justified, we asked? An attaché is not supposed to talk, but he conceded one word.

"No."

The Australian from the Cricket Club was also there. He had been around for a long time. We also asked for his opinion. He hesitated, looking out over the lawn and the sea beyond.

"Looking at the two sides, it's a pity there's got to be only one loser. But they probably won't find out who it is until 50 years from now."

38

A Good Man in Manila

Every year the newspapers in Manila used to print a list of the top-ten taxpayers in the country. It always contained, alongside the industrialists and film stars, the name of Dr Varwig. He was the only foreign doctor in the city.

I first saw him at the German Club, an incongruous *gemutlich* Bavarian retreat in the middle of a tropical Asian city. Outside on the street the fierce sun glared down from directly overhead, melting the asphalt of the road surface; while inside the German Club leather-shaded lamps suspended from the ceiling on heavy iron chains shone soft pools of light over old oak dining tables. The walls were decorated with Teutonic heraldic shields and the menu showed cabbage stew, schnitzel and goulash in Gothic script. At the entrance there was a large map of Europe on the wall showing German territory in red. It included Poland.

Most of the Germans who patronised the club were deeply conservative and lived a life more German than they would have at home. Some were social ruins, who had settled in the tropics for an easy life, and to be regarded as interesting simply by virtue of being different, being foreign. I used to notice a few shaking hands on the beer steins, and I was often disconcerted by what sounded like a reedy robotic telephone in the background. It was a desiccated old man with an eye patch who talked though an electronic microphone built into his throat. But the Germans are nothing if not an impressive nation, and there were usually a few distinguished figures there amongst the regulars. A handsome middle-aged man with silver hair stood out one lunch time. "Who's that?" I asked my German friend. "That's Dr Varwig." He was in a grey suit. Nobody wore a suit in the fetid heat of Manila.

Normally he dressed from head to toe in white, down to his white leather shoes. He would appear at the door of his surgery at the end of the waiting room, and, with a mildly ironic bow, take your hand and lead you into his room. He was rumoured to be gay, but respect precluded further probing, and when he led you in, sat you down, fixed you with his pale Nordic eyes and asked, "Vell, how can we help you this morning?" in his still heavy German accent, you felt as if you were in the safest hands in the world. I have always preferred my doctors godlike. I was usually there for skin problems, which are notoriously difficult to diagnose. He often confessed to being unsure of what to prescribe and told us to return in ten days if his intuition proved wrong, by which time he said he would have consulted the literature. I rarely had to go back – he was a superb diagnostician – but when I had to he did indeed have the literature at his fingertips. He always prescribed a double dosage of antibiotics. "Most of the drugs here are diluted," he explained. Pharmaceuticals in Manila were a monopoly of a crony of Marcos.

But it was our first meeting that cut into my memory in hard bright colours. It was a national holiday – one of the many Marcos used to give to his people to keep them happy. The Filipinos will happily confess to being lazy and the sacramental rituals of sleeping and shopping (both with the emphasis on the last syllable) on these holidays were precious to them. And that day was a day made for laziness. It was a beautiful sunny morning, with hardly a sound to be heard along the gardens of the street; and it was almost too hot to move. We had just finished the usual breakfast of papaya, mango, melon and pineapple on the patio, and the tea we had drunk had already reappeared as sweat on our foreheads.

My wife was pregnant for the first time and all had been going well – until that morning. It was about 10am when she came downstairs with an anguished look, bent double with pain. "I think it's a miscarriage, but I can't be sure," she said.

"What!" She described her symptoms, and if was not a miscarriage it would be even worse.

"I'll call the hospital," I said. The Makati Medical Centre was the best hospital in Manila, and it was close by. I found the number and dialled, but the phone just rang and rang.

"How can there be nobody there, at the country's main hospital? Does everyone get well just because it's a holiday?" I asked in frustration.

Her pain was getting worse.

"We'll have to try the doctor," I said.

"But it's a national holiday. And anyway we don't have a doctor." She was right. She had only been to a local gynaecologist for the baby checks.

We rang a lady who had been here for years and acted as mother hen to the young wives.

"You'll have to call Doctor Varwig," she advised.

"But we don't know him, and he doesn't know us; anyway, how could we ring him on holiday?"

"It doesn't matter. He's your best bet," said Eileen, and rang us two minutes later with his home telephone number.

My wife rang and a maid told her that the doctor was just about to go out for the day. But he came to the phone.

"Where are you?" he asked, after my wife had explained her condition.

"San Miguel Village."

"It will take you 10 minutes to drive to the hospital. It will take me 15 minutes. I will see you at reception."

We arrived at Makati Medical Centre, and found it deserted. There must have been nurses and doctors on the wards upstairs. But there was only a guard with a gun on the ground floor, and we wondered if we were at the wrong entrance. "Don't people get sick on holidays?" I said, repeating myself. A minute later Dr Varwig strode up the steps. Always correct, he had thrown a white coat over his sports clothes. I remembered his face from the German Club.

"Good morning. I am Doctor Varwig," he said. "Let's see, we must find a room." He led us upstairs, and seemed to select an operating theatre at random, as if the hospital was his own. He called my wife in, then a nurse to assist and closed the door.

A short time later he reappeared.

"It *is* a miscarriage. A small operation will be necessary... Are you allergic to anything?" he called back through the door. The anaesthetic took a few minutes and Dr Varwig and the nurse went about their preparations. As he finally closed the door to the operating theatre, he gave me not quite a wink but a small smile that said that it was going to be alright.

As I sat alone in that strangely empty hospital it was one of the few times since I was a child that I turned to prayer.

About three quarters of an hour later he walked out of the operating theatre, removing his mask.

"The operation went well. But the child had died some time ago," he said. He was very matter-of-fact. He lifted a bottle to the light. It contained the very tiny child that was never to be.

I thanked him effusively.

"And so sorry for ruining your holiday."

"I am a doctor," he said.

Then he added "Were you nervous?"

"Yes. Very."

"So was I," was his surprising response.

"Oh. . . Why was that?"

"I have never done that operation since medical school."

My wife was wheeled out on a trolley by a Filipina nurse, still asleep. Dr Varwig turned his head sideways to look down at her, then formed a fist and knocked her head very gently from right to left and then left to right. It flopped from side to side as if blown by a slight breeze. She seemed touched at that moment with a light unearthly beauty; she could have been far away in a different universe taking home the soul of her child. Dr Varwig noticed. "She is a very beautiful woman," he said slowly. "But it looks as if she'll be out for some time. I'll wait with her. You go for a walk and come back in about two hours."

As I came out of the fierce air-conditioning of the silent hospital entrance the sun was shining brilliantly on the bougainvilleas against the white wall outside. I heard the sound of traffic and saw ordinary people walking by doing ordinary things, and I felt one of those rushes of ecstatic happiness that recur only once every few years.

It was some time before he sent a bill, and it was very modest. We knew why Dr Varwig was a top taxpayer. The Philippines was one of those countries where all the real wealth was in the hands of 22 families. They are rich beyond imagination, and they have staff to deal with tax.

But we never knew what caused him to arrive in Manila as a young man, and never leave. He had arrived soon after the war ended.

39

Romania

"**O**h no," I thought. "Here they come again. Why me?" There were at least a dozen other people milling around outside the café in one of the leafy streets of old stone buildings that once had Bucharest known as the Paris of the East. But the predatory little eyes had locked on to mine, and a few seconds later one of them was walking alongside me.

"Money, mister."

I looked down at him. He was about ten, runty but with the rude health of a survivor. His eyes at close quarters had an animal brightness, and he had a scornful smile. I waved him away, knowing that if I were seen giving him anything a shoal of children would descend on me. But a few seconds later there were three of them, one on each side and one behind, one for each of my pockets. Their hands could dive like little fish and I remembered that I had put the credit card with which I had paid the restaurant bill in my back pocket. They were touching me now. They had probably found that this disconcerts their victims, and I was annoyed that I was starting to get flustered. I turned and shouted at them in a deepened voice. They looked startled and pulled back, but they regrouped immediately, guessing correctly that I had no more cards to play. Their sly smiles grew wider; and it was only when some locals spoke sharply to them that they turned and ran. My rescuers apologised on behalf of their country, but left me wondering why they had been able to scare them off while I had not.

It was the third time this had happened to me in my week in Romania. Before that week it had never happened in 30 years, and that last time became one of my ten or so memories that make me curl up in embarrassment. It happened on my first job abroad on my own and it was on the Sunday morning that I had arrived. The boy who offered to shine my shoes in the square had a smile like an angel but when he finished he asked for some enormous sum of money – at least I thought it was, but could not recall the exchange rate that first morning, and knew almost no Spanish. I said no; his smile turned to ice, and suddenly there were five of them. I waved them away. "OK," he said, "policia," and started to walk towards a policemen at the edge of the square. I called him back and gave him the money. After that I made one of those adjustments, a sacrifice of openness, that make you less vulnerable but also less alive. And it seemed to have worked. But here, 30 years later, they have walked through my defences.

As I walked back to the hotel I started to speculate that the street children could have been the notorious orphans of Ceauşescu. In the 1960s he wanted a larger population to build a better socialism, and banned contraception for women under 45 with less than five children, sending 'baby police' out to enforce his rules with monthly gynaecological tests. But Romania was poor and many families could not afford to bring up five children. Many of them were abandoned and ended up in state orphanages with no money, no food and, most corrosively of all, no attention. They lay silently in their beds for a few years and then were sent to institutes for the 'irrecuperable' – until their pictures flooded the Western television screens in the 1990s, with their dead eyes and scrawny vulpine heads. But, I thought, if that was almost twenty years ago, they could hardly be exactly the same children.

It was not only the street children that were getting to me. So were the packs of feral dogs that roamed the streets. They were another of the legacies of Ceausescu. Inspired by a visit to North Korea, he had built the second largest and arguably the dreariest building in the world, a massive, square, kitsch wedding cake, a tribute to the spirit of communism in all its pomp – full of marble, chandeliers, columns, gilt, gold leaf, vast conference chambers and the red carpets of three-star hotels. The locals called it the Madman's House. To make room for it he had to tear down thousands of homes in the centre of Bucharest and re-house the occupants in tower blocks where they had no room for their dogs. So their owners put them out on the streets where they bred fast and furiously. The first time I saw them I was alone on a long street. I heard the distant sound of yelping and barking, and turned to find about fifty of them running up the street towards me. They made my scalp tighten and as they came closer I racked my brains for what to do. What surfaced was 'walk slowly and look away', and it worked. They scampered past, barking dementedly at the guard dogs in the gardens they passed, and disappeared into the distance. They clearly could not smell fear.

I had arrived in Romania at the beginning of the week with a vague impression of a faintly Gothic country, drawn from photographs of the misty craggy mountains of Transylvania, deep forests full of wolves and bears, and the stories of Dracula. But Dracula is fiction, and what I had not known was that much of Romania's history makes the bloody fiction seem pale, and that Dracula himself was based on a real Romanian who made the fictional character seem congenial. Vlad the Impaler, who was the king of Romania in the 15th century, may have been the vilest ruler of all time. The fate that befell anyone who offended him was having a stake driven up between their legs, making its exit anywhere in the top half of their body. The stake was then driven into the ground, leaving the victim to die in full view of passers-by. Vlad would often invite his guests to eat with him in a room full of stakes and bodies writhing in agony, taking up to two days to die. His most famous victory was over the formidable Turks whom he terrified into retreat by planting a forest of 20,000 impaled Turkish prisoners on the road into Romania. He is also remembered for inviting the disabled and unemployed to a feast at his palace and afterwards asking them if they would like to be free from their sufferings. When they said yes he burned them all alive. The Romanians, though, regard him as a hero, and their school textbooks depict him as a strong ruler who stood up to the invading Turks, imposed law on the lawless and dealt with the weak.

And Vlad the Impaler, disturbing as he was, does not seem to be entirely an aberration. I was on my own that week and, down at the port town of Constantza, I sat out late in the open-air restaurants looking out to sea, and reading up Romanian history, which seems to have been persistently dark ever since. When they finally became a nation in 1918 the Romanians were so fractious that they had 25 governments in 10 years, and their own Romanian Fascist Party started to flourish around the same time as the Germans and Italians. They were the Iron Guard, or Green (sic) Shirts, who wore bags of Romanian soil round their necks and eventually decamped to Germany. When Romania came into the war on Hitler's side the Green Shirts were able to return to deal with the Jews. Their approach shocked even the hardened German SS, who intervened to stop the slaughter by methods that offended their sense of discipline. 'We use surgery, not butchery' said one of the German generals. Then their spell under communism was, on balance, rather nastier than in the other Eastern Bloc countries. Even their successes were rather odd. Perhaps their greatest glory came with the girl gymnasts – stunted elfin figures like the Lord of the Rings halflings, all full of chemicals.

It was my last night and, with my brush with the street children behind me, I went for a walk around Revolution Square, where Ceauşescu made his last speech from the balcony of the Central Committee building. The buildings around the square – the neoclassical Athenaeum and the University Library, and the little garden restaurants tucked into alleys – were almost romantic at the end of a warm summer evening with the walkers out in their summer clothes. But there were still the marks of bullets in the buildings from the two days of fighting 20 years before. The revolution in Romania had been lacking in style. Where Estonia staged their Singing Revolution and linked arms over hundreds of kilometres, the Ceauşescus were taken from the Kangaroo court that declared them guilty and shot as they left the door of the courtroom, without formality or even blindfolds.

There was one last attempt on my pockets. As I walked up to the hotel entrance they saw me coming, but I did not see them until it was too late. The charge was led by a handsome gypsy, with a pantomime villain's glittering white teeth, thick curly hair, a hooped sweater – but no legs. In fact he seemed to have no stomach. His body started around his bottom rib. But he moved like lightning on his little wheeled platform, and he had picked me as his target out of a possible twenty people walking towards the hotel entrance. His speed was frightening, and when I retreated to the side door he turned as if on a spring and almost caught me as I found refuge in the revolving doors, muffling the dying sound of his desperate cry, "Come back. Come back. I want to talk to you."

Upstairs in my room I could relax. The hotel was, as the guidebook had promised, opulent, the best in Romania. But there was more: it seems that between 1912 when it was built until 1989 it was notorious as a centre of espionage and intrigue. In the 1930s it was believed that almost all the staff and most of the cast of characters around the lobby were spies – for either the Gestapo or for British Intelligence or for King Carol's police chief to allow him to blackmail his own politicians. Later, in the 1950s it was refurbished as an 'intelligence factory' with bugs in all the rooms to supplement the work traditionally done by spies, informers and prostitutes.

I decided that I would not venture out again, although I was leaving for London the next day. I settled down to get my notes in order. I was about to do something that I never do. Although I may not be a sea-green incorruptible in my work, I will rarely bend the facts to please a client. But on this occasion, I was trying as hard as I could to get them the loan they wanted. It was because, despite everything – the dark history, the feral children lurking in wait outside the hotel and the sinister politics – the Romanians I had been working with that week, who were the only Romanians I really knew, were as nice and straightforward and intelligent a group as you could hope to meet.

40

Estonia

A few flakes of snow were starting to blow against the windows as the local businessmen trooped in. It was a room of glass and faded weathered timber, and outdated once-modern spotlights. A couple of well-positioned minimalist line drawings decorated the walls. The Estonians had been ruled by Moscow for 50 years, but never willingly, and, like their neighbours the Finns, they had never taken to the vulgar red carpets, gold-leaf chairs and poor lighting of the Russians.

Mr Volkov, the manager of the port, walked to the lectern. He was dressed smartly in his usual beige suit with a black shirt and tie. He tapped the microphone, and greeted the assembled businessmen with his bleak smile.

"Gentlemen we are here this afternoon to get your views on the work that our consultants have just completed. I consider the report, despite many errors, satisfactory, and we would like to have your feedback. . ."

I caught Jorn's eye, and mimed a sad clown face. This was unexpected. Mr Volkov had seemed pleased with what we had done until now. There followed questions which were not questions but whole paragraphs that had been heard many times before in their local chamber of commerce meetings.

Although they no longer worked for the Soviet government they were still finding their way in the new free economy, and thought in terms of 'reaching unanimous agreement' on all sections of our report and drafting a protocol.

Afterwards we tried to mingle with the guests over coffee and canapés of pikeperch and caviar, which were cheap in the local markets. But it was heavy going. They seemed distant. Most were still dressed in the thick jackets and dark woollen shirts of socialist times, unlike the reconstructed besuited young Estonians we were later to meet in Tallinn. Here in Parnu in midwinter the faces were parchment-grey, weather-beaten, wind-dried. They seemed weary and punctuated their conversation with little sighs. It was difficult to assess whether it was because the room was not so well heated, or because they were unsure of their English, or because we had made a bad impression. They gave us tepid smiles and eased away.

We eventually found the finance director, with whom we had spent a lot of time that week. He came up with a big smile.

"Well, you've done very well. Everyone, especially Mr Volkov is really pleased."

"Is he? He didn't seem so enthusiastic," said Jorn.

"Oh, no, on the contrary I know he really likes what you've done."

"Well, that's good to know," I added. "We *thought* he was happy enough as well – until his introduction. . ."

"Oh," he smiled, lowering his voice, "you have to understand us Estonians; we are known for being. . . let's see. . . unemotional, reserved and. . . excuse my English. . . erm. . . logical and methodical – and also grudging with praise. We are very different from our neighbours to the south in Lithuania. They are demonstrative, noisy and much more outgoing than we are. The Latvians next door are halfway between. We are the introspective ones, like most northern Scandinavians; especially in the winter when it doesn't get light until 11am and it's dark again by 3pm. We are also very cautious. We have a proverb, 'Measure nine times, cut once'."

"OK," I said, "I'll remember that. It explains a few things we have come across here."

"Are you familiar with our flag?" he continued. "It is black, dark-blue and white. And the white often looks grey. There you have the Estonians – maybe a little gloomy." The Estonians clearly enjoy introspection.

"By the way," he added, "have you been able to get out and see our beaches, or have you been working too hard?"

"Well, no, I'm afraid we haven't been out much."

"OK. You've finished now, so let's go for a walk. The sun has just come out and it'll be a couple of hours before it gets dark."

So we put on thick scarves and walked out into the biting cold, past the ice breakers moored in the river, the timber-clad port buildings painted in powdery Scandinavian greys and greens, and the yacht harbour, with its clean, bright navy-blue boats clinking at their moorings; then out along the shore. The Russians used to come for summer holidays on the beaches in Soviet times, but it seemed implausible that day. Although there was an austere beauty out there under the low watercolour sky with just a glimmer of a weak sun from time to time, the low dunes looked desolate and windswept and the beaches were stony and unwelcoming. I thought of old black-and-grey Ingmar Bergman films. We walked on towards the end of the promontory, the director breathing in deeply, savouring the fresh cold air. Suddenly, he raised his hand.

"Listen," he murmured.

We held our breaths and listened – to the sighing of the reeds in the shallow water, swaying and bending in the wind. He was listening for something else, but in the pale afternoon light that rustling, whispering sound will always be, for me, the sound of Estonia. The silence was fractured by the flapping of wings.

"Look," he shouted as the bird rose steeply, silhouetted against the low snow-laden sky. "A stork."

We walked further on, to the town's best-known attraction – a sanatorium first built 200 years ago and where people from all over the Soviet Union used to come to recuperate. Its speciality was, and is, its mud treatment. And, strangely, people still come. I never understood why. We met a young couple in their 20s who were staying there for a week. They showed us photos of their small functional bedroom with their jeans, rucksacks and CDs strewn over the floor.

"What do you actually do there?" we asked.

"We just chill out."

Our work in Parnu finished, we left the next afternoon for Tallinn, the capital in the north. It was starting to snow again as we left. The road was straight and flat and lined with silver birches, and as we drove on the snow fell more thickly, the large flakes flattening against the windscreen and slowly covering the road and the trees. We saw few people along the way, only the woods and neat wooden houses painted in muted Nordic colours, with dim lights in their windows barely visible through the falling snow, evoking that warm melancholic feeling with no name that I call snow sadness – a reverie that I could have lived at another time in another place in an eternal winter.

As we drove into the outskirts of Tallinn the landscape changed. The birches were left behind for a stark industrial wasteland of long, low, empty factories in the distance – metal and chemical plants that had been built to feed into the Soviet economic machine. Now abandoned they stood like tombstones in the snow; empty shells with see-through windows like tooth cavities They looked out of place in the landscape, as if transplanted from another country, as indeed they had been.

A few miles later we reached Tallinn – the jewel amongst the three beautiful Baltic capitals. Conquered for Christ by the German Brotherhood of the Sword in mediaeval times, then later by the Danes, Swedes, Russians and Poles, it finally matured as a wealthy Hanseatic city, with buildings from the 11th, 12th, 13th and every century up to the 20th, winding up the hill of Toompea. There is a story that Toompea was the tumulus for an ancient Estonian king, Kalev, built by his wife Linda who carried stones in her apron to build the grave mound, and that her tears formed the lake outside. But it does not need a Merlin-like legend to romanticise Toompea's narrow cobbled streets, courtyards, labyrinthine passageways, turrets, spires, merchants' warehouses, chapels and stained-glass windows – and after dark the shop windows with heavy amber jewellery glowing in the light of wax candles, fur-lined overcoats, warm restaurants and bars in centuries-old brick-lined cellars.

We had been working in Tallin in the previous week and had arranged to meet some of the local port staff in the evening, in a café housed under a fringe theatre in an old stone-walled crypt with a log fire and long, rough wooden tables dripping candles and the comforting smell of pork and cabbage stew – winter food, heavy and warm. We got there too early and sat over glasses of mulled wine watching the drama students from the theatre above coming in from the cold in thick scarves, their faces flushed from the icy wind. They were dressed in a refined art-student style that was now permitted with the departure of the Russians but with the advantage of the straight-backed deportment learned in the Soviet gymnasium.

Our friends from the port arrived and we ordered beers; and resumed the teasing banter that we had started the previous week.

"You know, you men are the luckiest males in the world," said Jorn.

"Why's that?"

"Well, you are mostly quite an ugly lot and yet you get to marry these princesses." He waved his hand in the direction of the girls all around us.

The Estonians permitted themselves little smiles.

"Do you realise how attractive your girls are," I asked, "or does it not occur to you, because you've always been surrounded by them?"

One of them gave the question some thought.

"No, come to think of it, it was only when I started to go abroad that I realised it. But it was the other way round. I thought how unattractive the girls in most places outside Estonia were."

Some say they are the most beautiful in Europe, with their ash-blonde hair, and limpid pale-blue eyes. Unlike the ice-eyes of the alluring but hardened Russian girls, the Estonians' eyes speak more of their lakes and forests than of nightclubs. These are the people who won their independence in 1991 after two million people linked hands and sang national songs banned by Moscow in a 375-mile human chain that stretched from Tallinn via Riga in Latvia to Vilnius in Lithuania.

Later in the evening the conversation turned, as it so often did, to how to get jobs in banking, especially abroad, where the salaries were much higher. All of the young wanted to work in banks. They asked if we had contacts in London, Hong Kong and Singapore who could help them with jobs, or entry to MBAs.

"Why do you all want to work in banks?" I asked. "You've all got good jobs in the ports. And anyway, aren't you missing a step? Only five years ago you were all working in industries to feed the Russian economy. I'm only a humble economist, but where is the money in the banks coming from?"

Next day, our local engineer called at our hotel and we walked over to his office through the morning's slush. The city looked different in the daylight – more faded and down-at-heel after 50 years of neglect by the Russians, who didn't care. But the redevelopment was already under way, to the international template. The historical buildings were being gutted and restored, not by conservationists but by the banks and international development agencies and schools of management. Behind the renovated stonework of the facades, the heavy, ornate wooden doors and new black-and-silver logos, we saw vast plates of glass erected, leading into white halogen-lit open 'spaces' with exposed beams and floorboards in grey decking paint, and displays in elegant Scandinavian graphics. And on the streets we saw the new tribe inhabiting the restored buildings, the young bankers that our friends from the night before were hoping to join – young, smart, black-suited and speaking almost perfect English. They worked even longer hours than the London bankers, with computer bags on their shoulders and stylish designer mobiles in their hands. Estonia had the second highest mobile phone ownership in the world after Finland. The port people had told us in the café that their babies are born with little pouches to hold their mobiles.

In comparison, the older people looked frayed at the edges. We stood in the slush at a zebra crossing, watching an elderly couple looking bewildered as the passing BMWs paid them no attention. Our engineer was in his 50s and had been doing well since he had started up his own company five years before. But he looked sympathetically at the old couple.

"There's nothing for the old here. They don't speak English and they can't use computers."

Estonia had been the fastest of the liberated Eastern European countries to adapt to the new post-communist world. They were called 'The Economic Miracle' and the 'Baltic Tiger', and they went on to invent Skype. They were not to know that they would be the worst hit in the recession of 2008. They had followed a now well-known path. The young bankers had queued up to lend money from their rich Scandinavian neighbours, inflating Tallinn's property prices: they had not paid attention to their proverb; they had not measured nine times before cutting once. And, as in Ireland and Iceland, the real-estate bubble burst. They will no doubt be even more introspective this winter, gazing out to sea from their grey limestone cliffs. But they will find a way through, and if nothing else they can console themselves that their ten-year experiment with a flawed banking culture had an unexpected windfall – that of rescuing their greatest asset, those beautiful buildings on Toompea Hill, before it was too late.

41

Kazakhstan 2

It was out there somewhere, past the greyness. We were standing on a bare hillock of fissured rock at the end of the road, looking out to sea. It was 18 degrees below zero and the wind was singing in the stunted scrub of the tundra, and tearing at our clothes. Down below, about a hundred tugs and barges were anchored in a bleak bay. They had been brought in to rest for the winter, while the sea was frozen. Out there was the costliest project since life began. The Kashagan oilfield is costing $150 billion to set up and it will produce oil worth $1,000 billion. To get it out they are having to build 34 islands in five metres of water that is frozen for four months of the year, with rock barged out from below our hillock. And it is not only costly, it is in hostile territory. The oil beneath the ice is mixed with poisonous sulphurous gas, and working conditions are vile. Geordies who had left school at 15 are said to be on £1,000 a day to speed up the work, which is now ten years behind schedule. I was with a group helping Shell with the shipping.

We stood there for a few minutes. The wiry bushes at our feet shivered as the gusts of wind whipped through them and then stiffened again.

"Jesus what a place," said someone from inside his anorak hood. Our cheeks were starting to go numb.

"How many people do you need to bring here?" I asked one of the Shell staff. "Thousands. . . but I won't be one of them," he replied.

It was too much even for the Russians in our group who had been brought up in Siberia and we retreated to the car.

The car was warm, and we nodded off one by one, knowing that the drive back would be no more pleasurable than the drive up. In the 100 miles from Aktau we had seen no trees, no hills and no people – only black camels, dwarfish ponies and tufts of dry vegetation in different shades of grey. It was like a planet without topsoil where only the hardiest mutations of life survived. The sea to the left of the road was a leaden grey and offered no comfort; it was known that you would die within five minutes if you fell in off one of the drilling rigs. But most dismaying of all was the mean ugliness of the scattered buildings that we passed. The atrophy of the soul that the great socialist experiment had added to this desolate barren territory seemed even worse than in other ex-Soviet countries. The few houses we saw under the low grey sky were like security cabins at gates of cement plants. They were built from unpleasant dirty-cream bricks and dark-grey mortar, with cast-iron window frames. We passed a necropolis – a traditional graveyard densely packed with forbidding concrete mausoleums – and a single tall block of featureless flats, both rising starkly out of a flat landscape otherwise populated only by skeletal telegraph poles lining the horizon. The least unattractive man-made structure we passed in the two hours was an almost completed gasoline station in hard ceramic blue and malarial yellow – the colour of poison in nature. A gas pipe painted a dirty lemon colour set back from the road followed our route all the way.

We arrived back in Aktau, the only town on Kazakhstan's Caspian coast, around dusk. Our hotel was plain but well heated, and the management had twigged that just a few red and orange lampshades could make it welcoming, like the early English motorway cafés. In the basement a smoke-filled billiards hall with ten tables made it a social centre, and at the end of each corridor there were little refrigerators with Snickers bars. After our journey north it was like coming home.

It is said that oil, the Devil's Tears, corrupts. But this was not so in Aktau, where the oil money had been good for the town, most of all in the restaurants and pubs that had sprung up.

Ten years before, when I first visited Aktau, the best restaurant was a damp stone-floored concrete bunker that smelled of fish and urine; and the nightclubs were seedy cavernous basements with gangsters with no necks on the doors – almost empty until midnight, when a few goodtime girls and hookers drifted in to dance with Mr Bigs over bottles of blue label Johnny Walker.

But with the coming of the oil money we now had a choice of warm pubs and clubs, filled every night with locals, foreign oilers, good food and concert pianists from the Moscow Conservatory. At least they had been, until their jobs disappeared and they turned to their real love, which was rock music. The lead guitarist and singer that night had started his career in tails and white tie, but now his blade-thin legs were visible through torn jeans, and his sculpted Asiatic features were three-quarters hidden under a baseball cap. He showed us from time to time that he could have played *anything*, but he was happy to churn out Credence Clearwater and Eric Clapton; and 'Living Next Door to Alice'. The chorus – "Who the fuck is Alice?" – dragged everyone up on the floor; and I was dancing with our Russian economist when a local girl pushed in. She was about three inches taller than me, around 30, athletic and very good-looking.

"Where are you from?" she shouted through the music.

"London."

Her mouth seemed to fall open.

"You come from *London*?"

She must have met a lot of foreigners in Aktau, but most probably came from Aberdeen, South Shields and Texas.

"What are you doing here?"

"I'm working with Shell."

This didn't surprise her at all, as most foreigners probably did.

Her name was Natalya and she knew enough English to hold a conversation, but her face had a continual look of mortification as she groped for the right words. This was endearing to me as I had put a lot of time into Russian and found it many times more difficult to pull out the right words. In between dances she pulled me to one side and kept a tight hold. Eventually the band stopped for a rest and she asked me to come over to her table. "OK," I said. "But I'll just find out what our group is doing." When I got to our table, they were all grinning. The girl, correctly guessing that one of our group, Elena, was Russian, started to talk to her in their language. After half a minute Elena turned to me and said,

"She's a little concerned that she is bothering you."

"No, not at all."

She added, "You go over and talk to her. She seems a very nice girl."

"Really?"

"Yes, I'm sure she is." So I went over to her table to where she was sitting with her friend, another Natalya. But the second Natalya's eyes narrowed as I arrived and she made it clear that she wanted to leave. My Natalya mimed a sad clown's face and asked me to write down my name and where she could find me, and she left. I returned to our table and feigned nonchalance.

What I did not tell them was that scattered over our long and fractured conversation Natalya slipped in the following sentences.

"How old are you?"

Then later, "Are you married?"

Then later, "Is your wife here?"

Then later, "How old is your wife?"

I think she probably *was* a nice girl, with an adventurous streak. But maybe she was desperate to get out.

So, although Kazakhstan is on the way up, it is still a hard, often cruel, country. The first identifiably Kazakh people were the descendants of Genghis Khan. At the feasts that followed the battles as his hordes swept though Asia, Genghis Khan and his generals would gorge themselves on semi-raw horsemeat as the captured girls were paraded for inspection. Genghis Khan took the best and most aristocratic and sent the also-rans down to the tents of his officers. He was explicit about the joys of conquest, saying 'The greatest pleasure is to vanquish your enemies and chase them before you, to rob them of their wealth and see those dear to them bathed in tears, to. . . clasp to your bosom their wives and daughters'. His genes are, according to the Russian Academy of Sciences, found in about eight per cent of the population between western China and the Middle East today.

Genghis Khan's direct descendants in Kazakhstan were the country's first aristocracy. They were called the white Bone, and known as 'Sultans' from birth, with the privileges of being 'above the law and immune from the corporal punishment'.

But for the next five centuries most Kazakhs were still nomads, wandering in tribes or 'hordes', where family ties were sacrosanct, the young respected the old and the grandmothers passed the family history down to their grandchildren through unwritten stories. It was for this reason they fell foul of Stalin who had set about the systematic extinction of national traditions and even family ties that interfered with loyalty to the socialist state. But of all Russia's colonies Kazakhstan was the least suitable for Stalin's solution – the collectivisation of the farms – and their response was to kill most of the animals and move on. Undeterred, Stalin brought in a new population, by exiling those who offended him in other countries to Kazakhstan's central plains to grow vast amounts of wheat – and so to become the breadbasket of the eastern USSR. But Stalin, The Great Gardener, as his sycophants called him, had not done his research. The topsoil was poor; it blew away and Kazakstan reverted to being an empty dustbowl.

There were minor revivals in Aktau's fortunes in 1960s when a uranium mine opened outside the town, and Russians were happy to be posted there, despite the radioactive dust in the air – for the high salaries. And the republic got more Russian dirty work when it was made the testing ground for nuclear weapns. But it would have gone into freefall when the Russians left, if it had not been for an accident. It happened in 1993, in a giant oilfield the Russians had discovered close to Kashagan. The oilfield was four kilometres beneath ground level and full of gas, and when the Russians drilled down the gas caught fire and the flames shot 600 feet into the air. It took a year to put them out. A few years later they decided that they had to bring the Western oil companies in.

There was a man we saw every day at breakfast who looked as if he had lived through all of this history. He was always the first to arrive and watched disapprovingly as the casually dressed oilers ambled in later. He was a slight, wiry man in his 70s with neat simian Asiatic features. He sat ramrod straight in his chair in a theatrical parody of pride, dressed immaculately in a grey suit with a very tight high collar and tie. But he did not look right; at best like a severe Norman Wisdom. He was accompanied by his wife, a tiny woman with a handsome lined face, also smartly dressed but with her head covered by an ethnic scarf. Both sat with their chins held high and mouths turned down at the sides. They never spoke. They looked lost in this new world, where the oilmen strolled into the breakfast room without ties or shoes polished. There was nobody to receive orders from these ageing Kazakhs. They may have noticed the last item on the menu, after the warming Russian soups. It was 'chewing gum', the badge of the brash American. Our proud man – a White Bone? – may have chaired meetings of his 'horde' as they discussed the pros and cons of allowing foreigners in to get their oil out and make them rich.

I had one last insight into the hardness we always sensed beneath the Westernising veneer. The only thing to buy in Aktau is caviar, and I had the maximum allowance in my bag as we drove to the airport. As the six of us went through check-in I was the only one that did not slip the caviar I was taking back into my suitcase. Instead I put my 200 grammes into my carry-on bag and gave the same amount to one of the Shell engineers who was travelling with us. All went well until the fourth and last scanner we passed though. As we headed for the departure gate, an airport official headed us off and screamed, "Come with me." He marched us to a room with a smoked-glass wall and no lights, pulled my companion in and slammed the door in my face. I hesitated for a moment, then walked in after them to find the man yelling in Russian, interspersed with a few word of English – "it is not permitted"... "a very serious crime". The crime could only have been that I did not have the required 'documentation' which was the receipt. It is perfectly legal to take out that amount of caviar. How he guessed that I would not have had my little receipt with me I have no idea. His face suffused with rage, he pulled the jars of caviar away from us and threw them in his bag. He then demanded our passports, clapped them together and stood up, implying 'Right, you are in big trouble now', and marching us out of the room. I followed him and said, "Look, our plane is going in five minutes." He switched off the amateur dramatics instantly, as if he had tired of them, handed us the passports and wandered off, no doubt to steal some more caviar from unwary travellers to please his wife.

It was a trivial event; I had only lost 50-pounds' worth of caviar. But it left more than a sour taste – because what was going through my mind as his brutish features contorted with rage, as he exercised his little sliver of power, was that 800 years ago they used to compete for who could cut off the most heads of their captives in a day. The target was around three hundred.

42

Latvia

We met our Russian client in his penthouse office on the South Bank, looking out over the Thames at the Houses of Parliament. He entered the room with the air of someone who knew exactly what he was doing, in command of a world of which we still knew almost nothing. It was three years since the Soviet Union had collapsed and he was one of the first of the new breed of private Russian businessmen that was quietly starting to buy up the country's industry.

Probably around 35, and overweight, he gave the impression not of going to seed but of bursting with surplus good health. It was difficult to read anything from his clothes – the blue blazer, grey flannels and highly polished shoes – as the Russians did not dress like Londoners but like Russians living in London, mixing mostly in their own clubs and restaurants. The man who accompanied him, his French financial adviser, however, was dressed and groomed immaculately.

We sat down and the Russian started to talk very fast about an ammonia and acrylonitrile export terminal he had bought at Ventspils in Latvia. His manner was cultured and amused. He spoke of his acquisition as if it were a plaything. His problem was that the plant was a long way from both Moscow and London, and the staff in Latvia was not cooperating.

"Right," he said. "Here is what I want. It's to know their costs, their revenues, their profits, why their prices are so high, and how many of the 800 staff they really need. Can you do it?"

I thought quickly for a few seconds: these countries were highly secretive; I did not speak Russian; I knew nothing about chemicals. . . But our client's question had been addressed not to me, but to David, the manager from Coopers & Lybrand, through whom I would be working; and I heard him reply, "Yes. I think we can do that."

"Good." He gave us a little more background, and ended by asking, "Any questions?"

I had two.

"If it's yours now, why can't you do this yourselves?"

He thought for a few seconds and gave a rueful look. "We have tried. And failed. Don't ask me why."

"OK," I said slowly with a questioning inflection on the K, hoping that he would elaborate. But he did not.

"And will it be safe?"

He looked straight at me, then let his gaze drift towards the window, thinking intently. Eventually he turned to his French colleague and raised an eyebrow as if to ask 'Have you anything to say on this?' By the time his eyes returned to mine 20 seconds of silence had elapsed. Then, in a level voice, he said, "Yes."

There was one last hurdle; that it was company policy if they were not familiar with a client to ask for 50 per cent of the fees in advance.

"Yes, agreed," he said and took out a chequebook.

"Oh," said David, "we need to invoice you formally."

"As you wish."

He paid by return of post.

A week later we drove into Ventspils – a windswept port on the Baltic coast where the oil and petrochemical pipelines from the centre of Russia reach the Baltic Sea. The town was covered, as always, by a low sulphurous cloud, and two per cent of the town's children were known to die in their first year of life. Its housing estates, with their grey tenement blocks named after the local industries – Petrochimica Building 6, and Metallurg Building 4 – stretched for miles along the pot-holed highway out of town. During our time there the sun never once filtered through the poisonous cloud and the rain and sleet slanted in from the sea.

I had been driven there by Kristina, an accountant from the office that Coopers & Lybrand had set up in Riga, Latvia's capital, soon after independence; and we checked into the only modern hotel in the town, also set up soon after independence, seemingly before the local architects had much experience of what a modern hotel should look like. The décor in the foyer was like a glittering ice sculpture in pale blues and steely greys.

Kristina went off to telephone a local agent who, we had been told, would be helpful, and he came to the hotel bar half an hour later. We sat down to talk, and he explained to us that the staff at the terminal company were nervous about their jobs and the new owner. He recommended whom to speak to in the company. As we talked we drank vodkas in quick succession. When I started to slow down, Kristina whispered to me, "You have to drink or he won't talk to you." She later turned out to be able to drink unusual quantities herself. She was in her early 30s, with crystal-clear pale-blue eyes, blonde hair and a brisk professional manner. Dressed in the regulation black suit of the management consultants, she spoke flawless English with a beguiling Slavic accent, and used her smile sparingly but to great effect, as she was unfairly blessed with a distant Nordic beauty. But her manner I found cool and a little disconcerting. I thought at the time that it might have been to maintain distance, as her work probably involved travelling alone frequently with men. It was only later that

I came to understand that speaking freely could have cost her her job just three years before, under the Soviet Union. And then there was the Baltic States reserve that I was to find that the Latvians shared with Estonians to the north.

The next morning we were picked up by an employee of the terminal in driving rain. As I got into the car I noticed that there were two handguns in the glove compartment. I nudged Kristina, pointing to them with widened eyes. She acknowledged them with only lukewarm interest. Then we were driven into the port at breakneck speed, for no apparent reason, and ushered in to see the acting manager.

The office was dark and un-showy like those of small companies in the north of England. The manager who greeted us, in his 50s, looked uncomfortable in his skin; heavily built and flushed, he exuded a dangerous charm. Around this time the life expectancy for men in the former Soviet Union had dropped under 60 years, mainly because of drink, and he was clearly a drinker. He spoke only Russian. We started on our discussion with Kristina translating. He was not hostile, but shook his head and shrugged his shoulders at each question, repeating that he did not have information in that form. We talked for about half an hour and seemed to have reached a dead end. It was what I had feared. We had come all this way and our only source of information was not going to cooperate. The conversation started to die. Then Kristina turned to me.

"Wait," she said. "I'm going to switch into Russian." Then she turned on the man and tore into him; until now she had been businesslike, but now she was talking fast and aggressively. He did not seem disconcerted. At the end of her attack Kristina asked, or more or less demanded, to see the accountant, and a heavy lady in a thick cardigan and unstyled hair came in and sat down, without a smile of welcome. Kristina started on the same questions, and the accountant listened patiently.

"How many people work here?"

"About 800. . . actually, 779."

"Do you have a full set of costs for the terminal?"

"Yes."

"Do you have a full set of detailed revenues?"

"Yes, of course."

"And do you have a balance sheet?"

"Of course."

She had everything we needed. But would she give it to us? Kristina avoided the question. She continued. "In what form can you give us this information?"

"Any form you like."

"And how long would it take?"

"You can have it tomorrow." All in front of her manager who had denied it existed.

And when we picked it up the next day it was pure gold – pages and pages of accounts, and everything else we had asked for.

The next day we drove back to the capital, Riga, a city that bore little resemblance to Ventspils. Originally a mediaeval fort for the Knights of the Sword in the 13th century, Old Riga has grown into a sprawl of old German, Swedish, Latvian and Russian buildings, cobbled streets, art nouveau, rattling trams, and candle-lit shops with chunky amber, leather and furs. It was only three years since the breakup of the Soviet empire and the city still had a sepia feel about it in the midwinter slush that evening. But it had always been regarded as the most Western of the Soviet cities, and Scandinavian blonde-wood bars and cafés were starting to appear amongst the old buildings. Coca-Cola and McDonalds had just selected Riga for their new Baltic base, and although the old Hotel Riga where I stayed was still state-owned it had leased off floors to private companies to run little boutique hotels.

The Coopers & Lybrand office in Riga was the first of many I was to see in the region – a long open-plan hangar with grey desks, banks of computer screens, white metallic lights and sections of the ceiling exposed as they were still installing the miles of wiring needed in the modern office. The staff were young and good-looking in the black suits that were the company's international dress code, but which they wore with a slight air of being in fancy dress. The few who still wore the dark shirts and thick woollen ties favoured by the old regime under their Armani suits looked somehow more real.

Most of the staff had been through a disciplined Russian education – they could all recite their metres of Pushkin – but parental circumstances had allowed them to spend time later in Ivy League, French or English universities. Bilingual, mostly with American accents, they had returned soon after independence, and a job with new management consultants was the best in town. Their general knowledge was startling. They told me that Ventspils had been built with dirty money by Armand Hammer, the American 'Comrade Billionaire' who had been a friend of Lenin, a secret messenger for American presidents, a spy for the Russians, a distributor of fake Fabergés to raise funds for communism, and the owner of Oxydental, one of the biggest oil companies in the world.

I sat there in the Riga office and wrote my report. It could not have been simpler. The reason for the high prices that our client had worried about was that they had profits of about 300 per cent. The terminal employed over five times as many staff as they needed, but their wages were low, so there was no need to dispose of them. A good result for all.

It had all been too easy, and my contribution had been limited. I did not know what Kristina had said down there in Ventspils, or the reason for the change of mind over giving us the information. I did not know whether it had been dangerous, or whether guns in glove compartments were normal. What I had done seemed too simple, and it was with some misgivings that we delivered the report to our client with the stiletto brain back in London.

He sent a note back saying it was just what he wanted and settled the final bill that week. I regretted not having met him again.

43

Tanzania

1991

The evening breeze blowing in from the sea was jangling the wind chimes on the roof terrace of the Kilimanjaro Hotel and ruffling the hair of the diners as they perspired in the humid night air. Across the bay, past the white tower of the Lutheran church, the lights on the ships were blinking in the harbour and shadowy black-sailed fishing boats were slipping silently out to sea. Up there on the roof it was as good as it got in Dar es Salaam in 1991. It was known for its fresh fish and the jam roly-poly the English had bequeathed it in colonial times. The one blot on that evening was the man I was sitting beside.

We had arrived on the roof terrace in the juddering lift that rattled its way up from the vast bar on the first floor of 'the Kili', the social epicentre of Dar es Salaam. It was a brutalist concrete monolith, built by the impoverished government and finished in funereal dark wood and thick-piled red carpets – seedy and fetid, and with a lingering smell of spilled beer. But it was the only place in Dar to be in the evenings. Up at the bar, government ministers could be seen bantering with glad-handing, back-slapping businessmen; teams of World Bank staff in safari suits, the men who were now calling the shots, were lording it over the locals; and Scandinavian aid workers who had arrived with high ideals were huddled in negotiations and banter with the girls. Everyone was there at least part of most nights. In the corner an elderly pianist in evening dress fought manfully against the clamour, playing Cole Porter melodies.

That night we were at the Kili to meet Torsten, a Dane who was our local manager. He was a striking figure of 6'4", almost too handsome to be a film star, had he chosen that calling. But instead he had gone bush in Tanzania. Throughout the evening he had baited us, "You whites, you just don't get it, you don't know how to live," his tawny yellow eyes dripping amused contempt for us. At his side sat his intimidating girlfriend, a powerfully built African woman with bulging haughty eyes that she rolled lazily to great effect instead of speaking. She sat slumped, bored and silent for half an hour until she could take our *mzungu's* ignorance of the real Tanzania not a minute longer, and made an icy observation about international aid policy in a throaty voice before lapsing back into the sofa. Yes, there were a few Conrad characters lost there in Tanzania, in their own personal variations of *nostalgie de la boue*, but most of the whites there were less impressive. More typical was the skinny, knowing man sitting at the edge of our group. He was from Wolverhampton and imported equipment for Shanks toilets. As we left to go up for dinner, I asked him, as a local, if it would be OK to give the pianist a tip for his efforts. "Throw him a banana," he replied, grinning lopsidedly at us, like a dog panting with its tongue out, seeking approval.

Up on the roof terrace the food took an hour to arrive, but was worth waiting for. After a few minutes the man from Shanks clicked his fingers.

"Bring me tomato sauce."

The waiter looked confused and returned a minute later to say that they had none.

"You don't have tomato sauce? So what am I going to put on my fucking chips?" His face started to twist in rage... "Anyway, take it back, it's shit."

The waiter cringed. His job could be at risk. Seeing the fear on the waiter's face, he smirked at us and at his pinch-faced wife, who egged him on. He had worked in Africa for 20 years, first in South Africa, but had been slipping down the ladder to end up in Tanzania, where he could get at least a little respect.

Tanzania, was now the fifth poorest country in the world, and Dar had become a city of shabby government offices, with everyone on safari – which meant out of the office and unlikely to return that day. The houses didn't have street numbers. The taxi drivers didn't know where anywhere was.

It was the legacy of a much-respected man, Julius Nyrere, the first African president after independence. He had come to power a prisoner of two overriding and highly contingent facts. They were that all independence movements were anti-imperialist, and all anti-imperialists were socialist, and therefore followed the Soviet model. And so, with the best of intentions, his first move was to set up a one-party state – and he then went on to nationalise everything that moved, confiscate private property, and herd the farmers into communal villages (or *ujamaa*).

Within ten years, production of their main crop, cashew nuts, was down to one eighth of what it had been, and life was a struggle for patronage, waiting in dreary offices for permits and licences, and giving tea – their name for bribes. Even worse, AIDS was cutting a swathe through the population. It seemed close at hand in that year; three men from our office had died of it.

From that first visit one small memory surfaces above all others. I had to pick up the national statistics from the Government Publications office, which turned out to be a group of concrete sheds, dirty and fly-blown. I found the girl at the main desk asleep with her head under her arm. I made a sound and she woke irritably, staring at me with bleary eyes, and said nothing. "Hello, is this the right place to buy the national statistics?" She waved her arm listlessly in the direction of another room, and let her head fall onto the desk again.

In the next room there were two girls braiding their hair. They didn't turn when I asked the same question. "Out of stock," said one, peering into her mirror.

2001

The Kili was empty, abandoned. Weeds were growing in the car park. They had been trying to sell it but there were no buyers.

There was now a new top hotel, the Sheraton. It cost $300 a night, and only the World Bank staff stayed there. This time I stayed at the New Africa, a recently built no-frills hotel, but still expensive.

The country was slowly getting back on track. I spent my days in the Parastatal Sector Reform Commission, where they were trying to re-privatise everything. I was sharing an office with a Tanzanian woman, who knew England well.

She told me that she often went over to London to visit relatives there, and that she was shocked by the way the English lived.

"I just cannot believe the way the children there behave. When they get to about fourteen they are so rude to their teachers and parents, who let them get away with it. And then they get in with bad company and drugs."

"It's not like that here?"

"No, absolutely not. I am forever telling my sister to send their children home for a few years once they reach about fourteen." She was very proud of her country.

On her wall there was a giant picture of Nyrere, who had died two years before. It seemed incongruous as her work was all about privatising what Nyrere had nationalised, undoing what he had done.

"How come his picture is still everywhere?" I asked.

"Oh, well, he's still revered. We call him the teacher. And even though much of what he did ended badly, he *admitted* that he had been wrong."

"Yes, that's certainly doesn't happen very often."

"And then he retired gracefully when he thought he couldn't do anything more to help, and went to live in his home village, very modestly. Yes, he was a good man."

It was what I heard in most of the offices. But it was not what I heard from the Sikh who was running our local post office in London. A few weeks after I got back I mentioned to him that I had just visited Tanzania and he lit up. "Oh, I was brought up there." And this what he went on to tell me.

"When I was young my parents used to own big stores up on Lake Victoria. We were quite well off, and one day a young Tanzanian came to ask for help with funds to take up an offer of a university scholarship. My father gave him a fair amount of help and he seemed very grateful when he returned. A few years later he had become the first Tanzanian president. He was, of course, Nyrere. After that we had no contact with him for a few years, until one evening we came back to our store and found soldiers surrounding it. 'What's happened?' I remember my mother saying. 'Has there been a robbery?' There hadn't; our stores had been taken over by the Government. So my father travelled down to Dar the next day to ask Nyrere what it was all about, and get it all sorted out. But Nyrere refused to see him. That was the last contact we had with him."

"Did you get any compensation?"

"No, we came to England a few months later."

"And you had to start from scratch again."

"Yes, and just look me now," he said, looking around his small shop. He had revealed a scar of bitterness that I'd never detected before beneath his cheery manner.

2011

The Kili has gone. The plot was sold, and on its site they have built the Kempinski. It is a square, modern building like a shiny fish-tank, faced with green glass. Inside it is full of marble and space, with icy air-conditioning that feels like an assault as you come in from the warmth of a soft balmy evening. It costs $350 a night, and the only guests are a scattering of men with Aquascutum sports jackets and women with sculpted hair, heads held high. The international civil servants who used to travel first-class and stay in very expensive hotels are now a dying breed. The bar is empty, and although the economy is now growing as fast as China's there is no replacement for the old Kili bar anywhere in Dar.

This time, though, I spent most of my time down in the south in a town on the border with Mozambique. It is dirt-poor, but even there things were happening. They had discovered gas under the sea, and their cashew nut exports had hit an all-time high. And there I stayed in a little hotel, the Southern Cross, with neglected rooms, dim lights and gaping holes in the mosquito nets; but it had a bar that looked out to sea, and was, in its smaller way, as much a centre as the Kili in its prime. By the second day, people I met in the Southern Cross were saying that they saw me in this or that office in the daytime, and people I met in the offices were saying that they had seen me at the Southern Cross the night before.

On my first evening, a woman in her late 30s, sitting alone at a table looking out to sea, turned and said, "Come and sit with me. I'm feeling lonely." It would have seemed like a come on in most places, but there it seemed just normal small-town friendliness. She was a doctor, working on keeping AIDS under control in the villages and had spent a quarter of her last 20 years in Tanzania. She lit up when I mentioned the Kili and she sat with her hair blowing back in the evening breeze coming in off the sea and told me the history of Tanzania seen through her eyes. She agreed that it was on the way up at last. "Look at these people here," she said. They were mostly young professionals, with healthy eager faces, sunburnt in the candlelight. There was nobody there like the Shanks salesman of 20 years before. She told me that AIDS had stabilized at last at seven per cent of the population;

it was still spreading along the main roads, although not away from them. But not all was well. She said that life was still hard especially for the women, who typically have about six children.

"There's a little exercise I often do when I meet them," she said. "I ask the girls what worries them most in their daily lives. The answer was always the same. It is that whenever they need something that depends on a decision from a man – say, high marks at school or a promotion in a government job – they have to sleep with him. They say it's a constant threat from day to day."

I watched her talk to the waitresses in Swahili and saw her personality adapt as she slipped into their la-la lilt, swivelling her eyes dreamily in a vague non-committal half-smile, watchful against danger.

"But, yes," she said, "it is still a good place to be. Why else would I have spent a quarter of my life here?"

Back in Dar on my last morning at breakfast, the light is flooding on to the tablecloths through the wooden shutters, and the white-painted Lutheran church is brilliant in the sunlight outside. There is a very old man at the piano, bent over and seeming to be half asleep. His eyes are glaucous and he is wearing evening dress. He plays sweet old melodies – 'Smoke Gets in Your Eyes', 'Tennessee Waltz' and 'Love Letters in the Sand'. His style of playing is elliptical; he often misses out half a dozen notes and picks up the tune again when least expected. A woman around forty comes to the table next to the piano, and he looks up and smiles, and starts to play beautifully, with feeling. She shares a joke with him and I overhear him asking her if she is still dancing. "No," she laughs, "I stopped years ago." I hear them mention the old Kili and wonder if he could be the pianist from that night 20 years ago.

Dar es Salaam actually means the haven of peace. For the first time on my visits over 20 years it is starting to sound right.

44
The Turks and Caicos Islands

I have never really liked small places. I prefer big cities where much is kept secret, including your own business. But Grand Turk looked like being an exception. The island I saw as we started our descent just south of the Bahamas was a tiny green jewel, rimmed by yellow beaches in a turquoise sea, and my spirits lifted further as we drove in from the airport along a shore lined by white cottages with painted wooden shutters and banks of flowers. When we stopped at the arched entrance to the hotel the scene was so perfect that I laughed. The arch framed a view over a stone-paved café leading out to a sunlit sea with a single palm tree in silhouette. We checked in and found rooms with calico furnishings and grey floorboards running out to little wooden gates to a beach of squeaky white sand studded with bushes bleached by the sun.

It was too late in the afternoon to start work, so we met in the cafe and sat watching the sun going down. It was empty apart from a woman sitting on a stool at the bar. She had wiry mahogany-coloured limbs, a lived-in face and a few coloured beads knotted into her hair that suggested that she might have been an artist. We asked if she was on holiday.

She laughed, and replied, "I think I've always been on holiday. I've lived here all my life." Her voice was deep and husky.

Her name was Purity Jones. "And what are *you* doing here?" Her look was friendly but implied that outsiders had to earn their right to be taken seriously.

We told her that the three of us were there to work on the islands' shipping.

"Ah-ha. So you'll be working on the cruise terminal?"

"Well. . . Yes. . . Amongst a lot of other things." We already knew from the local newspaper that Grand Turk was an island sharply divided by views on the cruise ships and that we should be careful about what we said. Most of its income came from tourism on an industrial scale on another of the islands. But Grand Turk itself was still unspoilt, It lived comfortably on huge grants from London that funded employment in the government offices. But some of the islanders thought that they would be better off making their own living – if they could get the cruise ships to call.

As the sun set, the bar at the end of the café started to fill up. It was becoming clear that it was the social epicentre of Grand Turk, and much of the talk that night was about the cruise terminal. We heard Purity airing her views across the bar.

"Lordy, when I see the first of those lost souls waddling up our streets clutching their little bags of souvenirs, that will be the day I leave my home of 50 years. I've nothing against most types of prostitution, but tourism will be the end of us."

"Oh, it's all right for you, Purity, with your widow's pension," said an elderly pink-faced Englishman, dressed in a blue blazer with silver buttons, beige slacks and well-shone brown shoes. "What about the rest of us who need to make a bob or two? We need tourists as well as government offices here." A Panama hat lay in front of him on the bar.

"Oh, dream on. *You* won't get anything," said Purity. "The cruise lines take all the profits. They'll knock up 50 little stalls at their terminal, import the silly souvenirs and sell them with their own staff. Most of passengers – poor dears with their blue hair – won't even get beyond the compound."

The banter continued, but then turned to local gossip. Later we got into conversation with a visitor who came every year, and knew all about the islands. When we told him what we were doing he said, "Ah! You should speak to Stanley. He's got his fingers in lots of pies but he's been in shipping here for 20 years. He knows everything."

"Sounds good. Do you have his number?"

"That's him over there."

It was the man with the blue blazer.

I waited for an opportunity to go over and introduce myself, but he was locked in conversation with a tall man, also English, who seemed unaccountably familiar. When I was up at the bar I overheard them talking about the congestion on the Guildford bypass and the M25. They were in agreement that anyone would be insane to live in England these days. Later in the evening I tried to catch Stanley's eye but in vain.

The office we worked in was a long bungalow near the shore. The first person I met was Delton. A heavily built man in his 30s, he was dressed in shorts and flip-flops which suited his slow walk. My first sight of him was at the end of a corridor as he passed a slightly older man, both raising their hands in high-fives and greeting each other with a "Zup, mun". The older man was the minister of finance and Delton was the islands' chief economist. There is a joke that if you place all the economists in the world end to end they would never come to a conclusion. But Delton was an exception. He knew exactly what was going on, what it meant and how it fitted together. The island was small enough for this to be possible, if you were as bright as Delton.

He filled us in on the local transport problems and gave us a list of the people he thought we should see.

And so began a fortnight of that sort of work that makes holidays seem a second best. We settled into a routine of early swims and flights around the islands in four-seaters to talk to anyone that had a view. We met a girl in her 30s who ran a local airport for small private jets. One of her regular customers was Bruce Willis who had a house on a small island nearby, and in her office I talked to a friend of hers who had danced with Keith Richard the night before. One of the islands didn't have cars, only electric golf carts. The day we visited they were celebrating Guy Fawkes' night, 4,000 miles from London.

On the second night we had arrived in the bar a little later, and found the same cast of characters as on the previous night. Stanley was sitting in the corner seat, in the same blue blazer, eating a pork chop. It was the seat I had occupied the night before. It emerged that the reason Stanley had ignored us was that I had been sitting in his seat. He never forgave us, and although he held court from his corner seat for the next two weeks he never addressed a single word to us.

At end of evening, however, we were approached by his tall companion of the previous night. He was a drunk, and I again had this feeling that I had seen him somewhere before. He seemed to want to be friendly, but found it difficult. He was a graceless man with the knowingness of a commercial traveller more suited to a Basingstoke motel than a Caribbean island. His plain-speaking manner, which seemed more affected than the affectations of those he disdained, fell short of charm. After a short stilted exchange he suddenly blurted out, "I know who you are and I know what you are doing. I want a meeting with you... When will you be free?"

Clive and I looked at each other and I said, "Well... now."

He said, "No. Are you free on Thursday at lunchtime?"

"OK. Where?"

"Here."

He gave me his card. His name was Paul Knight; and now I started to remember. I had done some work with an engineering company for him in a neighbouring country a few years ago.

I emailed someone with whom I had worked: 'Guess who I've come across out here? Paul Knight. Do you remember, the man we did that work for in Belize.' The reply came back, 'Yes, I remember. Very well, because he never paid us. And it wasn't a small bill.'

I met him on the Thursday. He talked for half an hour and he was angry. It seemed that his business involved routeing exports from other countries to the UK via Grand Turk – a UK dependency – so that they would not have to pay import duty. The benefits of this operation were to him alone. His explanations were Byzantine and his perception that we were out to ruin his business was as incomprehensible as it was unfounded. After half an hour I said, "Look, could you just write down *exactly* what you don't want us to put in our report, and I'll do my best to keep it out." He never did, and I later felt uneasy enough to mention his name in telephone call home – just in case.

Purity, however, turned out to be a goldmine. She seemed to know everyone, and how to do everything – not from lessons or education, but from having lived through a time when life was simpler. Although she couldn't use a computer she had seen how the foundations of her house had been built and she could mend a generator or a grandfather clock, pick a lock, follow electric circuits, supervise a birth, read time and directions from the sun, understand what different sorts of clouds presaged and when the sea breezes reversed from in to out; she not only understood but felt a part of the eco-system that directed them.

She told us that the islands were being sold to foreigners, plot by plot, under the counter; she hinted at who slept with whom; and she enjoyed feeding us stories to poison our thoughts about the passenger terminal. She told us about the debacle of the first call by a cruise liner. As the completion of the terminal was still a couple of months away, they had anchored the ship in the bay and brought the first visitors ashore in rowing boats. It was to be a great day, and the children had set up their own steel bands and rehearsed songs and dances of welcome for weeks. All dressed up in their Sunday best, their parents beamed as the children serenaded the tourists being rowed ashore. Purity's eyes shone as she concluded:

"They stepped ashore... looking like a flock of parakeets. The parents hadn't known that it was a gay power cruise, and, as the welcome song started to falter, they grabbed their children's hands and hauled them indoors."

Most nights I went for a walk up the coast just before sunset. Best of all were the Sunday evenings, when the streets were almost deserted, with most people in church – men in suits and ties and the women and children in pink and green taffetas and satins, bright against their black skin. I stood outside and watched them help the old ladies up to the front to sing in their Sunday best, in voices that were no longer what they had been. But it was when the choir sang alone, in their little mortar boards and robes, that the sound floating out along the shore – with the last of the low sun glinting on the water – was like an idyll from a past age.

I told Purity about it, and said that I would have liked to have gone into the church, but it was too full. She lowered one eyelid skeptically, like an ageing Motown diva.

"Dream on, my dear," she said, "just *don't go* into that church. I tell you, if you walk in that door you are in danger of being struck down by a thunderbolt from heaven. You know, the Lord picks up more gossip, slander and libel in that nest of vipers on a Sunday morning than in Hell's Kitchen on a Saturday night. The devil himself probably sits in, to learn a thing or two."

"So you're not a church-goer?"

She rolled her enormous eyes.

"Lordy. . . even if I was, I wouldn't be able to get in there on Sundays. You know, they all have to sit six feet apart, what with the diameter of their hats. If you think modern life is competitive you've seen nothing until you see those hats jostling up against each other on a Sunday morning."

The other reason she didn't go may have been that she knew almost everything that mattered already.

45
Mozambique

"Hello. It's great to see you again. What are you doing here?"

I turned to see a well-dressed Mozambican with an engaging smile. We were standing outside the supermarket – actually an iron-barred warehouse – in the centre of Maputo.

"Oh... just shopping," I replied, spinning out the three words. I was playing for time, combing the recesses of my mind to recall where I had seen him before. I am often embarrassed not to be able to place people who have been helpful. It is worst in Africa where hair colour and texture is much less varied. He seemed to detect my hesitation.

"You *do* remember me, don't you?" he said with a hint of mortification.

"Yes, of course I do."

"At the airport," he continued.

It was an own goal. We had been met at the airport by Danes who had steered us through the ordeal of the customs. We had not met any locals.

"Look, I wonder if you could possibly help me out," he continued, cheerily and just as plausibly, "my car has run out of petrol and I need to borrow $20 to buy some more to get home..." But by that time I was heading for the entrance to the supermarket.

"I am sorry," I said, "I have no local money at the moment. I'm going to change some inside."

Safe inside the supermarket I watched him through the window, bearding another foreigner, and then another. I waited until he was deep in conversation, and then slipped past him.

If only he could have put his ingenuity and persuasiveness to better use. But there was no better use, nothing else for him to do. There was no work in Mozambique in 1990 and no money. Twenty years before, Maputo, then called Lourenço Marques, had been an international beach resort for wealthy South Africans, but since the Portuguese rulers left in 1975, pouring concrete down the wells and sabotaging their abandoned cars, the Mozambicans had settled down to a long and bitter civil war. They lined up in the usual formations. The government, Frelimo (Front for the Liberation of Mozambique) were communists, supported by Russia; and their enemies, the rebels, were Renamo, a creature of the white South African Government. But after 15 years of downward spiral, the principles and politics meant little. The soldiers were little more than bandits looting and foraging for scarcer and scarcer food. They joined up with whichever side would feed them best. About a million people had been killed, and the countryside was empty of crops, in fact empty of almost everything apart from the hellish wandering bands. The average annual income in Mozambique in 1990 was only $80 and of this $50 was aid.

It had not taken long to detect clues that this was to be an unusual country. On the flight down, most of the hair visible above the top of the seats in front was not dark and curly but blonde. They were Scandinavian aid workers and their families. Their governments favoured the left-wing countries, and had set aside extraordinary amounts of money to help them. But there was nothing to spend it on, as there was no agriculture or industry left to build on. So, in the absence of Mozambican problems to tackle, the aid agencies imported problems that their staff was good at solving. Their greatest expertise was in transport economics, so they conceived plans to build rail corridors across Mozambique to the land-locked countries. They were to cost almost a billion dollars, close to the national income. Our mission, however, was more modest. We – two Danish engineers, Soren and Fleming, and myself – were there to arrange finance for a berth for a tug in the port of Beira.

"A berth for a tugboat?" I asked. "That doesn't seem a big deal. What would I have to do?"

"Show that it is economically justified."

"What! Surely it won't cost much? Three people to do the analysis would probably cost more than the berth."

"But can you do it?"

"Well, I can probably do it less badly than other people."

"Are you on, then?"

"OK." I liked working with them.

Our meetings with the Danish Embassy in Maputo took a day or so, and then we had to get from Maputo to Beira. It was 500 miles to the north, but no foreigners were allowed to travel on any roads outside the city of Maputo. To leave the city would be risking having your nose slit or being captured by passing soldiers. There were only a few foreigners who made the run to the border at the dead of night in four-wheel drives, and they were legends in the city. The only other option was the flights of Mozambican Air Lines (LAM). No foreigners ever used LAM; they used private chartered planes. But there were no seats on the charter planes on the few days that we able to travel.

"You're not going by LAM!" exclaimed one of the embassy staff.

"Yes, why not?"

"Well. . . they crash. In fact they only have three planes left now. And even if you get there you won't get back. They run out of fuel every month."

But we had no option; we took the plane.

The town we found at Beira had two parallel worlds. There were no real shops, restaurants, cinemas or decent hotels. They had all closed down; and so the aid agencies had built their own compounds with neat little bungalows, tennis courts and swimming pools full of blonde children, in an area flattened out of the tropical jungle. And in the daytime we worked in the pristine white building of the Beira Corridor Authority alongside the earnest young Scandinavians with their neatly trimmed beards and computers. They were hospitable and friendly, but they had no room in the compound, so we had to stay in a little flat outside. We asked them where to shop and find restaurants, but they were unfamiliar with the town outside their compound. In reply to our questions about Beira, they often said, "Carl may know."

By the second lunchtime we were hungry, and set out to trawl around the town in a borrowed car; and eventually we found a warehouse, full of large bins of rice, soap, cooking oil, electrical wire and other basics. Almost all of it bore the wording 'Made in Swaziland' or 'Packaged in Swaziland'. Swaziland was the tiny state on the border between Mozambique and the great enemy, South Africa; and 'made in Swaziland' really meant 'made in South Africa'. Almost everything in the warehouse was on an industrial scale, but Soren suddenly shouted, "Look at this!" He was holding a little jar of powdered cinnamon. Outside, we found some bread at a street stall and two tins of sardines, and we went back to the flat to make cinnamon toast, and share out the precious sardines. Fleming had also brought with him a traditional Danish drink called Gammel Dansk and we drank with ironic formality. Later, an old man who looked after the building arrived with some bottled water to allow us to make coffee. He showed us pictures of his children and grandchildren. He said that there was no hope for him in his lifetime and that he feared for his children. He was a lovely old man, with gentle manners and a few words of English. The next day he brought us some oranges.

We found Carl a few days later, helping to repair a truck. He was short and wiry, with gelid eyes and a direct stare. He looked what he was – a man who knew exactly what he was doing. He had passed no exams: he had been a stonemason in Denmark; but the staff in Beira deferred to him on most subjects, even transport economics. He was also one of the small group who dared to make the night-time dash to the border, where he picked up goods to bring back to Beira.

By the end of the week, we knew him well. He showed us the hole-in-the wall shops where we could find food, and took us to the only good restaurant, down on the shore, where we ate prawns with piri-piri sauce most nights, listening to the sea. When we wanted anything that was not available, he took us to the shed in his car-maintenance compound. It was dirty and damaged on the outside, but inside it was full of goods – from car parts to electrical equipment, pipes and food – all tidily stacked and numbered on modern shelving. In a corner of the shed he had set up a little lounge, lit like an old Italian restaurant with straw-covered chianti bottle lamps and soft couches. There we met his girlfriend, a regal Mozambican woman, several inches taller than him, and to whom even Carl seemed to defer. She was one of the few Mozambicans we came to know.

The other was our client, a white Mozambican. He was one of the foreign-educated 'golden children' who despised their Portuguese parents for their colonialist past and the way they left the country destitute, and had stayed on to work with the new revolutionary government. At first they wore beards and sunglasses in the style of Che Guevara, but later rose to be politicians and civil servants. Rui Fonseca was now the head of ports and railways, and was known for his high intelligence, arrogance and volcanic rages. At our meeting with him he tore into us for wasting money on a tiny project, and he reduced Fleming, who was our project manager, to a humiliated speechlessness. But both Soren and I had the impression that the great man had decided to act out one of his tantrums, for which he was known, before he entered the room, and, waiting until the end of the tirade, I started to argue: "It was your port that commissioned this report on a tugboat berth, not us." Then Soren, who was much younger, stepped in and continued our defence with such easy charm that Fonseca calmed down. I was told many year laters that Soren had risen to the top of his company.

Our last two days were spent at the airport, involuntarily. As we had been warned, the planes had stopped running when they ran out of fuel. By the end of the first day 300 passengers were sprawled waiting on the airport floor and on the second day there were 600. Even if the planes came that day it would take more days to clear the backlog. So we called Carl.

He came to the airport to introduce us to two American pilots in bandanas and fatigues who carried air freight between Beira and Maputo; and we walked out to a hangar to see their plane. It was the second oldest DC3 in the world, and had a jagged hole in the undercarriage. How did that happen?

"The propeller came off its bearings."

"What!? How along ago?"

"About five years." He looked unconcerned.

"And you still fly it?"

"Every day, man."

And so we hitched a lift, sitting on metal trunks amongst the bins and boxes, deafened by the sound of the old propellers, watching the rain stream in through the gashes in the roof and staring down at the dense jungle below.

The last few days were spent with Danes, whose hospitality and manners were immaculate. On one occasion the Danish chief of the local tug crew interrupted the table at a restaurant and said "Gentlemen" – there were about eight present – "I think we should remember that one of us is English, and it would be better if we stuck to the English language."

But I felt uneasy about their having to speak English all the time, and sometimes I escaped. Often after work I walked alone along the shoreline just before sunset, to a partly run-down jewel of a hotel, the Polana. Once the top hotel of Mozambique, it now had a seedy abandoned appearance, but it still had its cool marble floors and rich wood furnishing. I had come across it by chance one night when I had to send a fax, and found nowhere open. My last chance was the Polana. It cost me $47 to send it, the locals being so disconnected from the outside world that they had no feel for whether $47 was a large amount or a small amount to foreigners. But while I waited for the fax to go, I found a patio café looking out over the sea, and it was to this café that I returned to eat smoked salmon, capers and salad with an unidentifiable citrus sauce in the late afternoons. I was sometimes the only person there apart from a few couples on romantic trysts. It was the middle of the rainy season, and as the evening breeze coming in from the sea cooled the air and the insects began to whirr and buzz I looked out at the cosmic wreckage of the sunsets, their fevered orange skies and ominous gold-rimmed, black, storm clouds. When the rain came it was in drops as big as old pennies and we dashed for cover.

There were other signs of life carrying on in spite of the war, signs of little groups holding the torch. In the last week we stumbled on a restaurant run by a cookery school in a vast wedding cake of an old colonial building, where the young trainee chefs served wonderful food without any of the cultivated servility that often spoils expensive restaurants. And other cafés and restaurants were starting to open again, often with tables out on the street. There, eating *bacalhau* and piri-piri in the warm tropical evening air, the locals – Portuguese and Mozambican – mixed easily. Unlike the British, French and Belgians, the Portuguese colonials had worked alongside the Mozambicans, as plumbers, electricians, and mechanics, before independence, and there was no racial divide.

And then there were the sunny smiles of the children everywhere we went. When the war ends I think they'll be OK.